BEGIN WITH A
DREAM

BEGIN WITH A DREAM

How a Private School with a Public Mission
Changed the Politics of Race, Class, and Gender
in American Education

AUGUSTUS TROWBRIDGE

Acknowledgements:
Special thanks to Rosemarie Robotham-Arrindell
for her editing and encouragement,
and to Adrian and Elizabeth Kitzinger for all their help.

Photo credits:
Except where otherwise credited, all photos are from
the archives of Manhattan Country School. Michael Norcia p. 32;
Life, June 14, 1968 p. 52; C. Smith p. 96, 350; Mel Dixon p. 130;
Matthew Septimus p. 152; Richard Frank p. 187; Virginia Warner p. 296;
Jessica Agullo p. 304, 314; John McDaniel p. 354

To order additional copies of this book, contact:
Xlibris Corporation
1-888-795-4274
www.Xlibris.com
Orders@Xlibris.com
28399

CONTENTS

For Marty

The façade of 7 East 96th Street, Manhattan Country School.

If we—and now I mean the relatively conscious whites and
the relatively conscious blacks, who must, like lovers, insist on,
or create the consciousness of others—do not falter in our duty now,
we may be able, handful that we are, to end the racial nightmare,
and achieve our country, and change the history of the world.

—James Baldwin in
"Letter From a Region in My Mind," November 17, 1962

None of us is guilty for the
sins of our fathers, but we are responsible
for how we react to the evils that were done.

—Don Ross, Tulsa, Okalahoma,
quoted in *Riot and Remembrance* by James S. Hirsch

Marty and Gus Trowbridge, circa 1997.

INTRODUCTION

The Decks on Which We Danced

IN 1991, I TRADED a letter sent to my grandfather from Albert Einstein for a memento of the civil rights movement. It was a copy of *Playbill*, dated Sunday, April 4, 1965, featuring an exclusive performance at the Majestic Theatre entitled *Broadway Answers Selma*. The performance was to commemorate the historic march of the month before, when John Lewis and Hosea Williams, courageous fighters for civil rights, led a crowd of six hundred demonstrators across Selma's Edmund Pettus Bridge in protest of the South's discrimination laws. On the bridge, the marchers refused to be turned back by police on horseback wielding clubs and tear gas and trampling them. The horrific images were broadcast from Selma, Alabama, across the country, sparking more protest, and soon a full-blown movement. March 7, 1965, the date of the first Selma march, would come to be known as "Bloody Sunday."

The original owner of my *Playbill*, whose ticket stub was included with the program, had sat in the second-row center of the orchestra—seat B-16 to be exact—and during the evening had secured Martin Luther King Jr.'s autograph, along with that of Harry Belafonte, James Baldwin, and James Forman. When I view my treasured acquisition, now framed and hanging on my bedroom wall, I often imagine other details and connections associated with what must have been such a triumphant event. Who else did seat B-16 see that evening? Was John Lewis himself there? Did Dr. King and James Baldwin talk with one another? If so, what about?

April 4 would turn out to be an especially poignant date in American history. Two years following the date on my *Playbill*, on April 4, 1967, Martin Luther King Jr. delivered one of his most famous addresses at Riverside Church, opposing the Vietnam War. A year later, on April 4, 1968, he was shot and killed. In hindsight, Bloody Sunday in Selma, Alabama, was a high-water mark of the civil rights movement, described by President Lyndon Johnson as an occasion when "history and fate meet in a single time and a single place to shape a turning point in man's unending search for freedom."

It was indeed a turning point in my own life, and in the life of Marty, my wife of forty-nine years. Inspired by the goals of the civil rights movement so movingly articulated on August 28, 1963, by Dr. King in his "I Have a Dream" speech during the climactic march on Washington, Marty and I discovered an enduring dream of our own. Both educators, we dreamed of founding a school in which all children would be treated as equals, and in which there would be no ruling group based on race, gender, or class.

In September 1966, we opened the doors of Manhattan Country School, a small progressive private school in New York City, with a working farm in the nearby Catskill Mountains. "The first obligation of this school," I would later explain to the school's parents, "is to provide equal opportunity and equal access to students of a pluralistic society. Our objective is the achievement of a constituency in which there is no given, predictable majority, a working community in which achievement, power, and influence are self-earned, rather than the legacy of privilege, and certainly not at the expense of others. We must acknowledge and respect our separate identities and our collective commitment. We dare not lose our humanity by adopting an ethic whereby we assert that any one of us is obliged to live in the image of another."

In this sense, Manhattan Country School proudly shares its origins with the march on Selma and other seminal events of the civil rights movement.

As with the movement, Martin Luther King Jr. is our visionary, his life a powerful example of the potential in each of us to bring about change. Symbolized by Ben Shahn's towering portrait of the civil rights leader that has hung since 1969 in our school's reception area, Dr. King's presence at Manhattan Country School had always been larger than life. For us, he is more than a pivotal figure of the civil rights movement. His voice is prophetic, transcending history, enabling those of us who follow him to apply his teachings to each new struggle in the effort to achieve what he called the "beloved community."

Not that the seas of our endeavor have always been smooth. In almost forty years of our school's history, we have weathered racial tempests and philosophical storms. As the terminology of race relations changed through the decades, and our understanding of the true dimensions of our mission became clear, we learned to define our goals in the broader terms of multiculturalism. I was sometimes accused of being arrogant, and no doubt, sometimes I was. At certain moments, I despaired of ever achieving the "little Utopia" Marty and I had set out to create. But even during the days of our deepest despondency, we never once considered relinquishing our dream. Marty and I, and the band of dreamers who set sail with us, knew with unshakable conviction that we were charting a course worth charting, and all the storms and tempests were necessary if we were to arrive together at the promised shore.

SINCE FOUNDING MANHATTAN Country School, from which I retired as director in 1997, I have often been called on to explain the depth of my commitment to racial equality and my determination to create a community in which children could be judged, as Dr. King envisioned, not "by the color of their skin but by the content of their character." There are some who find my life's work an odd preoccupation for a White Anglo Saxon Protestant whose ancestors settled in New England and earned the family fortune as slave traders in the New World. Even my own next of kin don't always understand my fervor.

I recall one encounter with my brother, when I tried to convince him that racial prejudice in America would never be addressed until whites admitted and worked to change their own racism. Marty and I had walked a mile south to the Metropolitan Museum of Art from our house on 101st Street in East Harlem. It was the first year of a new century—indeed, a new millennium—and the occasion was our annual Presidents' Day weekend lunch with my brother Clint and his wife Elaine. Since their marriage three years before, Clint and Elaine had come to New York from their home in Maine every February to soak up some big-city culture.

After settling ourselves in the museum's cafeteria, Clint asked what Marty and I were up to now that we had retired. I mentioned we were getting ready to write a book. The topic, of course, would be Manhattan Country School. I told Clint and Elaine that we were debating how to tell our story. "I don't want to write a pedagogical tract," I explained. "I want to speak to white people about racism and about their need to change their ways."

Elaine spoke up at once. "I'm not interested in white racism," she declared. "I'm sick of all this white-guilt stuff."

Marty smiled and gave me a meaningful look, then changed the subject with Elaine. I turned to Clint to enlist a more receptive response. White people, I argued, don't even recognize their own racism. In fact, they see things upside down. I cited an example: The year before, I had been invited by the Friends Seminary to give a speech on diversity. I met first with their diversity committee, then a few weeks later addressed the whole school. Later, I was told that many white parents, and some black ones, were surprised to discover I was white.

"But that was a compliment," Clint insisted.

"At best, a back-handed one," I answered, because unlike my brother, I saw their reaction as a red flag. It exposed their ingrained perspective that whites weren't responsible for making integration work; that to be an activist for racial equality, one must be a member of the underdogs. Clint resisted my interpretation, so I tried a second example.

In 1968, after *Life* magazine wrote a story on MCS, optimistically titled "Making Prejudice Impossible," I was invited to be a guest on the TV show, *To Tell the Truth*. I declined because there had been a recent bomb threat in the school, and I didn't want exposure to further opposition. At the time, I didn't think about why I had been selected for the show. The program's format was to present three people, all claiming to be the same person, to a panel of celebrities. By asking a series of questions, the members of the celebrity panel had to identify the "real" person. "Now, I see their motives," I told Clint. "They probably would have had a black man there, a white hippie, and me, dressed in a blue blazer."

"Exactly, Gus, and that wouldn't have been a bad thing." Clint responded. "They wanted to show the courageous stand you took."

"But, Clint," I pleaded, "the show is supposed to be a comedy. They didn't invite me to break any stereotypes. It was the opposite. They wanted Kitty Carlyle and her fellow socialites to get a laugh out of who was the real Gus Trowbridge, at the expense, no doubt, of those who were deadly serious about racial equality."

I didn't tell my brother about when I was invited to submit my application to *Who's Who in Black America*, expecting that he would consider the story hilarious. At the time, I was momentarily amused, even joking with the lower-school director, Marge Trimble, who is black, about sending in the questionnaire with my résumé and her photograph. On reflection, however, I didn't find the incident quite so funny. It's not out of character for white people to presume my being black, but it's distressing that black people should also find it unthinkable that a white person could care about race relations in our country.

Leaving the museum that afternoon, I was prepared to accept Clint's interpretations on one level, hoping that he might accept my deeper misgivings. In an attempt to reach mutual ground, I said, "Clint, I know we came from a liberal family in the heart of the white establishment, and that our parents were social activists in their way. But you've got to acknowledge the degree of our own racist upbringing. Every night there were terrible jokes about Negroes and Jews. You remember the story about Freddy Warburg, who sent a Negro messenger over from his office at Kuhn, Loeb to Tommy Lamont at Mellon Bank with the note that read: 'Here's the Coon from Kuhn-Loeb.' It was always good for a laugh."

Clint answered mildly, "And that wasn't politically incorrect in those times."

It was getting late, and my purpose was not to accuse my bother of racism. He's not intolerant, but like so many of my old-line WASP background, he and I were raised to think of ourselves at the top of the social ladder. Our whiteness and rightness gave us the privilege to tell ethnic jokes all we wanted without giving a thought about their "correctness." After all, we were the "good" whites, innocent of any actual wrongdoings.

The Education of a WASP, written in 1970 by Lois Mark Stalvey, describes the generation of my upbringing and explains perhaps why we were able to feel oblivious to any prejudice on our part. "Singing 'America, the Beautiful' always made me cry and when I recited the Pledge of Allegiance with proud fervor, I was sure that 'with liberty and justice for all' was true then and always would be," writes Stalvey. "These were the conditions under which, I believe, most WASPs of my generation grew up. This should not excuse us, only explain us. The people I knew didn't practice discrimination; none of us suspected we were co-operating with it. We were like first-class passengers on a ship, comfortable with our privileges. We didn't know—or perhaps want to know—what went on below the decks on which we danced."

In founding Manhattan Country School, in embracing Dr. Martin Luther King Jr.'s dream of a "beloved community" of equals, indeed in writing this book, I am doing my part to dismantle the decks on which we, the "good" whites, have for so long danced.

Justin Dewey Fulton,
great-grandfather of
Gus Trowbridge,
circa 1853.

Gus, 1 year old,
with great-uncle
Robertson Trowbridge.

CHAPTER 1

The Making of a Liberal

WHEN MY MOTHER died in 1985, I realized with a pang that more of my close relatives were dead than alive. Being well past the halfway mark in my own lifetime, this should not have been a surprise. But what caught me unprepared was that my mother's dying put me permanently out of touch with my forebears, her death being the last of my previous generation. As I sorted through her papers and memorabilia, I found a wealth of unidentified family photographs, letters, and partial genealogical documents. Sifting through them, I longed for one more day with my mother so that I might gather the lost details of my family history.

From the photographs I could identify and from other records, I managed to assemble an album and a sketchy family tree, which I photocopied and gave to each of my mother's thirteen grandchildren. In my note I said I was sorry there was not more to tell them, particularly about my mother's side of the family.

My mother's father was DeWitt Clinton Whiting, whose wife, Lida Lowden, died before I was born. I have a carton of Whiting photographs, all unidentified. They were all I knew of her family history until 2001 when I received a lengthy legal notification concerning the clearing of a title to property once owned by my great-great-great-grandfather. The notice, which lists over two hundred heirs, traces the Whiting lineage from 1853 in Massachusetts, naming my grandfather's three siblings and his father's ten brothers and sisters. So, while I now have the names of the scores of people in my Whiting pictures, they will never be connected to the faces.

My Trowbridge ancestry, on the other hand, is well documented and traceable to the medieval French king, Charlemagne. Ancestors of my paternal great-grandmother include Lyman Hall, who signed the Declaration of Independence, and Jonathan Law, governor of the colony of Connecticut in 1741.

The first Trowbridge to come to America from England was Thomas, born in the 1590s. His son, by the same first name, settled in New Haven, Connecticut, where family records state "he engaged in prosecuting voyages to and from Barbados," a veiled reference to his occupation as a slave trader. His family business, from which all future Trowbridges gained a prosperous inheritance, was carried on by his son, Captain Daniel Trowbridge (1703-1752), and his brother, William Trowbridge (1684-1744), who was himself a slave holder. Perhaps out of embarrassment, my parents never told me of this, leaving me to learn this particular detail of my history through family documents. But my parents took pleasure in telling me the scandalous circumstances of a fifteenth century ancestor, George Trowbridge. His story had been related to them by my grandfather, Augustus Trowbridge.

Apparently, George had purchased a chapel that once belonged to Tavistock Abbey in Devonshire, England. With the help of friends, he tore the chapel down, using the stones to build his home. He gave the chapel's communion table to a neighboring ale house, which used it as their bar. Village historians relate that "the family of Trowbridge never prospered after this sacrilege, and that all concerned in it, particularly one who had the chapel bell for his trouble, died miserably." Two hundred years later, there was no sign of George's curse on the fortune of mercantilist and slave-trader, Thomas Trowbridge.

Unlike my Trowbridge forebears, my paternal grandmother, Sarah Esther Fulton, descended from Irish stock who settled in Upstate New York as farmers. Sarah's father, a Baptist minister, was Justin Dewey Fulton. I first learned about Justin in 1985 from a book in my parents' library, which was dedicated to him.

Entitled *History of the Negro Race in America from 1619-1880* and published in 1883, the book was written by George Washington Williams. Williams had served in the Union Army, attended Newton Theological School, and then started a newspaper called *The Commoner* with the encouragement of Frederick Douglass. Moving to Cincinnati, he became active in the Republican party of Abraham Lincoln, and was the first black to be elected to the Ohio legislature. In 1889, after a failed attempt to become ambassador to Haiti, Williams sought to abolish slavery in the Belgian Congo, which he visited just before his death.

Between the leaves of Williams's book was a page torn from the *National Cyclopedia of American Biography*, showing a sketch of my great-grandfather. Williams's dedication to my great-grandfather reads as follows: "To the Illustrious Representative of the Church of Christ: who for a quarter of a century, has stood the intrepid champion of divine truth, and the defender of humanity; during the dark days of slavery, pleading the cause of the bondmen of the land; during the war, urging the equality of Negroes as soldiers; during the reconstruction, encouraging the freedmen to noble lives through the agency of the church and the school; and evermore the enemy of any distinction based upon race, color, or previous condition of servitude."

I do not know when Williams and my great-grandfather first met, but most likely they already knew one another in 1853, when Justin Fulton delivered the first free-state sermon ever preached in St. Louis, Missouri. Although I know only a portion of my pedigree—a genealogy that includes slave traders and a man who demolished a chapel and gave the communion table to a house of ale—I take great satisfaction in knowing that at least one of my ancestors was an abolitionist.

I WAS NAMED Augustus Trowbridge after my grandfather who died three months before I was born on August 14, 1934. Father T., as my parents called him, was a physicist who had served in World War I as a lieutenant colonel in the Engineering Corps under General Pershing. He later became dean of the graduate school at Princeton University, where he was responsible for bringing Albert Einstein to the United States. When I later applied for admission to Princeton, and met one of the university's grand dames who had known my grandfather, she declared that she would rather shake the hand of Augustus Trowbridge than that of George Washington. Despite her honor in greeting me, the admissions department felt otherwise and turned me down.

My grandfather's scientific leanings were quite different from the preoccupations of his older bachelor brother, Robertson, a lawyer of independent means, who lived next door to the writer Henry James on Washington Square North in Manhattan. Though an atheist, Robertson Trowbridge was perhaps a stronger influence on my father's political and social views than his own parents. When not tending to his collection of rare books, he was an active civil libertarian. He became a principal financial supporter of Nicola Sacco and Bartolomeo Vanzetti, Italian-born anarchists whose involvement in labor strikes and antiwar protests famously led to their conviction on robbery and murder charges in Boston in 1920. Uncle Rob remained convinced that both men were innocent and had been railroaded by the legal system because of their radical activities.

Family records show that Uncle Rob also legally adopted a young man named Pierce Wetter, whom he felt had been falsely convicted of treason. In a letter carefully explaining this adoption to my parents, Uncle Rob assured the family that no share of his inheritance would pass along to Pierce. Uncle Rob went on to address another matter of probable family concern. "I should like to be equally explicit that the step I have taken does not involve any personal or social contacts between Pierce Wetter and my family or friends," he told my parents. "Although Pierce is well-born and on both sides of his family well-connected, he has, I imagine, disqualified himself for 'society' as we understand the term, by serving a sentence in a federal penitentiary under the Espionage Act. More detrimental still, from a social point of view (in New York, at least) would be the fact that he is married to a Jewess." Despite this reference to the prejudices of his immediate circle, Uncle Rob closed his letter saying, "I think the civil liberties of which I am so staunch an advocate should begin at home."

My own father's conscience led him down a different path: He became an Episcopal minister. Named George Augustus, born August 12, 1897, my father was the second of three children. His older sister Katharine died of influenza during the epidemic of 1918, only a year after her marriage to George W. Perkins, whose family estate, now Wave Hill, overlooks the Hudson in Riverdale, New York.

My father's younger brother was Cornelius, a name I've otherwise only heard used in one of the *Babar* children's books. The brothers' sibling rivalry lasted a lifetime. Though following in one another's footsteps through the same schools, colleges, and eventually the Episcopal ministry, they were always at each other's throats, especially after the cocktail hour. The only time I ever heard my father praise Corny was when, as president of Planned Parenthood, my uncle made a speech expressing indignation that anyone should oppose the giving of birth-control information to the poor in the name of religion.

Born in Berlin, Germany, where my grandfather was studying for his master's degree in physics, my father grew up in Princeton, New Jersey, leading a comfortable life in a prosperous, academic family. He attended the Hill School, a boarding school in Pennsylvania, and then entered Princeton University. In 1917, he left college to serve for six months as a volunteer ambulance driver for the American Field Service on the French front. Although later inducted into the United States Army, he never entered active service as the war ended weeks after he finished boot camp.

At Princeton, he starred as an athlete in track, and the year following his graduation, while he attended Oxford University, he won a championship race for the 120-yard hurdles, setting the record for this event in England, Ireland, Scotland, and Wales. Had he not been afflicted with appendicitis, he would have qualified for the American Olympic team of *Chariots of Fire* fame.

After returning to the States, he graduated from Virginia Seminary and entered the Episcopal ministry, and in 1924 was appointed chaplain at Yale University. He met my mother, Jean Whiting, on January 19, 1926, at a Princeton classmate's wedding, where she was a bridesmaid. Immediately smitten with one another, they were married less than five months later, and for years they celebrated January 19 as their most cherished anniversary.

Before meeting my father, my mother had never even attended church. And she had been involved with another man, Briton Hadden, who owned half of Time, Incorporated. She soon ditched her love affair with Hadden to begin her religious training with letters of instruction from my father. Her parents had insisted that she return to South Carolina for a month, to test her devotion to the man she had so impulsively determined to wed. At her parents' home, between riding and golf and tennis at a fashionable resort hotel, my mother exchanged daily love letters with my father, mailing her Friday ones special delivery so that they would be received on Sundays. And she dutifully studied her catechism. Before her June wedding, she was baptized and confirmed, though she declined my father's offer to perform the baptism, saying it would just make her giggle.

Born on January 11, 1900, my mother liked to say that she was conceived in one century and delivered in another, which may account for her weighing eleven pounds. She was raised in the Flatbush section of Brooklyn, which though stylish at the turn of the century, was across the river from New York's Manhattan elite. Her father was a self-made man who began as a shoeshine boy and later started his own coffee business, which provided him with an ample fortune. Though well-to-do, Grampa Whiting had none of the airs of the privileged. He had a big heart, a fun-loving manner, and as my brother liked to say, "He treated children as adults and adults as children."

My mother was my only known relative to have gone to public school, which she attended through eighth grade as a straight-A student. From the Brooklyn Model School, she went to Packer Collegiate, spurning the more popular Brooklyn Heights Seminary, or Cemetery, as she called it, which she considered "a finishing school where all they taught you was to say 'please' and to curtsy." Her college choice was Smith, from which she graduated in 1922, three years before meeting my father.

My mother was not your typical seminarian's wife. Her friend, my "Aunt" Zorka Oenslager, once described her as the "naughtiest girl I knew." It must have been difficult for her to break from her party-filled Roaring Twenties social life and become engaged to a minister. She told her friends that until my father proposed, she didn't know ministers married. "We were shocked," Aunt Zorka said, "when she decided to marry a man of the cloth."

Two years after she married my father, he was called to his first parish, All Angel's Church on West End Avenue and Eighty-first Street in Manhattan. He was rector there for ten years, serving a large congregation far more diverse economically and socially than parishes on the fashionable East Side. In 1928, my brother Clint was born, then two years later my sister Katharine, followed by me in 1934. When I was four, the family left New York City to live in Chestnut Hill, an upper-class suburb of Philadelphia. There, my father served as the minister of St. Paul's Church until 1956—the year that Marty and I were married.

Chestnut Hill was not the kind of place that I would have expected my parents to spend so many years of my father's ministry. It was an enclave of Philadelphia's high society, second only to the Main Line, which people in Chestnut Hill would never admit. It was a hub of snobbery, where those in the Social Register, or the "stud book" as it was called, lived, and the Episcopalians out-snubbed all other WASP denominations. The parishioners of St. Paul's, when not dancing to Meyer Davis or playing golf at the Cricket Club, to which my parents refused to belong, were in my father's church at eleven o'clock Sunday morning, usually leaving before Communion to catch a swim or a set of tennis before lunch. I thought it must have been terribly hard for my father to preach the social gospel to this crowd, but then he had been brought up with their kind.

As their years together in Chestnut Hill progressed through the atrocities of World War II and the decades following when racial segregation at home was put to the test, my parents grew more and more radical and united in their egalitarian views. The McCarthy witch hunts of the 1950s only helped solidify their position. In part, this may have been due to the differences in their personalities and upbringing, which drove them to find some common ground. They were not an easy match, but despite friction between them, they always voted the same ticket, supported the same causes, and took on the same adversaries.

In seeking to make their mark among those in Chestnut Hill whose company my father's ministry obliged them to keep, my parents grew closer and became a team. Although many considered them subversive, with my father even being forced to defend himself against charges of being a Communist, they were a formidable pair—he in the pulpit and she on the front lines as volunteer head of the Christian Social Relations Department of the diocese, and later as a delegate to the National Convocation.

Excerpts from the scores of speeches my mother gave to Women's Auxiliary groups throughout Pennsylvania and neighboring states show that she knew more about the problems of race relations than the Church acknowledged, and that, for one raised with no religious instruction, she could cite the theological grounds for racial equality, chapter and verse. At times she spoke like an evangelist, calling the struggle for justice "Bringing in the Kingdom." "If we believe in the brotherhood of man, we cannot believe in a superior race," she would declare. She would not rest her case, however, on spiritual conversion. The "converted heart" was not sufficient, she would say. "Don't just talk it; act it."

At one meeting, when she was assigned the topic "The Christian and Race," she began her speech by saying, "I should be talking about the Christian and racism. There is nothing in race that excludes it from Christianity, but there is everything in racism which precludes Christian participation." Speaking like this in the 1940s, even using the word "racism" in this context, put her years ahead of her white-establishment contemporaries. Probably her most progressive insight was her recognition that legislating racial equality would not automatically result in a trusting response among blacks. She viewed segregation as a caste system, "a negation of God's saving grace, which breeds cynical bitterness in the outcast race." As a consequence, speaking almost as if she were living in the 1970s, she warned, "If we set out to cross the color line, we will have to bear patiently the distrust and threats and alarms of our fellows and walk warily lest we inflame where we seek to bring peace."

Sensing the reluctance of some among her audience, my mother frequently closed her speeches on race relations with a quotation from *Color Blind* by Margaret Halsey. In it, Halsey wrote, "Improvement in race relations is not a matter of a few people having a great deal of courage. It is a matter of a great many people having just a little courage. Sometimes it is ludicrously easy. It only needs beginning. No heroes need apply."

For his part, my father did his most important work as an early civil rights activist when he was president of the Philadelphia Fellowship Commission, and in 1950 he was given the Inter-Faith Award from B'nai B'rith for "promoting understanding and goodwill among people of all races and religions." In the year he retired from St. Paul's, he and my mother were sent a farewell letter from their friend, Sadie Alexander.

Sadie Tanner Mossell Alexander, wife of Raymond Pace Alexander, whose two daughters were schoolmates of mine at Putney, was the niece of the renowned artist Henry Ossawa Tanner. A lawyer by profession, she was the first black woman to pass the Pennsylvania bar, and in 1946 she was appointed to President Truman's committee on civil rights, becoming the first black woman in America to sit on a presidential commission. She knew my parents from their work together for the Fellowship Commission. And on the occasion of my father's retirement, she wrote:

"Frequently when I have seen you in conferences or at meetings, my mind has traveled back to various times during my childhood when I sat on a stool hidden from sight, listening avidly to discussions among my elders in my grandfather's study. Grandpa was born in Pittsburgh in 1830 of free Negro parents, and married a free woman. They both secured an education and Grandpa entered the ministry, pastoring a Presbyterian Church in Washington, D.C., during the Civil War. Because of their long and diverse experience, my grandparents were called upon almost daily for advice on racial and religious matters. The event which repeatedly has come to my mind when I have seen or thought of the Trowbridges was a conference when my uncle sought Grandpa's advice on his efforts to have colored girls admitted to a nursing school in one of the Philadelphia hospitals. When my uncle stated that he had visited and conferred with all the managers of the hospital, Grandpa replied, 'I know well every one of those men. My son, you cannot expect action from any one of them. The God they serve so well with their lips has never reached their souls.'

"Approximately fifty years later it has been my great privilege to meet and know you, two white Protestants, whose religion has reached each of your souls. Your lives have been leaven in the lives of many more persons than you will ever know. There are moments when those of us born into the race problem become weary and wonder if the fight is worth the never-ending effort. But, when we see even one person, not to mention two, willing to face social censure in order to live in accord with his and her Christian convictions, we are strengthened in our determination and our faith in humanity is renewed." Reading Sadie Alexander's letter years later, I could not help but be reminded of George Washington Williams's inscription to my great grandfather, Justin Fulton, almost a century before.

THOUGH I WAS undoubtedly influenced by my parents' activism, I believe I truly learned to hate injustice not from them, but from my experiences at school. My parents chose to send me to Chestnut Hill Academy, an all-boys Dickensian school, rather than its coeducational competitor, Germantown Friends, which was run by Quakers. At Chestnut Hill, one of my classmates was a Quaker, as was my favorite teacher, Mr. Ambler, who allowed us to call him by his first name, Thomas. There were no Negroes, of course, and no Jews or Roman Catholics. Otherwise, we were all Episcopalians.

The school's dress code was gray flannel shorts, matching knee socks, a white Oxford button-down shirt, school necktie, and a blue blazer. Long pants were permitted only in eighth grade. I hated wearing shorts and had constant scabs on my knees. At home each evening, I changed to khaki trousers. Not even my parents would permit blue jeans.

Upon admission to Chestnut Hill Academy, the boys were assigned to one of two teams: the Light Blues and the Dark Blues. I was a Dark Blue because my brother had been one. Between these two teams there was no crossing over, not even in our seating arrangement in daily chapel. In the name of gentleman rivalry, the teams quickly grew to despise one another, and we were taught that mastery meant dominion, that success required defeating the other side. Everything we did—our athletic victories, our grades, our demerits—either added to or subtracted from our team's running score. The culmination of our year-long competition came in May when we engaged in a giant tug-of-war, with the headmaster hosing down the defeated team as it was dragged across the middle line of the schoolyard. At chapel the next day, the captain of the winning team was presented a silver cup to place in one of the trophy cases outside the headmaster's office.

I was never at a loss for friends at the academy; some of them were even Light Blues. Our principal pleasure was to break rules, making sure our infractions were blamed on someone else. One gambit I perfected was employed at meals when we were served brussels sprouts, which I loathed. We ate family style at large oak tables. I would take a seat at one end of the table, hold my nose while putting a sprout in my mouth, and then in a flash, expel it into my napkin. Beneath the table, I tossed it along the floor to the boy opposite me. During lunch, the masters patrolled the dining hall to catch boys with their elbows on the table. They would grab their wrists from behind and slam down their defenseless arms. At the end of lunch, they inspected the room while we stood behind our seats. It was then that the boy across from me would receive a demerit for each of my four discarded brussels sprouts. I was learning to hate injustice and was doing a good job practicing it as well.

We also tried to vex our teachers on every occasion possible. Mr. Wales, our math teacher, rearranged our assigned seats every week on the basis of Friday's quiz—the brightest boys in the front row, the dumbest in the back.

Mondays were free-for-alls, Spit Ball Days, we called them, because Mr. Wales hadn't yet memorized the new seating plan. Another teacher, Mr. Donner, who taught us English, had suffered shell shock in the war and was prone to brief episodes of deafness. When he blanked out, one of us would stand up and tell dirty jokes until Mr. Donner regained himself.

Mr. Cutler taught us Latin, first period, three days a week. Our caper with him was for two of us to arrive in class early, turn over his desk, put the top center drawer in upside down and return the desk to an upright position. The first time he opened the drawer and watched its contents rain to the floor, he blamed the cleaning service; thereafter it was demerits for the whole class. The only teacher who was spared our chicanery was our eighth-grade biology teacher, Tom Ambler.

Like most children, I acquired my politics from my parents, which made me an oddity among my mostly Republican schoolmates, who pronounced Roosevelt's name to sound like "rooster." At home I learned about the NAACP and met civil rights leaders Walter White and Ralph Bunche. Eleanor Roosevelt slept across the hall from me when she came to receive an award from the Fellowship Commission. On another occasion, so did Danny Kaye. Dinner conversations were about all the liberal topics of the times: the United Nations, amnesty for conscientious objectors; the World Council of Churches' program to assist displaced persons; labor cooperatives, efforts to overthrow McCarthy's loyalty tests, opposition to China's Chiang Kai-shek, and support for Alger Hiss. Once, my father took a return call during dinner from New York's Governor Thomas Dewey; he wanted to explain why he would not give clemency to Communist Party members Ethel and Julius Rosenberg, who had been convicted of espionage, and were to be executed the next day.

In the 1948 presidential elections, when Dewey was running against Harry Truman, with Henry Wallace running against them both on the Progressive Party ticket, I sang in a children's chorus on a program with Paul Robeson at a "Workers for Wallace" rally. The mock student election at Chestnut Hill

Academy the next week was a landslide for Dewey. At chapel the following day, the headmaster announced the expected results: "Dewey, 235 votes." The boys cheered. "Truman, nine votes"—a smattering of applause. And then, pausing to take off his glasses, the headmaster added, "And we have one boy who voted for Wallace." Mr. Ambler was smiling.

Joyce Dinkins, New York City's first lady, sings along with children from Manhattan Country School during a ceremony honoring Dr. Martin Luther King Jr. outside Gracie Mansion.

CHAPTER 2

The Company One Keeps

MY LIBERATION FROM Chestnut Hill Academy came in the fall of 1948, when I enrolled in ninth grade at the Putney School, a progressive boarding school in Putney, Vermont. There, I once again voted in a schoolwide mock election for president. The results made clear the degree to which Putneyites differed from my conservative classmates at Chestnut Hill: Although Dewey, the Republican, still won the election, it was by the narrow margin that his supporters had hoped for in the popular elections, aided by third-party interference from Wallace. The director announced the results: "Dewey, seventy-three votes," and the students groaned. "Wallace, seventy-one votes; Truman, thirty-six; and Norman Thomas, the socialist candidate, seventeen." After we stopped cheering, she added, "Seven students voted Vegetarian."

Finding Putney for my high school was my mother's doing. She had selected three schools for us to visit, saying it was up to me to pick the one I liked best. There was Putney, New England's most progressive school; Groton School in Groton, Massachusetts, which my brother Clint attended; and South Kent in South Kent, Connecticut, which I dismissed on sight, announcing that I would not go to a monastery.

Groton was the American archetype of the British public school. As far as I was concerned, its only attraction was that my godfather, Jack Crocker, was headmaster. Clint hated it and was nearly expelled the first week he enrolled. Students lived in cubicles which contained only a bed, a dresser, and a chair, with no pictures allowed except of their mothers and fathers. Clint protested this spartan décor by entering every cubicle in his dorm and leaving the window open. For this, he was given six black marks, the heaviest penalty short of black death, which confined you in a locked room for three days, provisioned with only a Bible, bread, and water. A student could erase black marks by running around the inner circle of the campus—an hour for each mark. When my father was summoned to Groton to account for his son's infractions, he could visit with Clint only by jogging alongside him. Fortunately, he was fit from his years as a track champion. Given Clint's experience, there was no way I was willing to choose Groton as my refuge from Chestnut Hill Academy.

My mother and I visited Putney last. Had we visited it first, I would not have looked elsewhere. My mother agreed that Putney was perfect: it was coeducational, teachers were called by their first names, competitive athletics were optional, effort marks took the place of letter grades, and there was no formal dress code. But there was a student council and a working farm!

Putney, with its emphasis on learning by doing, and its casual ambience, was my earliest exposure to progressive education. I loved the school from my first night, when we all slept out on Putney Mountain. But unlike other students who had come to Putney from progressive schools like Shady Hill in Cambridge, Massachusetts, or Dalton and City and Country in New York City, I was not well prepared for the progressive approach. My external transformation was easy, and I welcomed my new wardrobe of Levis', barker boots, and a checkered wool shirt from LL Bean. It took me longer to call Mrs. Holden, Anne. "It doesn't sound right," I said. "Then try 'Miss Anne' for a while," she offered, "and get rid of the 'Miss' as soon as you can."

The school was at the opposite pole from my life in Chestnut Hill. Socially, I'd never experienced an iota of diversity, to say nothing of being in school with girls. Academically, I had learned only by rote and had never been asked to think for myself. And given my complete lack of talent in the arts, which were Putney's forte, I was surprised I was even admitted. Despite the exhilarating sensation that I was "free at last," I was in fact only a seedling, and a transplanted one at that.

The school would leave its mark on me in more ways than I knew. It was at Putney that I met Marty, who arrived at the school the year after I did.

Born Martha Ann Dwight on August 15, 1936, in Jacksonville, Florida, Marty had been raised for the first three years of her life in the segregated South. She was cared for mostly by her maternal grandmother, who was left in charge while Marty's parents, both actors, rehearsed and performed. Marty's parents had met while studying theater at Black Mountain College in North Carolina, which then attracted world-renowned artists as teachers. Marty's mother, Sara Natalie Sylvester, was the first in her family to attend college, while her father, Everett Dwight, was the first in his family to attend a college that was not an Ivy League institution. Everett also declined to go into the family business: Church and Dwight Company, makers of Arm and Hammer Baking Soda. It was a decision that would cost him his inheritance.

Despite the wealth of her paternal grandparents, Marty grew up understanding that her parents had little money. Marty herself was somewhat cushioned from the effects of their financial insecurity, as her father's parents footed the bill for most of her schooling and summer-camp experiences, and she spent long lazy days at their spacious three-story home with its sprawling grounds in Summit, New Jersey. But that was after she and her parents moved from Jacksonville to New York when Marty was four. Before that, Marty had spent many happy days in the company of her maternal grandmother, whose two-story house in Jacksonville, now listed on the Historic Register, was run as a rooming house to help make ends meet.

In her Southern childhood, Marty saw few "colored people," and so had little context when a neighboring child announced that she had named her black kitten "Nigger Baby." For some reason the name unsettled Marty. Later, when she told her Nana about it, her grandmother's response was emphatic. "Nigger" was not a word Marty should ever use, her grandmother instructed her, adding, "Only white trash speak that way."

In an account of her life written at about the time I began work on this book, Marty recalled that occasionally her parents took her to the beach in Jacksonville. In town, she would ride on the swings and the see-saw in the playground across the street, blissfully unaware that black children were denied the same pleasure. "Years later, when I discovered that a former president of Spelman College, Dr. Johnnetta Cole, born the same year and in the same city, was not permitted to play in that playground or go to that beach because of the color of her skin, I wrote to her," Marty noted. "I wanted to make a belated acquaintance, and to marvel at the coincidences of our lives and the similarities in the work each of us had chosen to do despite the glaringly different worlds we experienced as children."

After moving to New York City, where Marty lived with her parents in a small ground-floor rear apartment in a brownstone in Greenwich Village, she attended Bank Street School, and later, City and Country School. From there, she went to high school at Putney, so that her entire school experience until college was defined by the progressive rather than the traditional approach.

I will always be grateful that Marty chose to attend Putney, and that we found each other there. By junior year, we were a couple, and her influence on me exceeded all others, as it would for the rest of my life. Without having met her, I doubt that I would have found my way to who I became.

My freshman year at college, while Marty was a senior at Putney, was the only year we have ever been separated. Poor college boards and an average academic record at Putney kept me from going to Princeton or Yale, but I was accepted at Oberlin and Brown. I chose Brown, in Providence, Rhode Island, because I wanted to put my newly acquired liberalism to the test in a more traditional setting. I joined a fraternity where my "brothers" were similar to the students I had known at Chestnut Hill Academy, but with my Putney training I aligned myself with the activist wing of campus life, joining the Students for Democratic Action and the civil rights committee of the Brown Christian Association. I tutored children in a segregated black neighborhood in North Providence, and worked in an orphanage for disturbed children. I rooted for Adlai Stevenson, booed Joe McCarthy, and applauded the *Brown v. Board of Education* decision in 1954.

Marty came to Brown my sophomore year, having been turned down by Radcliffe, Smith, and Wellesley. Warren Leonard, Putney's administrator in charge of college admissions, can attest that our both going to Brown was not a plot. Choosing separate majors, Marty's in music and mine in English, we both flourished academically, and our high-school romance led to our marriage in June 1956. A year later, after Marty's graduation, we moved from Providence to New York City, where we have lived ever since.

By my senior year at Brown, I knew that I wanted to be a teacher or a minister. The latter was appealing because I saw myself following in my father's footsteps, but I didn't have the religious conviction. The theology of the Episcopal Church in which I had grown up, while intellectually capturing, had little spiritual meaning to me. So I chose teaching.

My godfather, Jack Crocker, offered me a job at Groton, but Marty and I had no interest in returning to boarding-school life, and despite my affection for Uncle Jack, I could not muster the desire to work in a school that I had declined to attend eight years earlier.

In New York, my father introduced me to Wilson Parkhill, headmaster of Collegiate School, and my friend from Putney, Peter Buttenwieser, introduced me to Charlotte Durham, head of Dalton School, where Peter was teaching eighth-grade history. I was offered jobs in both schools. Collegiate's salary was $2,900; Dalton's was $3,000. Instinctively, Dalton, with its more progressive approach, was my preference, and the extra hundred dollars was a lure. I opted for Dalton and became a lifelong devotee of progressive education.

Over the years, I've often mulled over the differences between progressive and traditional education. Perhaps the most obvious difference is that progressive schools adopt a hands-on approach in which children learn by doing, whereas in traditional settings, teachers tend to lecture from the front of the classroom, with children learning more by memorization and rote. But this pedagogical difference is less significant than the political idea behind progressive education which is prophetic in nature—meaning it seeks to shake things up, to change the world. Traditional education, on the other hand, maintains the status quo. It is no surprise that traditional schools were originally single-sex, while the first progressive schools were coeducational. Of course, many traditional schools have since embraced coeducation and some other aspects of the progressive model as well. Still, their underlying goal remains the same: to prepare students to navigate traditional routes to power.

Given Marty's and my politics and our shared experience at the Putney School, it is no surprise that when we founded Manhattan Country School, New York City's first fully integrated private school, in 1966, we would adopt the progressive model of education, seeking nothing less than to change the world.

SEVEN EAST NINETY-SIXTH Street, the New York City landmark building that would become the home of Manhattan Country School, is uniquely located. East Ninety-sixth Street traverses a massive geological rift which occurred millions of years ago in the Precambrian Era. The bedrock of the Manhattan Ridge, which forms the western and central lengths of the island, contains a fault line commencing midway along 125th Street and extending diagonally across the island to the East River at Ninety-sixth Street. The fissure created along this fault is so deep that when the city built the aqueduct leading into Manhattan, it was necessary to dig 350 feet below sea level to reach solid ground. I'm told there is an underground river that still runs today, beginning at the Harlem Meer and flowing down to and across Ninety-sixth Street. Apparently, from the beginning of recorded time, the street on which we chose to situate our school has been a principal dividing line in the geological makeup of Manhattan.

The street became a conspicuous dividing line in sociological terms as well. To the north is El Barrio, or East Harlem; to the south is Yorkville, or the Upper East Side—two neighborhoods, adjacent but unalike in every way. In 1990, the median family income of East Harlem was twenty thousand dollars a year. It would have been lower were it not for the fact that the gold coast of the East Side extends north of Ninety-sixth Street along Fifth Avenue. Farther north, in sections of Harlem, family income levels were closer to six thousand dollars a year, the lowest in the United States, according to Susannah Lessard's 1997 *New Yorker* article, "The Split: An Intersection Where Opposite Worlds Collide." The intersection described by Susannah Lessard might be better understood as one where worlds fail to touch. In 1966, and still today, East Ninety-sixth Street was Manhattan's Berlin Wall.

Heading south from Ninety-sixth Street, one enters Yorkville, with a median family income of $120,000 a year. Below Seventy-second Street, apartment dwellers have average annual incomes of three-quarters of a million dollars, making the East Side one of the most affluent urban residential areas in the country. Garden malls, planted annually with spring tulips and summer begonias and decorated with lighted Christmas trees each December, run the length of Park Avenue, all the way to Grand Central Station. Once called Fourth Avenue, Park Avenue originated as we know it today when the New York Central Railroad replaced steam engines with electric ones and enclosed the tracks below ground. The garden malls were then built, and the avenue was closed to commercial traffic. In creating this stylish boulevard, the East Side asserted its territoriality, and in the same instance, ignored its northern neighbor, East Harlem. In what is perhaps a small gesture of hospitality, each year the Park Commission sets out one Christmas tree in the narrow wedge of park extending above Ninety-sixth street. Otherwise, this small appendage is unattended.

Ninety-sixth Street, from Central Park to the East River, is as visible a color line as would exist in any segregated city. This was not so in earlier periods of immigration when East Harlem was heavily populated by Italian and Jewish working-class people. By the eighteenth century, Harlem had become an elite region for summer homes, among them the Alexander Hamilton country house and the Morris Jumel Mansion, the latter built in 1765. In 1879, when the city constructed an elevated train line along Eighth Avenue, Harlem was rapidly developed by New York's upper class. Marty's ancestor, John Dwight, along with other fashionable New Yorkers, designed and built homes around Mount Morris Park just south of 125th Street. From there, he and others took a ferry to Wall Street.

Today, Dwight's house is occupied by the Commandment Keepers Ethiopian Hebrew Congregation. After 1904, when the Eighth Avenue subway line was extended to 145th Street, blacks began moving to Harlem from lower Manhattan, where real-estate prices had escalated. During the same period, the East Side north of Ninety-sixth Street, known thereafter as El Barrio, became a predominantly Hispanic neighborhood.

Anyone who has ridden the Lexington Avenue subway north from downtown in recent decades knows that, come Ninety-sixth Street, all the white people get out. Once, going home from an evening meeting downtown, I boarded the uptown subway. Reaching Ninety-sixth Street, the train barreled northward without stopping, as it did again at 103rd Street, my alternate stop. I had inadvertently taken the express train. I was able to get off at 125th Street, and as I walked the deserted platform to reach the downtown tracks, an elderly black man appeared before me. He kindly greeted me, saying, "Dr. Livingston, I presume?"

We have lived in four different places since we first came to New York. Our three children, Katharine, Stephen, and Mary, were forced to share a bedroom, not always peacefully, until Katharine, our eldest, was ten. Soon after starting MCS, we were able to purchase a home on 101st Street, east of Park Avenue in East Harlem. Though extensive renovations were needed, finally we had a home with ample space, a fireplace, and a workshop in the basement. More than that, we had cut a small passage through the city's equivalent of the Berlin Wall.

Our lives on 101st Street conformed to our principles. A white parent at MCS once argued with another about her assessment of Marty's and my politics. "How do you know what their politics are?" she was asked. "By the way they live," she answered.

I wish that we had found our home on 101st Street five or so years earlier, for the sake of the children who relished their own turf and took to the street so eagerly. The best thing is that we moved there at all, that we made a home for ourselves that was not solely defined by our likeness to others. A goal of ours for children at MCS is that they learn to live in different worlds, not only racially and culturally but financially as well. Once we moved to 101st Street, this happened naturally for our own three children. At MCS they qualified for half scholarships, on 101st Street we were probably the wealthiest family on the block, and when they attended high school at Riverdale Country School, they were among the poorest. My children's experience confirmed my belief that except for the extremities of class, to consider oneself rich or poor is a relative matter, and one should be able to move comfortably within different worlds regardless of economic circumstance.

Marty and Gus Trowbridge in the school's office,
circa 1966.

CHAPTER 3

Starting From Scratch

I HAD ALWAYS believed that every actor yearned to be a director and that a doctor's highest aspiration was to run a hospital. I'm told I was mistaken, but for me, after teaching for eight years, I wanted to be the head of a school. The precocious nature of my desire was fed by two influences: a growing disenchantment with Dalton, and my consuming awareness of the civil rights movement and the resulting social upheaval of American life.

Dalton was founded by a revolutionary educator, Helen Parkhurst. During the tenure of her successor, Charlotte Durham, Dalton remained wedded to Parkhurst's progressive principles, and the school became immensely popular as New York's best liberal educational alternative. The names of parents of children on my class lists included Alistair Cooke, Mark Rothko, Norman Podhoretz, Jacob Javits, Marietta Tree, Kermit Bloomgarten, James Wechsler, Max Lerner, Maria Riva, Louis Calhern, and Jacques Barzun. There were also Harrimans and Rosenwalds, Altschuls and Sterns, and Lehmans and Loebs.

When Mrs. Durham, as I called her, retired, there followed a fallow period when the school was headed by Jack Kittell, a Californian who, though pleasant personally, was truly a fish out of water. The school waffled. The faculty demeaned its leader as tasteless and not versed in progressive pedagogy; the old-guard liberals on the board, many of whom had served past their time, were replaced by a new and ambitious breed whose motives were to make Dalton the talk of the town. Kittell left amiably without carnage, and then began a pitched battle to redefine Dalton's persona.

At that time, I was a faculty representative to the board and one of five members on the faculty selection committee to appoint the new head of Dalton. Among the candidates was David Mallery, a well-regarded liberal voice among progressive educators in the National Association of Independent Schools. Mallery visited the school and won favor among its faculty. But he was not invited for a second interview, reportedly because the powers that be found his red sports jacket garish. Their candidate of choice was Donald Barr. The faculty selection committee met with Barr, and finding his manner unlikable, unanimously voted against him. Two hours later, the trustees appointed Barr the head of Dalton. So much for faculty representation!

Barr's first speech to the faculty the following fall confirmed our misgivings. He recalled being in kindergarten, describing himself as one who always sat outside the sandbox looking in upon his classmates, never joining them. He said, "Ever since, I have lived in my head." He sounded unreasonably smug about it.

The combination of a board of trustees that was apparently selling out on Dalton's progressive past, and a new head whom many of us disliked, led to faculty revolt and at least a dozen resignations in the spring of 1965. For a number of years after we started MCS, the school was regarded as an insurrectionist offspring of Dalton. This characterization might have been sufficient were it not for the compelling force of the civil rights movement, which gave MCS a deeper and more proactive purpose.

MCS students frequently ask me if Martin Luther King Jr. was a friend of mine, if I had been one of the freedom marchers, if I was ever put in jail. My answer is none of the above. This surprises them, perhaps disappoints them, as it does me, until I remind myself that with three children under six I didn't feel at liberty to be an activist. Yet some revolutionary spirit in me stirred as we experienced the movement vicariously. The world in which I lived was turned inside out. My life with my family and my students at Dalton was subsumed by the daily events we followed in the news, most especially on television, which historians would later recognize as the most powerful force in aiding the success of the civil rights movement. It was Walter Cronkite, almost as much as Martin Luther King Jr. himself, who aroused the conscience of America. But the defining vision of the school that I wanted to run was Dr. King's.

In founding MCS, my goal was to dismantle the exclusivity of the white establishment and to create a truly integrated school, one that celebrated rather than shied away from people's differences. Indeed, the unifying concept of the school would be to embrace those differences. Our school would be racially integrated and economically diverse. And, drawing upon Marty's experience at City and Country School and our joint one at Putney School, we wanted to have a farm, a place where, regardless of background, all children would begin on an equal footing.

While Marty and I talked about the prospect of starting our own school, my initial approach was to see if I could direct an existing school, where I would work from within to accomplish my objectives. I had applied to be head of Town School, and in the winter of 1963-64, I was offered the job. I accepted, boldly stating my intention to turn the school into a microcosm of the American Dream. Shortly thereafter, the outgoing headmistress, Margaret Crane, changed her mind, no doubt cold-footed at the thought of my declared aims for "her" school, perhaps encouraged by a faction of trustees who shared her reluctance in voting for me. Whatever the cause, I was asked to withdraw, and I politely did so without even considering the inequity of the matter.

Marty was relieved. She had always preferred the idea of starting our own school. I decided to stay on at Dalton another year to give us time to make a plan. But, it now being known among private schools that I might be an available candidate for head of school, Emerson School sought me out, as did the Walden School. The latter was a particularly tempting option to me, given Walden's distinction as a progressive school and its alignment with the civil rights movement. The prior summer, Andrew Goodman, who had been a student at Walden, had been one of the three young men killed in a voter-registration drive in Philadelphia, Mississippi.

I was torn between the awesome challenge of going our own way and the safer and more financially secure route. During the time I was wrestling with whether to accept the Walden job, I took my father for a drive to the Jamaica Bay Wildlife Refuge. He had initially been opposed to Marty and my starting fresh, going so far as to promise, "If you do it, I won't give you a nickel." Unfazed, I had retorted, "That's fine. I don't want a nickel; I want a million dollars."

Now, as we headed out to the wildlife sanctuary, I asked my father, "When does the devil stop tempting you?" Being a minister, my father answered thoughtfully, "When you give in; that's when he stops." Moments later, he said, "Why did you ask me that?" I told him about my lunch meeting earlier that week with three trustees of Walden. "Don't listen to them," he declared. "Don't take a cushy $22,000-a-year job." His change of heart clinched it for me. In one of those priceless moments between father and son, we enjoyed the spring migration of ducks, and I treasured the pleasure of his company.

IN RETROSPECT, OUR timing was perfect. A decade earlier, in spite of the Supreme Court's mandate for integration handed down in the *Brown v. Board of Education* decision, a school like MCS could not have garnered sufficient support from affluent whites. And as few as six years later, during the Nixon administration, which openly reneged on integration, the establishment was running scared. But in 1965, the national stage was set to usher in our embodiment of the American Dream.

I was thirty-one, far too young in my father's judgment to be taking on such a challenge, but I was in step with the youthful spirit of the decade, which cried out for change. John F. Kennedy had become our nation's youngest president, and Martin Luther King Jr. was only twenty-five years old when he took on the Montgomery Bus Boycott and formed the Southern Christian Leadership Council. Age didn't seem a factor in joining the new frontier, nor did class. Indeed, Mrs. Malcolm Peabody, mother of the governor of Massachusetts, joined freedom fighters in St. Augustine, Florida, in 1964, where she was sent to jail.

The same month that I left my job at Dalton, President Lyndon Johnson spoke at Howard University's graduation. More than any other public address, Johnson's message that afternoon clearly outlined the course that we had set for ourselves, and coming from a Southerner it resounded even more urgently. Extending the mission of the civil rights movement beyond legislation and into the personal care of all Americans, Johnson proclaimed that the country's "next and more profound goal [was] not just legal equity but human equity, not just equality as a right or theory, but equality as a fact and result."

Although resolved to start a new kind of school and strengthened by Marty's shared determination, we faced a steep learning curve. I had never taken a course in education; I had no administrative experience, no knowledge of finances, and knew nothing about fund-raising. I had a small sum of capital, perhaps enough to provide for our personal needs for a year or two but nothing sufficient to underwrite the costs of the school's preoperational year.

We also had few acquaintances or friends of color. My volunteer work for the Union Settlement House's college-readiness program and my being on the board of Franklin Plaza Nursery School had introduced me to the people of East Harlem, but we were a long way from having the contacts we needed to promote an integrated school among people of that area. Most pressing was our need to find at least two people of color who would serve as charter trustees—not titular representatives, but people who believed deeply in the school's mission and with whom we would have a lasting association.

Our one advantage was having friends and colleagues at Dalton who were either ready to join us when we opened the school or prepared to help us in other roles, as consultants or trustees. Ruth Cooke, Dalton's admissions director, signed on from the beginning and became my associate director. Martha Norris, a kindergarten teacher from Dalton, who was black, was prepared to join our staff when we were ready, and Marge Trimble, also black, agreed to teach our second grade the following year. Other Dalton supporters included Estelle Meadoff, our physical-education teacher; Sally Kallem, who became our lower-school director; Louise Carpenter, who taught middle-school science; and Jim Perkins, our first farm director.

We were also fortunate in knowing where we would start our farm program. Jim Perkins had property in Roxbury, New York, several hundred acres on Plattekill Mountain, and he had offered to give the school some of his land where we could build, using his own house for farm trips in the meantime. Jim's property met the two criteria we had set for the farm's location—that it be in New York State and that it be no farther than three hours from the city. The countryside of Roxbury reminded Marty and me of the area around Putney School where we had first met: dirt roads, rolling hills, dairy farms, pastures with stone walls, maple woods, and clear, cold streams. The area was still mostly rural farmland interspersed with a few second homes owned by city folk. Like our choice of Ninety-sixth Street for the school, Roxbury seemed a perfect location for our farm program.

We had identified the school building and the farm, and we had several teachers waiting in the wings. But there was still the need to find people, especially people of color, who would serve as trustees and sponsors of our school. We needed individuals who were well-connected socially or professionally, who would be willing to function as honorary advisors, introducing us to donors, and otherwise lending distinction to our efforts.

In the early spring of 1965, after the pivotal birding trip with my father, Marty and I began weekly planning meetings with our Dalton associates to discuss the school's educational programs and to identify sources of support. In July, we dispersed for the summer. Armed with copies of the Foundation Directory (which a family friend had purloined from the Metropolitan Opera Development Office), my mother's Social Register, and lists of potential donors gleaned from alumni directories from Putney, Dalton, and North Country School, Marty and I left for my parents' house in Maine to do our homework.

Marty poured over the Foundation Directory, identifying those organizations with an expressed interest in education and race relations. My chief assignment was to write the school's prospectus. My first draft, which ran twenty-four pages, was heavily influenced by contemporary critics of education such as John Holt and proponents of nongraded schooling. In the jargon of the day, it dwelt also on the needs of the "disadvantaged" and argued that the inclusion of "culturally deprived" students would not lower the school's standards. Finally, it declared my belief in progressive education and my preference for the methodologies of Putney and Dalton.

As an explication of who I was and where I was coming from, it served its purpose for the relatively small and familiar group to which it was sent. By November, I had condensed my lengthy prospectus to a few pages called, "First Principles," which thereafter, together with periodic progress reports, we used to promote the school.

To underwrite our projected costs of $15,000 for 1965-66, we enlisted pledges of $5,000 each from three of our Dalton friends: Peter Buttenwieser, Margie Lang, whose children I had taught; and Trudi Pratt, a former Dalton administrator and trustee. It was agreed that their pledges would be paid when we became a not-for-profit organization. I would maintain my teacher's salary of $7,000, Sally Kallem would be paid only for the interviews of applicants that she conducted, and Marty and Ruth Cooke would begin as volunteers—leaving the balance of our budget for office and promotional expenses.

In September, for $85 a month, we rented a basement apartment at 1165 Park Avenue, only a few blocks from Dalton, which our children Katharine and Stephen attended. The apartment, formerly janitor's quarters with access through the service entrance, had the singular attraction of providing us with an address that prospective donors would find reassuring.

But we had yet to come up with a name for our school. "Name this child," my father had solemnly said to us at each of our children's baptisms. We had mastered this parental duty three times, but we had never named an institution. Most schools are called by denotative names, signifying their locations or their principal benefactors. We wanted ours to be connotative, suggesting the school's goal of embracing differences. City and Country School would have been ideal, but it was already taken, so we searched for alternatives. One suggestion was Gus's Schoolhouse, which I vetoed. Another suggestion, the Manhattan Farm School, sounded like a reform school. The Bridge School almost made it, but I didn't like its reference to my last name. When I suggested the Uptown Community School, one of our sponsors chided me, saying, "Ninety-sixth Street uptown? No, Gus, Ninety-sixth Street is the beginning of downtown."

Our final choice, Manhattan Country School, satisfied us all. Its initials flowed naturally, and its apparently contradictory name conveyed the goal of bringing together people of different backgrounds, which was exactly what we were about to do.

A month after the 1968 assassination of Martin Luther King Jr.,
fourth and fifth graders planted five hundred trees
at the MCS farm in his honor.

Chapter 4

Beyond the "Symbolic Negro"

WE WANTED TO be ready to announce our plans in the fall of 1965. To do this, we needed to spell out our vision for MCS, the makeup of the school, and its methodology. The purpose and educational philosophy had already been determined, but many questions remained unanswered. Among them: How were we to define integration? How much of a scholarship program would we need to support the school's goal of economic diversity? And what would be the farm's curriculum?

We tackled the issue of integration first, knowing that our central purpose required a clarity of definition for which there was as yet no precedent. Since the influx of the first European immigrants, America has always been confused about diversity. We take pride in our heterogeneity, yet we speak of the country as a melting pot. We claim to value our differences, yet we practice assimilation. Our confusion is even reflected in our nation's motto, *E Pluribus Unum* (From Many, One), and today the debate over the meaning of multiculturalism still rages, resting largely on whether the *Unum* overrides the *Pluribus* or the reverse. In creating a racially integrated school, the challenge that faced us was how to achieve unity without forcing the assimilation of any racial group.

Historically, private schools, notably the religious schools, have always attracted people with common bonds. Nonsectarian independent boarding and day schools in the Northeast were also exclusionary, but more for elitist reasons. Traditionally all-white, the more established schools enrolled few, if any, Jewish students until the 1940s. Negro students were not admitted until a decade later, and those who attended were from old-line, middle- and upper-class families.

In 1965, among all but three of New York City's forty-odd private schools, black students constituted 1 to 2 percent. In most of these schools, the administrations had no statistics available concerning minority enrollment. Interestingly, the three exceptions were among the most liberal, progressive schools in the city: Elisabeth Irwin with 9.7 percent students of color, New Lincoln School with 14.2 percent; and Downtown Community School with 20 percent.

I attended a conference at Downtown Community School in 1963. It was chaired by the school's principal, Norman Studer, and the keynote speaker was Dr. Robert Coles, the respected Harvard child psychiatrist. Coles spoke forcefully about the need for Northern private schools to join the cause of integration. "I see rage up here," Coles said, "a reaction of shock on the part of white people to the cruelty perpetuated on Negroes in the South. But I haven't seen white people at our key northern universities and prep schools actually subjecting themselves to scrutiny on matters that are at the center of this whole moral crisis . . . . Actually there's no better way for independent schools to justify themselves than to take leadership like this."

The audience, consisting primarily of New York City private-school teachers, welcomed Coles's call to action, and four teachers from an all-white girls' school even shared their fruitless attempts to persuade their administration to admit Negroes. Leading the discussion period following Coles's speech, Studer listened sympathetically. The teachers pleaded for advice, and Studer gave it to them bluntly: "Leave," he said. "The situation you describe is hopeless." His honesty was a breath of fresh air. Coming from the head of an independent school, and on the heels of Coles's persuasive delivery, it empowered many of us in the room to consider our roles anew and to recommit ourselves to the ideals of the civil rights movement.

In the fall of 1965, Marty and I visited Robert Coles in his office at Harvard and enlisted his help in starting MCS. He agreed to be a sponsor, sending us the following unsolicited letter in the spring of 1966, five months before MCS opened its doors:

"I think the proposed Manhattan Country School will have an impact on education far beyond the scope of the specific situation at the school. I say this because it is quite clear that truly integrated education, public or private, in Northern cities is still something of a rarity. Particularly does this hold with the kind of first-rate private education that I know the Manhattan Country School aims to offer. We know very little about how Negro and white children from different classes, as well as obviously different racial backgrounds, will get along. Most education is both class and race bound and also tied down to the specific limitations of the public school system. In essence what you are trying to do is transcend a number of confinements, including even the rural-urban dichotomy. It seems to me that in my experience in both the North and the South, and by the way both rural and urban situations, that your school in many ways is totally unique, and therefore offers an incredible richness of future information for all of us who are interested in children and their education. Frankly, if I weren't tied up with other things I wouldn't mind sitting in and watching what goes on there from the very beginning because I suspect that there is a lot that will be important to anyone who is concerned with what is going on in the country today."

Although Robert Coles did not actually visit the school until 1997, when he came to receive an award for his children's book, *The Story of Ruby Bridges*, he was a powerful advocate through the years, making overtures to many of our critical funding sources.

On our same trip to Boston to meet Robert Coles, we had also made an appointment to see Katharine Taylor, another outspoken proponent of racial integration in independent schools. As director of Shady Hill School in Cambridge, Massachusetts, KT, as she was known, was an eminent progressive-school educator. As a long-time trustee of the New World Foundation, which played a leading role in supporting the civil rights movement, she was highly regarded among many of the foundations we would be approaching.

Shady Hill was not known to be in the forefront of school integration, but Katharine Taylor, like her mentor, Eleanor Roosevelt, was wedded to social change. Defining the benefits of integration, she wrote: "If children from different backgrounds learn to live together, work together, play together, classmates are realized as persons, co-citizens, not stereotypes. Thus the danger of their growing up into adults who succumb to prejudicial generalizations about one another or another group in society is averted, and the will to understand and to take one's part in social issues is strengthened."

What particularly drew me to Katharine Taylor was her sense of the urgency for change. "The times have more than caught up with us," she had said. "We as citizens need to exert strong new efforts to make up for the neglect and omissions of the past. In this effort, I believe that the independent schools can become a major influence." KT kindly embraced our plans for MCS, coming to see us often on her regular trips to New York, teaching us how to run a school, and offering constant encouragement. She also introduced us to Frank Jennings, her cotrustee at New World, through whom MCS landed its first major gift from the Kettering Foundation.

My experience with Norman Studer and Katharine Taylor aside, whenever I spoke with the heads of private schools about their Negro and Puerto Rican enrollment, they typically stated that they did not keep count. "We accept any qualified applicant, regardless of race, creed, or color," they would say. How familiar that expression became to me! Given my liberal upbringing, which taught me to shun intolerance, I initially took comfort in hearing this answer. I quickly realized, however, that it failed to explain the overwhelming absence of minority students unless, of course, the loaded modifier was the word "qualified." Did the schools whose heads said their admissions policies were nondiscriminatory actually have no applicants of color? Or did they have no *qualified* ones? If so, I found this very hard to believe in a city of millions of minority children and ample referral sources. The problem obviously rested elsewhere. Either these schools were quietly opposed to integration or, to give them credit, they were doing nothing to attract or recruit minorities, naively presuming that to say race didn't matter was sufficient to open the doors to integration.

The Francis Parker School in Chicago, Illinois, was perhaps the only private school in the country committed to racial integration well before *Brown v. Board of Education*. Founded in 1901 by Colonel Francis Parker, who called his school "an embryonic democracy," FPS admitted its first Negro students in 1944 and adopted the most progressive and successful admissions policy used by any private school prior to MCS. According to Cleveland A. Thomas, the school's principal, two factors governed their admission of Negroes from the start: 1) that no Negro child would be admitted to a grade in which he would be the sole representative of his race; and 2) that no Negro child would be admitted to the school above fifth grade, where social groups tend to be established. "The school was unwilling to expose a Negro child simultaneously to all the difficulties of adjustment to a new school, to possible exclusion from established cliques, and to the problems of adolescence," said Thomas to explain the school's wise rationale. But despite the school's distinguished reputation, its example was never heeded by others.

While not a pioneer in racial integration, Wooster School in Danbury, Connecticut, accepted its first Negro student in 1955, and by 1962, its enrollment of blacks had reached 5.5 percent, a percentage which the school's headmaster, John D. Verdery, claimed to be higher than that of any other independent school in the country at that time. Verdery's no-nonsense views on integration were instrumental in developing my own thinking, particularly his recognition that numbers counted. "I have come to believe that what I call the 'symbolic Negro' is a kind of smoke screen behind which old prejudices can still hide," he explained. "I speak neither from cynicism nor self-righteousness. It is just a devilish convenience when someone says, 'Do you have any Negro students?' to be able to answer, 'Certainly, there goes one of them now. I don't know where the other one is, but he's around here somewhere.' A single Negro student, I think, represents a feeble gesture. The presence of only two is still open to suspicion. If not just one or two, then how many?"

In his article published by the National Association of Independent Schools, entitled "Finding Qualified Negro Applicants," Verdery traces Wooster's gradual increase in its black enrollment and acknowledges his own trepidations about how many was too many. His honesty and insight posed questions to the heads of independent schools that had simply never been raised before from within the establishment. "In institutions where the color line has been broken," he warned his colleagues, "much more thought and searching of conscience must be given to the question of numbers. Morally, the symbolic Negro, except as a first step, is a dishonest gesture. The question of whether or not there should be a Negro quota is one which no private educational institution has yet to face. No school can seriously defend the proposition that it had a quota of two. If this is their claim, then they might better have a quota of zero."

Among my contemporaries in the private-school scene in New York City, Andrew McLaren was the most outspoken integrationist. I first met Andrew in 1966 when he was teaching at St. Bernard's School, two blocks north of MCS. To scrape up a little income, we rented three apartments on the fourth and fifth floors of MCS. The rent was cheap, as we had made no improvements to the rooms and provided no heating on weekends, although each apartment had a working fireplace. Andrew took the fourth-floor flat; being from the United Kingdom, he didn't mind the cold.

St. Bernard's was an Etonian all-boys private school with a dress code nearly identical to mine at Chestnut Hill Academy: blue blazers and a blue cap, gray flannel shorts, knee socks, and Buster Brown shoes. There were no students of color, of course, and apparently, very few boys who were not blond. The school's headmaster, Dr. R. I. Wilfred Westgate, called me only weeks after we opened MCS and invited me to lunch. As we entered the dining hall, the boys stood in silence at their tables. They remained so until Westgate finished grace and introduced me properly to those assembled. He couldn't have been more friendly and welcoming. "Like a tugboat captain being dined by the admiralty," is how I characterized the experience to Marty afterward.

Westgate was accustomed to conducting only one faculty meeting a year, the day before school opened in September. The day after Martin Luther King Jr. was assassinated, he called a special gathering of his faculty. After speaking of his sorrow, he announced that given the tragic turn in America's racial problems, it was time to seek a new level of relationship with Negroes and to discard the old solution of their removal to Africa. This startling revelation of the headmaster's white supremacist attitudes did not surprise Andrew, who was part of a group at St. Bernard's that had unsuccessfully pushed for the admission of students of color. "The school," Andrew said, "accurately stated that it treated all applicants alike. That was easy to do. The applicants were all alike."

Westgate believed there was a purpose to be served by not pursuing racial integration at St. Bernard's. The week before his solemn address following Dr. King's death, the *Wall Street Journal* had published an inflammatory article subtitled "Private School's Aid to Poor Negroes Burdens Middle Class." The article reported on Collegiate School's "slum program," launched four years earlier in order to enroll students from "the city's dismal Negro slums." Quoted in the article, Westgate explained St. Bernard's lack of interest in Collegiate-type efforts, saying, "A good school should be the extension of the boy's home. The effects of placing a child in a totally new atmosphere for eight hours a day and then returning him to his own environment can be shattering."

When I was invited to speak about racial integration at Collegiate School in 1969, I shared my own negative reactions to the *Wall Street Journal* article, but expressed agreement with Westgate that no integration was better than integration based on patronage alone. Schools which enroll minority students from inner-city communities ought not to consider their actions as charitable. "If enrolling Negroes in Collegiate has any charitable purpose at all," I told them, "it is to benefit you, not to upgrade blacks."

Twenty years later, Andrew McLaren had become principal of New York's most integrated private high school, Elisabeth Irwin, and I was the director of MCS, the city's most integrated private elementary school. Together, we were invited to cochair a conference entitled "Black and Latino Students in Independent Schools: How Are They Faring?" at the Cathedral of St. John the Divine. In attendance were private-school educators, administrators, and parents. Andrew was the keynote speaker and I gave the opening remarks. In commenting on the mission statement for the conference, I expressed support for its acknowledgment of the problems encountered by black and Latino students in our schools, and of racial biases within the private-school sector. I stated my objection, however, to the title of the conference, saying, "My uneasiness is with any statement that poses a 'we-they' relationship."

Andrew's speech was an impassioned and astute critique of the nature of prejudice and its accompanying lines of defense among whites who dominated the private-school sector. "The greatest enemy of any valid reform," he observed, "is not malice, but the placid ability of decent people not to think or not to feel, or both. Denial, repression, suppression—call it what you will—when you're unconscious of something, you cannot blame yourself for it; so ignorance, if not bliss, is at least temporary comfort." Recounting his own upbringing, Andrew continued, "I imbibed as a child what I was given to drink—undiluted prejudice. It is a comforting drink, soothing, reassuring—and the most frightening thing in the world is to know how easily it goes down."

To Andrew, the chief reason diversity was lacking in the private schools was neither demographics nor dollars, but instead a desire "to have diversity reside at the level of intention rather than action." As he explained it, "St. Augustine prayed that most human of all prayers: 'God give me chastity, but not yet.' Certainly, with regard to diversity, there are trustees and parents of some of our schools who want diversity, but not so much of it that this 'won't be our kind of place anymore.' Give us diversity, but gradually."

Andrew's final advice to our group of private-school educators struck the moral funny bone of his predominantly white audience. "It is said that you're either part of the problem or part of the solution. I would assert that this is not true. It's not true for family differences, institutional issues, or international conflict. What's true—and the easiest thing to forget—is that you cannot be part of the solution unless you know that you're also part of the problem. In that recognition lies hope."

As Andrew pointed out, being "color-blind" is not the virtue I was taught it was. The term is the invention of white people, often coined with best intentions. When school segregation was abolished in 1954 and the races were put on a more equal footing, white people had to begin relating to blacks as their legal equals. Bigots refused to do so. White liberals who were not ready to practice what they preached had only one line of defense. So they clung to the assertion of color-blindness as a protection from having to deal openly with race.

No black person in America can ever be color-blind. Clint Ingram, a teacher at MCS, told me that the only time in his life he was not constantly thinking of his own blackness was when he went to Africa. Blacks in this country live daily in two worlds: their own, where perhaps they can feel at home, and the white world, where they must be on guard at all times.

In his book, *We Can't Teach What We Don't Know*, Gary R. Howard contends that "the declaration of color-blindness assumes that we can erase our racial categories, ignore differences, and thereby achieve an illusory state of sameness or equality." Howard goes on to recount the story of a white teacher who told him that God was color-blind, to which Howard replied, "If God is color-blind, why did she create such a beautiful array of skin tones among the human family?" To prove his point on a more personal level, he asked his black associate, "Jesse, if I tell you I don't see your color, how does that make you feel?" Jesse replied, "You don't see me."

Why is it that liberal-minded white people say, "I have a friend, who happens to be black"? They think that they should not appear conscious of race, that to do so would expose their prejudice. A color line in America has always existed, and there is nothing inherently the matter with it unless color is used to distinguish the superiority of one race over the other. Ironically, white people who espouse color-blindness apparently do not consider their own countenance to be of any color at all. In viewing themselves as colorless and in asserting their blindness to the color of others, they aim to establish equality, but in fact their message to others is that only whiteness matters.

In contrast to other schools opening their doors to black students in the 1960s, MCS was to be an experiment in affirmative action. With the goal of equal relationships among races, we decided that an integrated school would have to enroll students not "regardless of race, creed, or color" but by deliberately seeking out these attributes.

A little more than ten years later, when the Supreme Court in the Bakke case declared that the law was color-blind, the tide of national politics began to turn against our vision. Only two dissenting justices recognized that the decision marked the end of the civil rights movement. Justice Blackmun insisted that "in order to get beyond racism we must first take account of race." And Justice Thurgood Marshall wrote, "We cannot let color-blindness become myopia which masks the reality that many created equal have been treated inferior." Their minority views echoed the founding principles of MCS.

Workshop participants use cube exercises to illustrate degrees of racial integration.

CHAPTER 5

Alone in the Canoe

NATURE'S DISTRIBUTION OF an equal ratio of males to females dictates the numerical equation for coeducation. It establishes the benign quota system that all coed institutions follow. No coeducational school would be content to enroll one gender in gross disproportion to the other. At times, some imbalance may occur, but that doesn't alter the stated goal. In practice, schools and colleges with a shortage of applications of one gender do not revert to substituting one sex for the other. Instead, they give preferential consideration to students of the category for which they require more applicants. Thus, it was common among girls' colleges converting to coeducation to recruit male students in order to guarantee a balanced enrollment.

Similarly, in defining what we meant by racial integration, Marty and I determined that it had to have a numerical base to it. I used the example of coeducation to help me formulate a working definition of integration. Like coeducation, there had to be a quantitative way of measuring the conditions that defined integration.

The formula for integration was not as apparent as it was for coeducation. Racial demographics, national or regional, did not seem to be a useful basis for defining integration. A school reflecting the population of Augusta, Maine, for example, would be 99 percent white; one in Augusta, Georgia, would be its mirror image. In 1965, the nation's racial composition was 10 percent black. This could, perhaps, have been our point of reference, but we believed that mere proportionality would not produce the numbers needed for real integration.

We viewed the linear progression from segregation to integration in terms of the children's perspective, asking ourselves what number of children of a given race in a class of eighteen boys and girls was needed to make a child comfortable. One was unacceptable; one of each sex was no better. Ten percent was not only "tokenism," it was damaging to the self-image of the minority child, and placed upon him or her the intolerable burden of representing the entire Negro race. To white students in an integrated school attempting to counter racist views and nourish attitudes of equality, a token 10 percent black enrollment could do more to reinforce stereotypes than to eliminate them.

We announced our quota of 30 percent students of color in our original prospectus. The decision to do so seemed natural, yet it set us apart from every other private school in New York City, and for all I know, the entire country. Not only were we to be the most racially integrated school, we were also to be the only one that had set a numerical goal for racial representation. In years to come, we would increase our quota to 50 percent students of color, with the goal that the student composition would include no racial majority.

In an article about MCS published in April 1969, first in the *Southern Education Report* and then in the *New York Post*, Bernard Bard acknowledged the radical and experimental nature of MCS, quoting my views about integration in private education. Some, I'm sure, found my voice on the edge of arrogance. In truth, given the monumental need for the white establishment to join in the struggle, I was in a furious state to challenge those who gave only lip service to racial equality. My anger was aggravated by my intimate personal acquaintance with the establishment and its deep resistance to change.

Bard had reported this incident in his article: One "lily white" girls' school had recently asked me for assistance in locating ten black children to be blended into its enrollment of four hundred. Their plan was to place the black children one or two to a grade. I told them, "You can't integrate your school with ten Negroes. You can perhaps integrate your first grade, and can do well by it. But to do it the way you're proposing would place an unbearable burden on the black children, each of whom would be a token piece or a house Negro. It would be a burden on the white children too, forcing them to formulate their racial attitudes on the basis of a single experience. I personally would be more content to have your school remain totally segregated than to be tokenly integrated."

Brash as it was, my response was intended to underscore the unacceptability of racial isolation, which was the norm in private institutions in the 1950s and '60s. Jenny, a white fifth-grade girl at MCS, shared this feeling when she related to her classmates the story of Angela, the only black child in her camp the previous summer. One morning, their counselor told the girls to go to the lakefront and prepare for canoe instruction. The girls put on their life jackets, selected paddles, chose partners, and went to their canoes, followed by the counselor. Jenny looked around and noticed that Angela was sitting alone in a canoe. The counselor joined Angela, and the event passed by unnoticed. But Jenny couldn't stop thinking about it. "Imagine being alone in a canoe," she told her classmates. "I suppose no one meant to hurt Angela's feelings, and of course she got to paddle with John, the counselor, but I couldn't stop thinking about how rejected she must have felt." I'm sure Angela's experience was not her first of this sort. I'm sure also that it pained her deeply, although she apparently showed no visible discomfort.

Being alone in a canoe is an apt metaphor for the experience of black people in white America. For those who have entered white schools to obtain a better education, and for those during the movement who sacrificed themselves to secure the rights of others, theirs has been a valuable and necessary exercise. Too many private schools, however, have unnecessarily repeated this experience for black children in the name of integration. Desegregation requires only one person. But desegregation, no matter how welcoming to the newcomer, does not equal integration, and unless desegregation is sufficiently surpassed, the experience can be more damaging than productive to all involved.

Despite this, many private schools, when they first admitted black students, did not really consider racial integration as their goal. They were more concerned with image, wanting not to appear discriminatory. For these schools, enrolling minority students was seen as a one-way street to their assimilation. This view was shared by a group of white parents in a conference held by the Parents League of New York City in 1972. One presenter, Diane Hockstader, in her paper titled "Integration: On the Road to Reality," observed: "Integration appeared to work better when there were very few black students in a class. In that situation, the blacks were absorbed, didn't separate themselves from the group, didn't actually change the status quo. In other words there are some white parents who are awfully happy to have one or two black children around, provided they don't make waves. Except for some show of external skin color, the black children would be no different from anyone else."

Stephen Davenport, a teacher from Kingswood School in West Hartford, Connecticut, held the opposite view. In his article "Farewell to the Old School Tie," published in 1968 in the *Saturday Review*, he wrote, "When there are only one or two Negroes, there is a tendency for them to feel pressure to become 'white' like the rest of the school. When there are six or seven, there is sometimes a tendency to stick together as the black group. When there is a greater number, there usually is no pressure either to fit in or to relate exclusively with one another. They can play whatever role comes naturally."

Davenport, an early advocate of school integration, had been educated and taught in all-white private schools. He had witnessed the beginnings of integration from within the establishment. A graduate of Pomfret School, he remembers attending an alumni meeting in 1956 at which the headmaster, speaking of the school's future, mentioned the need to consider accepting Negroes. "As soon as he was finished," Davenport recalls, "one alumnus made clear that he did not like the idea of his old school 'opening the gates.' The crisis came when this man asked for a show of hands to determine the number who favored the proposal. Somehow this incredibly gauche idea was accepted and the count was made. The tension was awesome. The faces of the trustees, sitting like patriarchs in their blue suits around the head table, were of stone. The vote turned out to be a draw."

Schools which chose to "open the gates" under such circumstances did little to help their entering minority students. In an effort to avoid any disturbance, they focused principally on the readiness of white students to tolerate minority presence, ignoring the needs and sensibilities of the newcomers. Davenport tells a chilling tale: "In the beginning, Jay Milnor, Pomfret's headmaster, used to send out a questionnaire to incoming students and families, asking if they would object to their child rooming with a Negro. One evening at Pomfret, a Negro boy and his white roommate got into an argument which developed into a pretty hostile thing. In the heat of the moment, the white boy blurted out, 'You know, I didn't have to room with you!' There was a tremendous moment of silence in which it is safe to guess that anger was replaced by a kind of grief, certainly regret. And then the Negro boy stated with amazement, 'They didn't ask me.'"

The struggle to achieve authentic racial integration in private schools continues to this day and will last until schools recognize the radical extent of the change they must be willing to undertake. In 1988, when Shady Hill School in Cambridge, Massachusetts, reached its goal of enrolling 20 percent students of color, its director, Bruce Shaw, spoke directly to this point. "The question any school asks when wishing to change is how to make the transition toward inclusiveness while maintaining the traditions that have defined its culture and shaped its purposes. The answer is that it is impossible. To be successful, an institution must forge a new identity."

TO DEMONSTRATE MY theory of the relationship of numbers to the attainment of integration, I developed a series of exercises that I still use in teacher-training workshops at MCS and other schools. I have found that the response to these exercises follows a distinct pattern depending on race and gender.

I use a math material called Unifix cubes, which are three-quarter-inch attachable plastic cubes of bright solid colors. With a group of ten people, I offer a bin of over a hundred cubes, including a majority that are black and white, red and blue. As an introductory exercise, individual participants are asked to select ten cubes, and attributing a racial characteristic to each cube, arrange them so that they represent a grouping typical of their childhood school or neighborhood. This is task number 1. Participants then briefly tell one another about the groupings they have composed. These configurations generally reflect a background of racial separation. Sometimes, a black participant will construct a group of nine white cubes with one black one, saying, "That's me when I was in school."

Following this, there are six more tasks that are done in small groups of three or four people. Each group is required to arrive at a common decision and then to report to the other participants how their solution was reached. The tasks, done in incremental steps, are presented as follows:

Task number 2: Participants are asked to place fourteen white cubes in two equal groups. For the purpose of this exercise, white and black cubes represent white and black children in school.

Step 1: Participants are then asked to add one black cube to either group. This step poses no options.

Step 2: Participants add another black cube to either group. If desired, they may rearrange the cubes at any time during the exercise, but groups must be kept of equal size, within one number. This step can be most problematic. To add this cube to the all-white group is the typical choice of most white participants. Their response to the alternative—creating one all-white group and one with two black children—is usually, "That looks bad. It looks like we're segregating the black children." In contrast, a black participant will most often opt for this alternative, arguing in favor of having the two black children together.

Step 3: Participants are instructed to add a third black cube to either group. Now the debate over step 2 escalates. Some remain in favor of avoiding having a single black child in a group. Others become increasingly uncomfortable seeing one group remain unintegrated.

Step 4: Participants add a fourth black cube to either group. Generally, this relieves the pressure and most participants welcome creating two groups equally constituted of seven white and two black children.

Steps 5, 6, and 7 are designed to retrace the exercise's central problem. Participants are asked to rearrange the eighteen cubes into groups of six each (step 5), then to remove one black cube (step 6), and finally to remove another black cube (step 7). If the group has arrived at its earlier choices without disagreement, these steps move uneventfully. Otherwise, the debate resumes. On occasion, some participants, usually the white ones, will change their minds. When this exercise is conducted with all-white participants, generally one or more will assume the perspective of the isolated black children.

A 1979 article in the *New York Times* partially bears out the findings of this exercise. In a race-relations poll conducted in Detroit, 95 percent of black participants said they would prefer not to live in an all-white neighborhood. The poll asked whites if they would live in a neighborhood that was majority black and 84 percent answered no.

In task number 3, participants are given blue and red cubes, representing boys and girls, with instructions to follow the identical steps of task number 2, first using fourteen red cubes and adding blue cubes as in the prior exercise, then using fourteen blue cubes, adding in red cubes in the same sequence. When the core problem of isolation recurs along gender lines, the same debates arise around steps 2 and 3, although the gender-based responses vary in the degree of feeling expressed. Men, whether black or white, are apt to be resolute in not allowing a blue cube (boy) to be alone in a group. Women are far less concerned about a red cube being alone in a group of blue cubes. Asked why, women will reply, "We've been there before."

In task number 4, participants return to racial groupings, again following the steps of task number 2. But this time, they begin with all black cubes, to which white cubes are added. The most notable difference in the response of participants is that white participants cannot tolerate seeing white cubes in isolation. They are even resistant to distributing the four white cubes provided in step 4 into two groups of two each. They would rather all four white cubes be in the same group, even though it means leaving the second group unintegrated. Black participants in this task tend to be fairly indifferent to the distribution of the white cubes, though they often express amusement at the consternation of the white participants.

The lesson learned from these first four steps is as elementary as the Golden Rule. When the table of inequality is turned around and white people (or men) experience isolation or being in a minority, they invariably seek solutions that they had declined when they were in the majority.

A transformation of the Golden Rule, stated in the negative, "Do not do unto others as you would not have them do unto you," apparently struck President Kennedy when he abruptly mobilized the National Guard on June 11, 1963, to enforce the admission of Negro students at the University of Alabama. In a rare departure from his cool stance on the civil rights movement, Kennedy made an unscheduled address, speaking without a prepared text passionately and directly to white Americans, asking them to put themselves in the place of the American Negro. "Who among us," he asked, "would be content to have the color of his skin changed and stand in his place? We preach freedom around the world, and we mean it. And we cherish our freedom here at home. But are we to say to the world and much more importantly to each other, that this is the land of the free except for the Negroes; that we have no second-class citizens, except Negroes; that we have no class or caste system, no ghettos, no master race, except with respect to Negroes" (*New York Times*, June 12, 1963).

Like so many millions of Americans who had seen on television police with cattle prods, hoses and dogs physically assaulting Negro children on the streets of Birmingham, Kennedy responded to the nation's racism in a more emotional manner than he had ever publicly expressed. It seemed, to me at least, that he had seen the light and for the first time threw aside politics, taking a moral stand of extraordinary force and imploring all Americans to do likewise. It was a dreadful shock when the following day Medgar Evers, a field worker for the NAACP, was murdered in Jackson, Mississippi. There would be countless more such tragedies, including the president's own assassination five months later. Kennedy's speech that night, however, was a critical turning point in the movement's progress. I remember hearing it and thinking, "This man is angry at last and rightly so. At last he has personally identified with the victims of racism and pointed the finger of his moral indignation squarely where it belongs."

In my Unifix cube exercise, task number 4 ends with an additional step, done individually by each of the participants, who are now asked to create two groups of up to ten cubes each, using only black and white cubes. The results, of course, vary, although given the potential for an equal number of black and white cubes, some participants go for a 50-50 distribution. Many will integrate their groups with three black cubes to seven white cubes. Once, I observed a black participant begin by creating an all-black group and then a mixed group. I asked him why he didn't make an all-white group as well. "The black group is where I went to school, and it's what I want for my son," he answered, "but I don't like seeing an all-white group."

It struck me that separatism, whether defined by race or by gender is a two-edged sword. I can appreciate the need for building positive identity as a rationale for black colleges and for all-girls schools. But being an integrationist and one committed to coeducation, I shudder at the possible effects of a single-sex school of boys or a segregated school of whites only.

Task number 5 deals in part with this issue by introducing the effect of the race of the teacher upon the self-image of a student. Participants are asked to select two white cubes and combine them to make a figure representing a white teacher. Then they do this again, making another white teacher. They do the same with black cubes, making two black teachers. They are asked to set up three groups of cubes as follows: ten white cubes, ten black cubes, and ten cubes half white, half black. These groups must remain intact throughout the exercise. If participants wish, they may think of these groups as classes in separate schools. They are told to consider the teachers to be equally qualified and the students of equal caliber as well.

Step 1: Participants are asked to assign three teachers to the groups as given. Although the white and the racially mixed classes may be assigned either a black or a white teacher, invariably black participants will put a black teacher with the all-black class. White participants will yield to this choice.

Step 2: Participants are instructed to remove one white teacher and replace it with a black teacher. Then, if desired, they may reassign teachers. Generally, most participating groups opt for assigning the second black teacher to the racially mixed class.

Step 3: Participants are then asked to select and combine a new white-and-black cube, representing a biracial child, and assign this child to one of the three groups. All participants identify with this problem, and none chooses the white group for the biracial child. White participants are more likely to select the mixed class, while black participants favor the all-black group.

Step 4: Participants must then reassign the biracial child to one of the other two groups. Again, the white class is not considered a viable option. The mixed class is generally acceptable to all participants, although some black participants will state their desire for placing the biracial child in the all-black group even more firmly.

Task number 6 is a bothersome exercise for everyone. The scenario is an admissions officer's nightmare. Participants are asked to set up four blue-and-white combined cubes, representing white boys; three blue-and-black cubes, representing black boys; eight red-and-white cubes, representing white girls; and two red-and-black cubes, representing black girls. They are told to consider this group of seventeen children to be a class of five-year-olds.

Step 1: It is the day before school opens and the admissions office has learned that the three black boys will not be attending. Participants must remove these cubes.

Step 2: On the waiting list are two white boys and three black girls. There are no black boys available. Participants are asked to admit up to three new students. The group may not exceed seventeen children.

The imbalance of boys and girls and the dearth of black boys cause the participants such trouble that they will direct their discussion to the unfairness of the problem itself: "Why aren't there any black boys on the waiting list?" "The school should find some fast." "How come the admissions office enrolled three more girls than boys in the first place?" "If the school can't find any black boys, then take the whole waiting list and enroll a class of nineteen. At least the girls will be well integrated racially. To heck with a limit of seventeen. The admissions office should never have gotten us into this situation in the first place."

When told they must stick to the rules, some participating groups begrudgingly settle for admitting one black girl and two white boys, arguing that the gender imbalance takes priority. Other groups, favoring the overall racial makeup, will sacrifice gender balance and admit the three black girls, creating a more integrated class of thirteen girls and four boys.

The unsatisfactory nature of this task demonstrates to participants the importance of controlling numbers in both gender and race according to a benign quota system, which, of course, is one of my principal goals for the workshop.

There is one final individual task, which complements the opening exercise. In task number 7, participants may use as many cubes as they wish, selecting any colors available to make up their ideal group. When they are ready, they describe their group to their fellow participants and tell what it is their group is doing together. The opportunity for personal expression offered by this exercise invites participants to share their outlook on diversity and to alter their circumstances, imagining a better world. These are some of their responses: "This is my family. The black cube is my father. The white and yellow one is my mother. Her father was Polish and her mother was Korean. I'm the cube of three colors." "This is where I'd like to live, somewhere like New York City. I've used every color in the box." "This is my daughter's school. It's not all-black like the one I went to in the Bronx. It's a private school. Last year my daughter was the only black child in her class. This year there are two more. I've made her group the way I hope it will be in the future, adding more cubes of color." "This group is on a bus in August 1963, going to Washington, DC. I'm one of the white cubes. It was the first time I had ever been together with so many black people. When we heard Dr. King speak, I thought his dream was really going to become true."

The cube exercises are excellent gauges of the numerical relationships that underlie the attainment of racial equality. Of course, they do not attempt to deal with qualitative relationships; fellowship among races does not derive from proximity alone. It requires years of closeness and sufficient familiarity with others to recognize that friendship is not connected to race, or conversely that race ought neither be a defining source of camaraderie nor a natural cause for enmity. I did not acquire a close friendship among my acquaintances of color until I was able to overcome my racial self-consciousness and develop an allegiance based on personal affection and shared values. It took me even longer to acknowledge that just as there were white people with whom I shared no common bonds, the same could and did apply to persons of color.

Manhattan Country School Farm, Roxbury, New York.

"The school's Ninety-sixth Street building was chosen to bring together two neighborhoods that would not otherwise have known each other. Similarly, the farm has been in the position to bring together two other worlds, rural and urban."—Farm director Ginny Scheer

CHAPTER 6

Crossing the Great Divide

BEFORE US, IN the fall of 1965, was the awesome task of raising the funds we needed to open our doors the following year. We would have to cover not only salaries and the purchase or lease of a school building, but we would have to underwrite the most generous scholarship program of any private school in the country, as well as the operating expenses of a farm.

Setting the extent of our scholarship program was a matter of pure grit. Most schools applied 5 percent of their budget to scholarships; one standout, New Lincoln School, had committed 15 percent. Given our commitment to doubling their proportion of minority students, we chose to double the allocation for scholarships as well. Private schools seldom offered students more than a half scholarship. Whether this was to spread their funds to a larger number of students or to deliberately bar admissions to poorer families, I can't say. In either case, their policy precluded applications for most black and Hispanic children.

We decided that, within the 30 percent of our budget we planned to commit to scholarships, we would reserve 20 percent for students in the lowest-fee category and assign the remaining 10 percent for partial scholarships. Ironically, I soon found that the very schools that had told us they could not attract students of color were now referring them to us because they were "too poor."

In addition to adopting an unprecedented commitment to financial aid, we modified the application procedures used by other schools in order to simplify the process for families with low incomes. In place of the standard "Princeton form" put out by the Educational Testing Service, we made up our own scholarship form, eliminating questions about second homes, makes of vehicles, and yachts owned, if any. We also did not require families to submit copies of 1040 forms.

Our generous scholarship program meant that MCS could not be a self-supporting institution. Until it acquired its own endowment, MCS would be dependent upon charitable giving, largely from sources outside the school, for 30 percent of its annual budget. Fiscally, our decision appeared reckless, although no trustee ever doubted its importance. My staunch belief was that financial support would follow institutional initiative, not the reverse. The choice we made in forfeiting our financial independence was an even more radical one than our decision about the racial composition of the school. It meant that, to survive, MCS would have to prove that it warranted outside support. It would have to be an exemplary institution, which, in addition to providing an excellent education, would have to achieve and sustain recognition as a school which served a higher purpose.

From the outset, we knew we wanted a farm program to help us achieve that purpose, and we were fortunate in easily determining where it would be located. The original prospectus for the school clearly identified three overriding goals for the farm:

1. The farm will expose children to many aspects of life which their intensely urban environment precludes. Children will live close to the land; they will work the soil to maintain and develop the operations of the farm. Using simple tools and drawing on the endless resources of nature, they will apply their knowledge in practical and responsible ways. Children will also come to know firsthand the seasons, the elements, the designs, and the economies of nature. Hopefully, as they

grow older, they will gain both a rich measure of self-reliance and a strong awareness of the interdependence of life.

2. To children of broadly divergent racial and socioeconomic backgrounds, the farm will provide a natural setting, enabling children to know and respect one another by living together and by sharing in the responsibilities of a highly interdependent community. The farm offers a distinctly new learning experience to all children, thus putting individuals on a far more equal footing than they would find themselves in their city environment. Differences among individuals will not, and should not disappear. Rather, they will emerge as assets, hopefully ceasing to be viewed as causes for estrangement. In every way, the farm should assist in breaking unhealthy barriers, allowing for freer development of common interests and fuller exposure of uniqueness.

3. The farm, which should always be considered an integral part of the entire school, will serve as the school's most valuable laboratory. The open expanse and the wide resources of nature will liberate the school from a conventional view of curriculum, making it possible to narrow the customary gap between learning and living. Knowledge will no longer be artificially separated into such subjects as art, biology, geography, and mathematics. Experiences like caring for chickens, maple sugaring, or harvesting will expose the child to a broad set of practical and abstract concepts which transcend the confines of separate subject matters.

Our initial problems in defining the farm's agricultural and educational programs could not be foreseen, although they derived in part from differences of opinion among the school's early supporters regarding the relative importance of the farm's three stated goals. Was the farm chiefly to be a place for children to live together away from home? If so, need it be a farm at all? Was the farm chiefly an extension of the school curriculum, where children could gain new and different experiences? If so, why not offer tennis or photography? Was the farm to be MCS's Walden Pond? If so, in place of a domesticated agricultural program, why not follow the model of Outward Bound and give courses in wilderness survival?

Our "place in the country" prompted a spree of suggestions from those MCS teachers and parents who were frustrated city dwellers, would-be farmers, or naturalists. There were proposals for raising bees, for and against horseback riding, and designs for a high school and an adult retreat. One person even advocated the farm as a place for children "to go wild."

Somehow we needed to restrain ourselves and get down to the first order of business—setting up the farm. I had worked on a farm at Putney, signing up for farm jobs every semester, but the fact was, I didn't know how to run one. And facing the simultaneous task of starting a school, I definitely needed help with the farm. Our solution was to establish a farm council as a standing committee of the board of trustees. The farm council would be in charge of overseeing the farm's development. Its members included trustees, parents, teachers, and most importantly, experts in operating small working farms, such as Walter Clark of North Country School and Peter Pratt, a fellow Putneyite who had managed a family farm in Connecticut.

Guided by the farm council, we soon decided that the farm's operations should be kept to a size simple enough for children to understand and in which they could usefully participate. We also determined that the farm should be income-producing. No one was suggesting that the farm be fully self-supporting. Its major expenses were educational and should be viewed as one would regard the cost of teaching a child to read or write. However, for the farm to have integrity as an agricultural operation, it should bear income and operate year-round. We were committed to underwriting expenses related to farm production and educational costs, but we concluded that our farm produce should supply sufficient income to support a single farmer and his or her family.

IN ENLISTING FINANCIAL support for MCS, our first step was to assemble a group of sponsors, people with recognition in their professional fields or social circles, whose names would lend distinction to our effort. Our sponsors would serve as honorary individual advisors and would not be required to meet formally. Those who could provide financial support would be approached for contributions, but this was not a condition of their sponsorship.

Ruth Cooke secured eleven sponsors; Sally Kallem, two; and Marty and I, with my parents' help, provided the balance—totaling thirty-three. Five of our sponsors were Dalton connected and eight were well-known educators, including the presidents of Bank Street, Barnard, and Goddard Colleges, and the heads of Phillips Exeter, Groton, Putney, and North Country Schools. Two of our sponsors headed community agencies in East Harlem: the James Weldon Johnson Community Center and Union Settlement House. There were fewer black sponsors than I had wanted: Preston Wilcox, a professor of social work at Columbia University; Dr. Kenneth B. Clark, the psychologist whose evidence had helped secure victory in the *Brown v. Board of Education* case; and Constance Baker Motley, Manhattan Borough president, who later withdrew when she was nominated to be a federal judge. The largest number of sponsors were those in a position to help raise money or to give it themselves. Five sponsors, who had their own family foundations, contributed to MCS for the rest of their lifetimes. At least two of our sponsors qualified as bona fide celebrities: Robert Motherwell, the artist, and actor-comedian Zero Mostel.

I have always regretted that I never actually met Zero Mostel, particularly after reading the following story in Seth Cagin's book, *We Are Not Afraid*. "Zero Mostel used to tell a story about a train journey he made through the Deep South," Cagin wrote. "He got off at a station and, thirsty, approached the segregated drinking fountains. Sipping from the whites-only fountain, Mostel, an ungainly man who could not help but draw attention to himself, spat out the 'white' water as if it tasted of mud. Then he sampled water from the 'colored' fountain. 'Much better!' he exclaimed, and with comic officiousness switched the two signs, while the locals whose custom he was mocking laughed right along with him."

I'M SURE THAT all fund-raisers would agree that most money raised by charitable organizations comes through personal connections. In my case, the prime source of money was my parents' address book, which led me to my mother's lady friends at the Cosmopolitan Club. We lunched there together again and again. After my introduction as "Jean's little boy," I followed up with each friend separately to cultivate support and to be put in touch with others.

Most of the school's major donors have been women of a generation older than mine. Apparently, it fell to the women to look after the more nurturing charities and to take care of the education of children. The men attended to higher education, and typically they were less protective of the underdogs. But women born at the turn of the twentieth century had had their own experiences with disenfranchisement. Coming of age in the1920s, they were the first to vote in a national election.

The Zinsser sisters, Peggy and Ellen, were among my initial connections. Peggy was Mrs. Lewis Douglas, wife of the former U.S. ambassador to Great Britain. Ellen was Mrs. John McCloy, wife of the former U.S. high commissioner to Berlin. They took me on as their protégé. I'm sure they approved of my plans, but more important were their loyalty to my family and their pleasure in teaching me the ropes. Mrs. Douglas was especially helpful. She had raised millions of dollars for Rudolph Bing at the Metropolitan Opera, and she tutored me on all the dos and don'ts of fund-raising. "Never give up, not even on those who turn you down," she instructed. "Write them a letter immediately saying you understand, that you will keep them in touch. When someone gives you a check, write them back by hand. Don't use a typewriter. Make your correspondence personal and use the word 'generous' at least three times. Foundations are harder to crack. Don't expect to get more than one out of twenty, but keep working on the other nineteen." To my mother, Peggy would say, "Go after your friends for Gus. Tell them if they don't give, you will scratch their eyeballs out."

Her sister, Mrs. McCloy, paved the way for me to see Frederick Warburg, the man who sent Tommy Lamont "the Coon from Kuhn Loeb," and whose partner was Ben Buttenwieser, Peter's father. The secretary answering the phone said, "Oh yes, Mrs. McCloy said you would be calling." Mr. Warburg took my call and flatly stated that if I wanted to see him about money, he wasn't interested. "I understand," I replied. "I just want to meet you and tell you about the school I'm starting." When we met, he repeated his gruff overture: "The only reason I'm seeing you is that Ellen keeps batting her eyes at me saying you have to do something about Jean Trowbridge's boy, Gussie." He was very busy, he said, "So let's make this painless and quick."

Halfway through my description, he showed interest. "You're not just taking a few Negroes," he commented. "You're on to something different." He then pumped me with numerous questions, which led to an extended discussion. Finally, he said, "I just gave Millbrook School a quarter of a million dollars, so I'm broke. I don't know why I gave them so much. They don't need a hockey rink seating two thousand people, and they never even mentioned to me anything about having a scholarship program. That's something worthwhile, isn't it?"

Before I could respond, Mr. Warburg said, "All right, how much do you want me to give?" Mrs. Douglas had not coached me on this.

"How about matching the Buttenwieser Foundation? Ten thousand dollars," I said.

"Christ, what do you think I am? I thought I'd give a thousand. Let's make it $5,000 and you can name a toilet after Ben."

Overhearing our conversation, Ben Buttenwieser came in from the adjoining room. Mr. Warburg was telling me he needed to wait for some more dividends before he could give me a check. Ben assured me Freddy's credit was good. They exchanged another joke or two, and I stood up to leave. "Wait a minute," Mr. Warburg said. "This list of donors you've got. I hadn't noticed it before. You're not playing around with fly-by-nights. These people give some pretty serious thought before they cough up, and when they do, their support doesn't disappear overnight."

That's your cue, I heard Mrs. Douglas say. "Does that mean, Mr. Warburg, that I can think of your gift as sustaining?" He smiled warmly, saying, "You mean you can't come down next year and spend another hour with me?"

Mr. Warburg did give again, every year, and after he died in 1972 his wife, Wilma, gave even more generously. I never met Wilma Warburg, but for twenty years we corresponded. From the beginning, she addressed me as Gus, signing off at first "Yours," then "Cordially," then "With warmest good wishes," and thereafter "Affectionately," except on one occasion. I never called her "Wilma." She was my mother's age, so she was "Mrs. Warburg," and I knew not to use the popular honorific "Ms." Once, though, when writing her about her niece, Joan, I addressed her as Mrs. Wilma Warburg. She replied: "When you write her, I urge very strongly you address her as Mrs. James P. Warburg, and not Mrs. Joan. I suspect she, like most of my friends (and especially me), hate being addressed as if we had been divorced. Please, I am not Mrs. Wilma Warburg." She signed off: "Plaintively, Wilma."

The family foundation for the Warburgs was called aptly the Wilfred Fund, for Wil(ma) and Fred. When Mr. Warburg died, Mrs. Warburg moved from New York to live on her family estate on Snake Hill in Middleburg, Virginia. I wrote her a hand-written condolence note, and under separate cover, sent her a container of maple syrup from our farm, something I did regularly with all major donors. For the next few years the Wilfred Fund continued their annual support. Wilma's letters lengthened and her giving increased to $10,000. In response to one of my thank-yous, she replied, "Your letter was very heartwarming and of course made me feel I'd like to do more." She enclosed another check for $5,000. Peggy Douglas's tutelage was paying off!

In 1988, after thanking her for her annual gift, I received the following letter from Snake Hill, typed by Mrs. Warburg's secretary and signed "Wilma" in shaky handwriting. When I collected the mail, I had immediately spotted the Tiffany envelope with her return address embossed with red ink.

"Dear Gus, Thank you for thanking me for thanking you for thanking me for my September gift! Unlike you, I do propose to extend our correspondence, if not indefinitely, at least a little further, by awaiting happily your next thank-you letter for the enclosed cheque. I have recently redone my will, which is one of my favorite indoor sports, and since your letter mentioning the proposed Endowment Fund had just reached me, I thought it a good idea to remove my bequest to the school from my will and send it to you now. Hence, here it is." Her check was for $50,000.

I replied at once: "Dear Mrs. Warburg, Hallelujah! What an incredible surprise. I opened your letter while ascending the elevator with two other passengers. I contained my glee, befitting elevator manners, until reaching the office where I summoned Marty into a conference room to share my jubilation. Let me tell you what's gone through my mind since yesterday's windfall. First of all is the thrill of getting a check for $50,000, which is the second biggest gift we've ever received. Next, is the untold pleasure in being so generously disinherited, a twist of fortune that sets my head spinning. Years ago I heard a story about the founder of Chock Full of Nuts who gave a building to Lenox Hill Hospital. He spoke to an audience of big givers saying what a satisfaction it was to see his name imprinted above him and not be looking up from the grave. You have not only done the supreme act of generosity in giving away an inheritance before its time, but also you have allowed me the privilege to say my thanks while you are here to hear and appreciate it. Lastly, your gift is my dream-come-true: that every MCS supporter would endow their annual giving! My instinct was to pick up the phone and make direct contact. I resisted this, preferring to preserve a priceless correspondence. Your letters are worth as much to me as their contents, and I will forever treasure their affection, advocacy and humor. It is a rare thing to be the recipient of such encouragement and support from someone I've never even met face-to-face. Although I wish this were not so, I am nevertheless proud to say I know you well and you are a very good friend. Yours, Gus."

Wilma carried on her generous support for five more years until she died. Contrary to her promise, her will included a bequest to MCS of $35,000.

Another lifelong supporter was Katherine E. Hendricks, whom I also never met. Miss Hendricks was from La Connor, Washington, and her envelope and enclosed letters were always hand typed using a brown ribbon. She first wrote me on February 25, 1968, donating $100, saying, "I read about the school and the theory of diversification in a recent copy of the

Saturday Review. I believe that one of the functions of the small private school in addition to the education of children is to experiment. I wish you every success."

Over fourteen years, she sent twenty-eight gifts of increasing size, two each year. Our correspondence did not develop beyond formalities until one year, so struck by her loyalty, I asked her to tell me why she had been so faithful to a school so far from her home. She answered: "There have been shifts in attitudes for achieving equality since I first heard of your theories, but still I believe in an unsegregated living experience and quality education. The school system in the small western city I grew up in was not segregated but provided no experience with minorities as there were none. When I spent a year in Cleveland after the War, I met a Wilbeforce graduate who had problems as she was having her first contacts with a white group. I wondered if I would have been adaptable if I had made application to Howard and been accepted. I realized that no education can be equal that is separate. When small children are in a group it is obvious that they are color-blind. Intolerance and prejudice are learned reactions and once established are difficult to change. The problem is complex with no simple answer, but our culture should be sufficiently flexible to allow experimentation."

My last letter from La Connor, Washington, came from Miss Hendrick's attorney in 1982, notifying me that she had left MCS $5,000 in her will. Her only other charitable bequest was in the same amount to the NAACP. At her death, her entire estate was less than $150,000, making her gift to MCS proportionately larger than that of many of our wealthier donors.

I wonder if Katherine Hendricks would have ever contributed so generously to us and to the NAACP had she not befriended a Negro student from Wilbeforce, or if Wilma Warburg would have poured forth her support had she not taken Jean Trowbridge's son under her wing? Beyond the obvious connections that determine one's charitable giving—one's alma mater, one's place of worship—there seems to be something deeply private that motivates people, a need on the part of the donor to connect to some personal experience.

This was the case with Margie Lang. An early sponsor of the school, she had been one of its three founding contributors, and thereafter a loyal supporter whose gifts increased annually, reaching $50,000 in 1991. Margie and her brother, Arthur Altschul, were two of the principal trustees of the Overbrook Foundation, established by her father, Frank Altschul. On October 27, 1992, Margie became a hundred-thousand-dollar donor; she maintained this extraordinary level of generosity until she died in 2002 at age eighty-seven. I first met Margie and her husband Dan, a noted journalist on the staff of the *New Yorker*, when I taught their daughters, Francie, Niki, and Cecily, at Dalton. The girls' adolescent crushes on their English teacher and house advisor had led the Langs to invite Marty and me for frequent dinners. Their other guests included John Hersey and Lillian Hellman, causing me to be the one to fawn. Dan, I suspect, had arranged the company in this manner to release me politely from stage center.

Like many of the bright and privileged students I taught at Dalton, the Lang sisters were overprotected children—intellectually aware of the world's problems, but out of touch. On two occasions, I seized the opportunity to give them a taste of the real world. Francie's "house" (Dalton's term for their daily advisement groups) had decided to collect food for the annual Thanksgiving drive. When the children arrived, proudly bearing their Gristede shopping bags containing small jars and tins with SS Peirce labels, I said, "Put on your coats and meet me downstairs. We're going across the street to the supermarket to do some comparative shopping." I asked them to choose two items they had bought—peas, beans, whatever—and find out what they cost at the A&P. "And be sure to ask the storekeeper to tell you about number-ten tin cans," I added, referring to the large store-brand cans that were so much more economical than their little SS Peirce containers. The lesson learned, the children were refunded for their Gristede purchases, and the next day we went back to the A&P, returning to Dalton with several full shopping carts.

On another day, one of the Lang sisters, I think it was Niki, told me she had never ridden the subway. The next morning I posted her name on the eighth grade list of students who were required to stay after school. When she begrudgingly showed up, I said, "Come on. I'm taking you home on the subway. I called your mother and she said it was fine with her." We left Dalton and walked three blocks south on Lexington Avenue to the Eighty-sixth Street IRT station, where we took the downtown local two stops. Her family's apartment was half a block away.

Margie Lang would occasionally visit MCS, but more often I would go to see her. On the first available Thursday following the arrival of her first $100,000 donation, I dined with her at the Cosmopolitan Club, next door to her apartment building. I was itching to know what made her double her giving, but she was typically reserved about the matter. I pieced together, however, that she did it in part to spite her brother. Margie and Arthur were poles apart in their politics and in the causes they chose to support. Arthur enjoyed the kudos derived from his philanthropy and thus supported the more socially prominent charities; Margie was modest, declined high-profile charitable functions, and concentrated her support on liberal organizations committed to reform, such as the Environmental Defense Fund and Human Rights Watch.

She described foundation meetings to me as family contests: Margie's choice of a charity countered by Arthur's and then Arthur's trumped by Margie's. While Margie felt her own support of MCS appropriate, she set out in 1988 to win Arthur over to our cause, succeeding finally in persuading him to visit the school. He was not impressed and told me so, adding that a study we had recently done on our alumni confirmed that we were not preparing our black students to enter top Ivy League colleges. "If I'm going to give you money for scholarships for ghetto kids," he said, "I want to see them going to Harvard and Yale, not state universities or Negro colleges or second-string places like Wesleyan."

But Margie was determined to increase Overbrook's commitment to our school one way or another. In 1992, after it became clear to her that Arthur would not be converted, she played a wild card and announced that she had decided to double her own gift to MCS!

The last time I saw Margie was in December 2001, a few days before she left for her winter home in Key West, where she died less than a month later. Waiting for our cheese soufflés at the Cos Club, she told me she'd just called the Overbrook office, instructing them to forward her annual contribution to MCS. After extending my thanks, I said, "Margie, I know you don't want me to sing your praises, but do me a favor. You are MCS's largest and most loyal donor. Can you tell me what's made you so devoted and generous all these years?" She replied, "Because I like you." I had no cause to doubt her answer, but it was too simple to explain the depth of her attachment to MCS. Taking a circuitous route, I reminded her of the occasion I took her daughter Niki on her first subway ride, hoping this would spark some closer connection between us. Margie drew a blank; then she abruptly changed the subject and told me a story, one she had related to me several times before. Obviously, I had previously missed its importance to her.

Margie had attended Brearley School through eighth grade, after which she was sent to Emma Willard boarding school. In her first weeks there, she did something wrong—"Nothing really bad," she said, "just naughty." After scolding her, the headmistress said, "Now, Margaret, I want you to know that you are very lucky to be at Emma Willard. You are one of the first Jewish girls we've had, and I want you to be sure to set a good example."

This exchange set the tone for the years of humiliation Margie would endure at Emma Willard. Her never-forgotten experience as the object of prejudice in an elitist, exclusionary school determined the direction of her life and the company she thereafter chose to keep, which so generously included MCS.

In contrast to Margie Lang, there are donors whose choice to support institutions committed to social justice may be based on guilt or the desire to make restitution. I have known many such donors, and being on the receiving end of their charity has often been terribly discomforting. The most shocking example was when we received a $10,000 grant in 1966 from a foundation known to be among the principal supporters of the civil rights movement. I knew the director of the foundation quite well, and when I called to thank him the following day, he told me that when the trustees had met the prior week, the chairman—I'll call him Mr. H.—had brought the meeting to order, saying, "Well, what are we going to do for the niggers tonight?"

Stunned at the time I heard this comment, I have struggled with it ever since. It was so low and mean and hurtful that I've wanted to avoid revealing it. Yet it happened, and comments like it were more the norm than a behavioral deviation. How, then, did one explain it? How could such a liberal foundation be headed by one so overtly racist? Why did the trustees even give a damn about the movement? And most of all, what did such a shameful comment tell us about white people?

Louis Harris, reporting on a nationwide poll conducted in *Newsweek* in October 1963, helped to answer my questions. "The white American is divided within himself," he wrote. "He is biased against black skin, yet a sense of justice tells him he is incontestably wrong. He is pulled one way by his intellect, the other way by his emotions. Conscience whispers 'Equal rights, freedom for all;' convention says, 'But a Negro is different.' The white man is eternally torn between the right that he knows and the wrong that he does. And for most Americans, it is as hard to give up prejudice as it would be to deny openly the democratic ideal of equality."

I never knew Mr. H., but it seems he matched Harris's description of a person "torn between the right that he knows and the wrong that he does." The horrible contradiction between his deeds and words suggests not only the depth of his racism, but also that he was either paying his dues or searching for moral conversion. We know that donors who have suffered from physical causes or whose loved ones have been victims of dread diseases actively support charities that seek to remedy such conditions. It would follow that for some who contribute generously to the cause of racial equality, the motivation to obtain a cure for such a malady could be a personal one as well.

Among my Cosmopolitan Club lunches, my meal with one Mrs. Muir was a hard one to swallow. She was a trustee of North Country School, so I was sure she would like the idea of our farm and that she favored progressive education. On that much I was on fair ground, but when I spoke of racial integration, she stiffened, asking what were my views on interracial marriages. I said I hadn't given them a thought. "Well, it's time you do," she said, "because that's what you'll be producing having all those Negro children around." Mrs. Muir drove me home in her Rolls Royce, and gritting my teeth, I followed Mrs. Douglas's orders—I wrote her a note thanking her for lunch, and she responded with a check for $500, delivered by her chauffeur.

Many of my mother's Cos Club ladies had lived such isolated, privileged lives that the notion of racial integration was unreal to them, too remote to be considered seriously. One generation away from these people, and sharing a common social background, I understood their circumstances, even though I did not agree with their views. Some, like Mrs. Muir, had awakened to stirrings for racial equality. They probably supported the NAACP and took pride in welcoming Negroes of the likes of Walter White, Ralph Bunche, and Marian Anderson. They were not ready, however, to see the color line crossed any further, and certainly not to the point of having their children marry "one of them."

Thanks to the Mr. H.'s and Mrs. Muirs, I could see more poignantly the need for our school to help create a new generation of white people. The story of MCS is not simply about the integration of people of color into a dominant culture. It is as much about whites crossing the great divide.

Seth Milliken was one who expressed a desire to cross the divide. He was the brother of Alida Camp, a classmate of my mother's at Smith College who, like my parents, had lived in Chestnut Hill and who owned a home in Maine not far from ours. Alida had a small foundation, and she had promised to make a grant to MCS if I could make a winning case to her trustees. Named for her summer estate, the Blue Hill Foundation gave away only six thousand dollars a year, the tip of the iceberg of the Milliken fortune and barely enough to warrant the costs of quarterly dinner meetings at the New York Yacht Club.

We gathered in the walnut-paneled Afterdeck Room, which featured a moose head on one wall opposite the America's Cup, locked behind glass. Alida, joined by five other trustees, was the hostess, the chair, and the only woman. Three of the men were in matching blue suits and Princeton Club ties. One wore a tweed coat and plaid tie. I figured he would be on my side. Alida's brother Seth arrived late, three sheets to the wind. After chitchat about sailing, New York social events, and the state of the stock market, the conversation turned to an obscure discussion about whether the social order of America was circular or pyramidal with the President in the center or at the top. By either definition, Negroes, called "Nigras" by the man in tweed who I was beginning to realize I had misjudged, were at the bottom or the outside. Seth favored the circular theory and pointed out that I was perhaps trying to broaden the perimeter. At this point, Mr. Tweed demanded, "Is it true, Mr. Trowbridge, that you're advocating mixing the races?"

"Yes," I replied.

"Then you're proposing the ruination of our race," he declared, "and I don't understand, Alida, why we're sitting here talking about this man's proposal."

Alida apologized for the outburst, and Seth, trying to mend fences, asked his sister, "Alida, how many of them do you know? More than I do, I'm sure. You're on the board of the Urban League. I don't know one, and I'm ashamed of it. I swear before I die to do something about that."

The dinner ended, and Alida escorted me downstairs before returning to vote on our proposal. She urged me not to be too upset, promising she'd call in the morning. She phoned promptly at nine o'clock to say that the foundation would give $1,000. I didn't ask her how Mr. Tweed had voted. In addition to my letter of thanks to Mrs. Camp, I wrote Seth Milliken a note telling him how much I appreciated his support.

Carl Flemister—founding trustee, first chairman of the board, and MCS
parent and grandparent—on the occasion of MCS's thirty-fifth anniversary:
"I remember the turbulent 'sixties when we organized the Manhattan
Country School. Who would believe that the dream would unfold as it has
today? We dream dreams, and we live to see our dreams come true."

CHAPTER 7

Miracle on Ninety-sixth Street

WHEN OUR TWO older children, Katharine and Stephen, were at Dalton, I would take them to school in the mornings. Coming home, I would walk past 7 East Ninety-sixth Street, a handsome town house that stood vacant. On a tattered green awning leading from the building to the curb was written "Nippon Club." A sign posted to the side by Douglas Elliman Realtors read For Sale.

As our plans for our school solidified, I would stop in front of number 7 and gaze at it longingly, each time becoming more convinced that this was the building we wanted. The fact that it was, by some enormous good luck, available, seemed fortuitous. Its location between the predominantly black and Hispanic neighborhood of East Harlem and the almost exclusively white Upper East Side was symbolically perfect, and it was less than a block from Central Park. Originally the ornate private home of Ogden Codman, its size seemed just right for a small school of about two hundred students. Of course, as we were still raising funds there was nothing I could do but keep my fingers crossed that the For Sale sign would stay in place. As if reserved just for us, the building remained on the market for nearly three years.

Ogden Codman Jr. (1863-1951), whose ancestors had owned the wharf in Boston Harbor famous for the Boston Tea Party, was among the country's most fashionable architects and interior designers. His Social Register clients included John D. Rockefeller Jr., Cornelius Vanderbilt III, and Edith Wharton, with whom he wrote *The Decoration of Houses*. Today their book is still considered a leading treatise on the architectural merits of classic design. Codman and Wharton rejected Victorian excess and proclaimed that the "good breeding of architecture" was proportion, and its "supreme excellence is simplicity."

In 1904, not long after moving his offices from Boston to New York City, Codman married Leila Webb, the wealthy widow of a controlling owner of the New York Central Railroad. Prompted by his marriage and new financial fortune, Codman in 1908 embarked on a bold project, purchasing property on East Ninety-sixth Street between Fifth and Madison Avenues from Andrew Carnegie. He planned to build a row of four elegant townhouses, which he speculated would transform this undeveloped area into a "frontier for millionaires' homes."

The first lot at 7 East Ninety-sixth Street had been selected by Codman as his residence. Despite his wife's untimely death in 1910, Codman proceeded with the construction of number 7, altering its layout to include a downstairs private office and an adjoining place of work for his draftsmen, with a separate exterior entrance. In 1912, Codman assumed occupancy of the townhouse along with six servants and his chauffeur.

While Codman preached simplicity of design, the execution of his own residence was costly and relied on European craftsmen. Every detail of his interior was custom-built in France, including the yellow bricks for his courtyard. Imported to New York, they were then installed by American laborers under a French foreman.

The four-story Parisian façade of Codman's dwelling began at ground level with a huge double carriage-door entrance leading to a courtyard and a garage equipped with a turntable in the rear. On the second floor, three high arched windows open to a stone balcony with a wrought-iron railing extending across the entire forty-foot width of the building. The windows on the third floor were square with carved stonework beneath. There were large wooden shutters on each floor. Finally, the fourth floor was designed with arched dormer windows, above which rose a slate Mansard roof.

The interior of the building was Codman's forte. The grandest rooms, some with eighteen-foot ceilings, occupied the front and center of the building, with the entire rear section, which consists of an extra floor due to its lower ceilings, reserved for domestic help. A white-and-black checkered marble floor and sweeping semicircular staircase, exposing the double-height ceiling, decorate a foyer which connected the stately front room within.

The drawing room, which spans the width of the building on the second floor, parodied the Hall of Mirrors in Versailles. For his dining room on this floor, Codman chose the ideal shape, a circle, adorned with floor-to-ceiling French windows opposite two niches, presumably for sculptures. Its floor is crushed pink granite inlaid with a circular band of white marble. (A building inspector, rusty in his math, required a little assistance in determining the area of this room, though he recovered his composure with the comment, "So this is where you will teach the well-rounded child.")

Like the drawing room below, the third-floor master bedroom occupied the entire front of the building, with marble fireplaces in different colors at either end. Above the mantel on its east side was an eighteenth century oil painting, which I had appraised in hopes of securing the school's endowment. The expert from the Metropolitan Museum of Art said, "It's very good decorative art, not great, but good."

Believing that America was becoming too garish, Codman left the country in 1920 to live in France, selling his home for $250,000 seven years later to the great-great-grandchildren of Clement Moore of *A Visit from St. Nicholas* fame. There were approximately a dozen subsequent owners of the house before it was purchased by the Nippon Club, a Japanese social organization. One owner was apparently a Russian princess, who sold her jewels to purchase the house, and rented rooms to provide income. Another owner was a New York socialite. He had proposed to a woman whose condition of marriage was that he arrange for her picture to appear in the society section of the *New York Times*. He took her to the Metropolitan

Opera, where during the performance he stood on his head in his fourth-row center seat. A photograph of the two of them was displayed in the morning edition.

IN JANUARY 1966, THE board took a leap of faith and decided to open the school the following September. We still hoped that MCS would be housed at 7 East Ninety-sixth Street, though it was more likely that we would be forced to use temporary, leased facilities. The Nippon Club's asking price was $300,000. We had asked for an option to buy, but had been refused. To date, we had raised only $18,000. The prospect of having enough backing to buy our building was dim, although we were awaiting word from some foundations that were actively considering us. Whatever the outcome, we were determined to move ahead with launching the school. We had a committed staff and the promise of many parents wanting to enroll their children.

On March 11, 1966, the miracle on Ninety-sixth Street occurred when we learned that the education committee of the Charles F. Kettering Foundation in Dayton, Ohio, had made a recommendation to its board for a $60,500 grant to MCS—$18,000 for scholarships and $42,500 as a challenge grant toward purchase of the Nippon Club building. Frank Jennings of the New World Foundation had taken an interest in our school, and offered to use his influence as a consultant for Kettering on our behalf. His support put us in their favor, together with a little luck. Evidently, at their January meeting the committee members spent so much time talking about the upcoming Super Bowl game that they failed to approve sufficient grants to meet their quota. In a rush to catch up on their work at the next meeting, the committee approved our proposal on the basis of Frank's endorsement.

In the same month, we learned that a real estate investor named Fred Hill had made a down payment on the Nippon Club with the intention of making a quick resale. Mr. Hill, we were told, was a "man who ate brownstones for breakfast." Anxious to sell, he was willing to give us a six-week option to buy at $3,000, money we would forfeit if we failed to enter a contract. Our architect and engineer examined the building and told us it was sound and could be handsomely converted into a school of the size we had specified. Encouraged by the promise of the Kettering grant and our feasibility study of the building, we took up Fred Hill's option and faced the challenge of matching Kettering's offer within forty-two days.

My stomach churned each Monday morning when we delivered our $500 installment check to Fred Hill. As it turned out, we met our deadline, and with the help of two mortgages added to funds raised, we bought the building on June 1, 1966, for $265,000. Across the table from me at the closing, which took place on the fifty-sixth floor of a midtown office building, were officers, lawyers, and accountants from the Nippon Club, the Bank of Tokyo, which held the mortgage, and Fred Hill's corporation. Also present was Mr. Haquabard, the agent from Douglas Elliman, who stood to make a double fee from the sale. Negotiations were conducted with the help of a translator, and calculations by the Japanese were done with an abacus.

After the meeting, I noticed some of the lawyers conversing quietly while waiting for the elevator. On the way down, my lawyer turned to me, and said, "Would you like to sell it?"

"Sell what?" I asked.

"The building. Mr. Hill has another buyer, and he's hoping for more profit. I think you could stand to make $20,000."

With the keys to number 7 safely in my pocket, I took a taxi to Ninety-sixth Street without a second thought to my possible career as a real estate investor. The next day, I wrote Fred Hill, asking for a contribution. He responded that he was pleased to help, and sent us $100. I still see Mr. Haquabard on Ninety-sixth Street, and he never fails to remind me how fortunate we were in purchasing the building.

Codman's elitist manner and his preference for Old World order do not lead me to believe he would have been comfortable with the thought of his former home becoming a racially and economically integrated school. Yet I take some special satisfaction in our school's affiliation with one whose forbears unwittingly hosted the American Revolution.

WITH OUR SCHOOL building secured, Marty and I turned our attention to filling its rooms. We were keenly aware that if MCS were to achieve true racial integration, our most urgent initial task was to win the support of people of color for whom the promise of equal opportunity had never been a reality. I therefore set about getting to know my East Harlem neighbors. Every person I met led me to two or three others. Some of my most useful sources were the so-called "gray-shirt clergy," young white Protestant ministers assigned to local churches from their downtown parishes, wearing white collars and otherwise casual dress. These modern-day missionaries were committed integrationists and saw themselves as part of the civil rights movement. The older guard social workers and directors of community agencies were less outspoken about social change, but they too were helpful. After six months of pursuing each lead, I began to find the web closing in on itself as people referred me to agencies and people with whom I had already established contacts.

My first "discovery" was Carl Flemister, a program officer at the James Weldon Johnson Community Center. I was on the board of Franklin Plaza Nursery School with his wife, Gracie. Carl and I met for lunch in an Italian restaurant on 106th Street. I liked him from the start, and he showed great interest in our ideas. But he deflected my inquiry about his being a trustee, saying I needed someone of the stature of Whitney Young, then executive director of the National Urban League. Months later when I saw Carl again for the fourth time, I said, "Carl, forget about Whitney. Dozens of people have said to me, 'You should see Carl Flemister.' I want you to be on our board." This time, he agreed.

My hope was to persuade some of East Harlem's more established organizations to help underwrite the portion of our scholarship program which would be devoted to East Harlem students. Bill Kirk, director of Union Settlement House, and especially his wife, Mary, welcomed a school that would enroll children from East Harlem. But despite Mary's urging, Bill was impossible to pin down. He agreed to be a sponsor, which gave us an overture to nearly every agency in East Harlem, but he wouldn't give financial support.

Bill Kirk's blessings led us directly to Bill and Dibby Webber, who had founded the East Harlem Protestant Parish. When we had lunch with the Webbers and told them of our evening with the Kirks, they laughed and said they were not surprised. "When you're running the oldest settlement house in East Harlem, you don't take risks very easily," they said. Meeting the Webbers was another stroke of enormous good fortune. Over the next thirty years, Bill would become a trustee of MCS and serve as chairman of the board during one of the school's most critical periods. The Webbers were also sponsors, and they sent their youngest daughter to MCS. When their older son's boy later enrolled, they became MCS grandparents as well.

The Webber's first gift to MCS was to get the parish to support three scholarships. In the end, our idea of twenty such groups putting up $1,000 each was not a success. Peggy Douglas's warning applied not only to foundations. We were lucky to find one Webber among twenty. Peggy had also told me about the unpredictably of enlisting support. "You never know what's going to happen," she said. "So don't leave a stone unturned. There will be many disappointments, but every now and then you will land on something wonderful and totally unexpected."

That happened to me after my visit with Father Voleker at the Church of St. Edwards the Martyr, where I had observed their preschool program, run by Diana Dent. Diana worked as a volunteer at St. Edwards and lived in Greenwich, Connecticut, with her mother, who I'm told was a very wealthy woman. A few years later, she called me to recommend a boy she had taught, named Marco. She said the church's nursery school had folded and that she would see what she could do to get its principal benefactor to help MCS. Not much later, we began receiving anonymous annual gifts through a trust officer at the Bank of New York, amounting at one point to $40,000 a year. Diana acknowledged that the gift must have come from her source, but she was not at liberty to tell me anything further. The generous gift of our anonymous donor came in February every year. Without it we would not have met our operating deficit. I called our mystery donor "the lady in sneakers." I don't recall Diana's footwear when I first met her. Wearing sneakers or otherwise, she was, I believe, one of those extraordinary, unpredicted windfalls that enabled MCS to come about. Marco, by the way, graduated from MCS.

Northside Center for Child Development on Central Park North was a gold mine of another sort. Through Mamie Phipps Clark, its director, I met her husband Dr. Kenneth B. Clark, a professor of psychology at City College, who was then the sole black member of the New York State Board of Regents. A strong integrationist whose testimony in the *Brown v. Board of Education* case had been pivotal, Clark was also an advocate for community control of public schools. He agreed to become a sponsor of MCS, and over the years, he was a mentor with whom I had shared many conversations that encouraged and shaped my views, especially on race and prejudice.

Preston Wilcox, a professor at the Columbia University School of Social Work and an activist among educational organizations throughout Harlem, was also pivotal in helping me to clarify my ideas about race relations in America. Peter Buttenwieser at Dalton had introduced me to him. Outgoing and unguarded, Preston talked with me about the struggle for equality, not as an idealist but as a political strategist who never stopped testing the playing field. His candor and willingness to speak so honestly prompted me on my first visit to ask, "Am I being the white knight of the Ajax commercials? Is MCS going to be opening Pandora's box?" Preston laughed warmly, and said, "Yes to both questions. But do it, knowing it won't be easy. There's only one way out of the ghetto, and that's out. It's painful, but the alternative is worse. You can't wave a wand and have it all come out perfect, but do it because it's right and nobody else is sticking their neck out."

Preston became a sponsor as well as a charter trustee. He also became my compass, guiding me when I veered off course. While committed to integration, he was wary of white paternalism and the danger of blacks losing their racial identity by merging with the dominant group. He accepted my belief that equality derived from a numerical balance of power but argued, quite rightly, that an integrated school run by an avowed racist like Governor George Wallace of Alabama would remain a white racist institution.

He defined integration as "the sharing of a mutually self-reaffirming educational experience by students of a variety of ethnic, religious, social and economic backgrounds . . . . designed to enable students to establish co-equal relationships and to understand the true nature of society." To Preston, the achievement of integration rested on "curriculum modification, changes in the school's organization, a redistribution of decision-making roles, and a confrontation of the track system." During his close association with MCS, which lasted for fourteen years, Preston would tenaciously, often aggressively, hold the school responsible for meeting these tests. But when the militancy of Black Power overtook the nation in the 1970s, Preston aligned with the separatist cause.

Fortunately, this was not the case with most of the charter black families who enrolled their children in our school. Our first meeting with the families of prospective students of color at MCS was organized by Faye Edwards, who was in charge of the East Harlem Prostestant Parish's tutorial program. Martha Norris, who would be our kindergarten teacher, Ruth Cooke, Marty, and I were there. The gathering was quite large and the reception of us was initially cool, bordering on hostile. After listening to our goals, a parent stood up, and said, "All right, Mr. Trowbridge, where do you live and what's your background?" Recalling this moment, Marty has often remarked, "I'll never forget Gus's sigh of relief as he recited our East Harlem address. We qualified as legitimate locals!"

Next, someone asked if our staff was going to be integrated. She was answered by Mrs. McCoy, whose daughter was the first African American girl to join our oldest class. "Well," she quipped, "look at Miss Norris and you can see for yourself." The meeting went on for two hours, and the group became more and more vocal and enthusiastic. I told them of my need to raise money before we could open the school, and Mrs. Foy, sister of Mrs. McCoy, asked, "What can we do to help?" By then, parents were speaking of MCS as if it was their school. Of the sixty-six children who attended MCS in its first year, the largest delegation of students from East Harlem came from among this group of parents.

Another source of applicants was the Wilhelm Weinberg Nursery School, a private, cooperative preschool of predominantly white families from Yorkville, who were dissatisfied with their local public school and were seeking another option. These parents, who had already had some experience with racially integrated education, would turn out to be among the most solidly committed charter families of MCS.

THE SPRING BEFORE we opened our doors, I went to the New York Public Library to find a book on how to start a school. Of course, it wasn't there, so I turned to a lawyer. I soon learned that in New York State at that time the process of establishing a private nonprofit school required the following steps. First, you formed an association—a simple legal step needing five trustees who would assume personal liability for the association's fiscal operations. Until the school was incorporated by the Board of Regents in Albany, each trustee was unprotected should the school fail financially. Once established as an association, the school could file with the IRS for tax-exempt status, which only required its bylaws to state its purpose as educational.

In addition to Carl Flemister, Preston Wilcox, and myself, there were two other charter trustees, both white. Warren Leonard, who was then headmaster of Storm King School in Storm King, New York, had been my algebra teacher at Putney, where he later served as academic director. A skilled administrator, Warren brought us the knowledge of how to run a progressive school program.

The last of our all-male board was Philip T. Zabriskie, whose family I had known from childhood. Philip was a 1950 graduate of Princeton. He then went to Oxford and was ordained an Episcopal minister after attending the Virginia Seminary, where his father had been dean. In 1954 he had served as assistant chaplain at Amherst College, after which he worked for the National

Episcopal World Christian Federation, overseeing student activism in colleges across the country.

By the end of our opening year, the size of the board would grow to sixteen members, half of them women, including Marty. Two trustees were staff representatives, and two were elected from the parent association. Eventually, the board would reach its current composition of approximately thirty members, but it was the charter trustees who bore the greatest personal risk in the school's early days, especially given that getting incorporated took longer than expected.

The Board of Regents stipulated that a new school must have a two-year track record of fiscal independence before applying for a provisional charter. The Regents' educational standards applied principally to the school's physical plant and its library. We had to submit a written curriculum and a listing of teachers and their credentials, but when the Regents team visited our site, little notice was given to academic instruction. One of our teachers recalls returning from the park with her class and seeing the Regents team with me in the front lobby. Walking up the stairs, she thought to herself, "Flash cards. Forget block period; I'll give them flash cards." Not long after, in her classroom, one of the inspectors turned to me and commented, "I see you have a real school here!"

Our provisional charter was granted in 1968. Perhaps the best example of our trustees' faith in the school is that not once did any board member ever squawk about personal exposure to financial loss. And this was during a period when the trustees made bold and daring budgetary decisions. Had our board of trustees been made up of millionaires, I doubt that it would have taken such risks.

Gordon Parks, recipient of MCS's Living the Dream Mentor Award in 1999. In tribute to Parks, Gus Trowbridge said: "You have known the fury of racism, and have not faltered in pointing the finger of disapproval where it belongs, but, too, you have bridged the boundaries of racial division; you have transcended them, and been, if I may say so, to the mountaintop."

CHAPTER 8

Our Little Ark

BEFORE DAWN ON the morning of September 21, 1966, I dreamed that Marty and I were giving a dinner party. It was to be a lavish affair, for which we had prepared laboriously, cleaning house, shining the family silver and cooking our favorite recipes. An hour before the guests were due, we had set and arranged place cards at our dining table. At six, the door bell rang, and I sprang to greet the first of our guests. It was a false alarm, a neighbor delivering a parcel. By seven, no one had arrived. "Perhaps we got the wrong night. Are you sure it was this Saturday?" I asked Marty. By eight, still no one was there. Indeed, our guests never came.

A few hours after my dream, Manhattan Country School opened with sixty-six children on the day of one of the century's heaviest rainfalls, and everyone was there save one child whose family called in that he was sick. That evening, after 5.4 inches of rain, parents, teachers, sponsors, and donors gathered—like Noah's shipmates—for the first and most celebratory of parties in the school's grand room. Our little ark was afloat in high spirits. Marty remembers crying with happiness. I remember my sense of wonder at the birth of a perfect child and my fear that at any moment something terrible would happen. These mixed emotions have defined our whole lives since, but they were especially strong in the first two years of the school's existence.

Our initial enrollment of sixty-six children, who had been chosen from 140 applicants, included thirty-one boys and thirty-five girls. Of the thirty-three students on scholarship, fourteen qualified for the lowest-fee category, paying 10 percent of the tuition. As promised, a third of the school was comprised of black or Hispanic students.

Personal reasons as well as educational ones determined the school's four groupings: a nursery class of three- and four-year-olds, which took care of our youngest child, Mary; a kindergarten; a first grade, which included our son Stephen; and a combined third and fourth grade, which accommodated our older daughter Katharine. Beyond insuring that our own children would be with us, we wanted to begin with a broad range of ages, allowing the school to move more deliberately into becoming a full-fledged nursery-through-eighth-grade elementary school. Our third-fourth grade meant that we would be graduating students in four years' time and would experience right from the start a school with older children, more clamorous than their early childhood schoolmates, but more filled with the school's pioneer spirit. One family enrolled their fourth-grade son solely because the father, who had been in Putney School's first graduating class, wanted his son to repeat his frontierlike experience of helping to build a program that was entirely new.

Our third-fourth grade would also allow us to offer a trip to the farm in our first year. I did not want the farm program to be a dream deferred. Parents were generally very positive about the farm program, but I sensed that any postponement might cause some people to have second thoughts. My worry about this was based on the example of City and Country School, whose original concept of a country experience was the basis of our plan. However, City and Country's program was offered in the summer as an add-on to the academic year, when the entire school would move into the country. The program unfortunately failed. Teachers were not enthusiastic about committing themselves to extra work, and no doubt there were parents who had other plans for their children's summer. I didn't want the word "Country" in our school's name to be without the program for which it stood. To insure that the farm experience would not be optional, trips would take place during the school year and we would launch the program right away.

Measured objectively, our success was rapid. By January 1967, 150 applications were on file for the following year. The final number in June was 407, including twelve siblings. Two hundred and seventy applications were from families able to pay full tuition, dispelling the worry that MCS would not attract affluent whites. Such a record of popularity among upper-income parents was a reflection, I believe, of the new frontier spirit of the times. In this sense, MCS was proving that the civil rights movement was changing the lives of some New Yorkers, rich as well as poor, white as well as black.

As pioneers in racial integration, there was so much to discover together, so much to learn, and for many of us, so much to unlearn. Preston Wilcox had commented that it might be harder to integrate "the Negro with the Negro" than blacks with whites. Preston's observation was apt, particularly in the first years when some black families enrolled their children primarily because we were a private school, and they had assumed that, like other private schools, MCS would welcome only children of "good" family backgrounds. Marty encountered this view one afternoon when a black parent advised her, "Now, don't take too many Negroes into the school or you will lower the standards."

Dr. Kenneth Clark had proven the destructive effects of racism on the self-images of African Americans. His evidence, presented before the United States Supreme Court in the 1954 *Brown v. Board of Education* case, had demonstrated that segregation contributed directly to a sense of inferiority among black children. Clark had conducted experiments which showed that young Negro children, offered black dolls and white dolls, invariably chose to play with the white dolls. Similarly, it was common for black children to draw themselves as white, usually with blond hair.

And there were other lessons in those early years. A 1965 *New York Times* article by Robert Coles, titled "The Poor Don't Want to be Middle-Class," had cautioned affluent do-gooders who would offer aid to the poor, saying, "Money and work are what the poor people I know demand and need, but

I am not so sure that some of the qualities they already have are not in turn needed by the rest of us: the unmasking humor, and the caustic distrust of fake morality, hypocritical authority and dishonest piety."

Coles's warnings were clear. We were determined to bring different racial, economic, and social groups together, but we could not claim that we were prepared. In the eleven years since the Brown decision, few people had experienced true integration in America's schools. Many of our early encounters illustrated how far apart and unacquainted we were and how deeply we had been misled. When a white five-year-old told her mother that she had seen a classmate in the bathroom who was "brown all over," I knew that MCS would become a myth-breaker. In my thirties, the summer before school opened, I had been surprised at myself one day in Maine when the Flemisters had visited. In preparation for our picnic, Grace applied sunscreen to her children. Until then, I hadn't known that people of color were subject to sunburn.

This made me think of my nephew, Peter. When he was two years old, and introduced to his parents' dinner guest, the former *Life* magazine photographer Gordon Parks, Peter announced, "You're dirty." "No, I'm not," Gordon replied calmly. He then took Peter to the kitchen sink, where he washed his hands. "You see, Peter, I'm not dirty." Peter answered with a smile. "You're *not* dirty," he agreed. Recently I saw an early twentieth century lithograph advertising a brand of soap. The image depicted a black man scrubbing his hands. His fingers were white. I thought of Gordon Parks and of all the others who have been subject to assumptions based on their pigmentation, even by uninformed, white-skinned youngsters.

One of our first teachers, Marge Trimble, recalled such an experience. She shared with me a story about a white three-year-old she had taught while at Dalton, where she was, for a while, the only staff member of color. After the first day of school, the child's mother inquired how she liked her teacher, to which the child replied, "She wasn't there, only the maid was there." Marge is a wonderful conversationalist, humorous and gentle, and in coming to MCS she welcomed the opportunity to have discussions about race with her second-grade students. She was often able to help white students dismantle their preconceptions about race, curbing their budding prejudices.

In one discussion following an incident the children had observed in the park, a white student asked, "Why do Negroes steal coats?" prompting some of his classmates to say, "Yeah, why do they do that?" To Marge, such racial slurs were not occasions for a sermon from the teacher. Instead, she would let the discussion flow and join in later when her voice was a natural addition to others. The six children in the class who were black objected vehemently to their white classmate's remark, and when one of them said, "What do you mean? I'm a Negro and I don't steal coats," Marge chimed in, saying, "Well, I'm a Negro, too, and I don't steal coats either." The class was dumbfounded, and then one of the children said, "But you're not a Negro. You're a grown-up."

I wonder how this conversation would have transpired in an all-white classroom with a white teacher. There's little else the teacher could do but moralize, saying something like, "It's not nice to say things like that." And what if the class had only one black student? The teacher's remark might be the same, or perhaps the offense would be deliberately overlooked. Either way, the toll would be paid by the lone child who was not white, and more sadly so because the original question had never been intended to inflict injury.

The more samples one has of anything, the less likely one is to generalize inaccurately and the more likely one is to cease stereotyping. In applying this reasoning to race relations, I cite the example of a white ten-year-old's discussion with her mother. The mother told me, "My daughter and I were talking about Negroes, and I asked her how many Negro friends she had at school. Using their names, she counted up to about ten when she came to the name Nancy, whereupon she paused and said, 'And I don't like Nancy.'" It is fair enough to dislike a person not because of race but for strictly personal reasons. To be free to do so, however, one must be in sufficiently mixed company. In schools with only one of two children of color per class, it is virtually impossible for white children to judge their black classmates "by the content of their character," and the damages incurred from this circumstance affect those of both races. Black students in nearly all-white schools commonly complain that they seldom feel the relief of being themselves, of being other than a label to their white classmates. Conversely, white students experience a hyper-consciousness of racial difference, and finding themselves leaning over backward to be nice to their token black classmate, they rarely establish more than an artificial relationship.

Given enough diversity in a group, children who are in conflict are better able to avoid racial polarization. I observed this in a third grade classroom which was discussing black protests in the South. When a white girl said, "Negroes are mean to people," she was challenged by a black boy, who said, "Listen, you're the one who's been picking on Michael." Michael was a new white boy in the class. The other children, whites included, joined in, chiding the girl for having been nastier than anybody else to Michael. The issue raised by the white girl was skipped over to address a more pressing matter of group dynamics, effectively dismissing the original generalization. Had the group been 90 percent white, I doubt that the black child would have had the courage to speak out as he did, nor perhaps would the white children have been so ready to accept a confrontation on the part of the black child.

IN OCTOBER 1966, CBS television ran a three-minute story about MCS on their evening news which sparked an array of press inquiries. Some local news stories followed. In our second year, we were deluged with national coverage, beginning with Peter Schrag's January 20, 1968, article in the *Saturday Review*. Entitled "Experiment on Ninety-sixth Street," the article positively characterized the school's mission and prospects. "Manhattan Country School," wrote Schrag, "is private, but in the way it is integrated—racially, economically, culturally—and in its educational promise, it represents what the public school in America was ideally supposed to be but rarely managed. The school does not preach integrated education or human relations, but the diversity of backgrounds of its pupils is one of its great curricular assets." Schrag generously closed his article by saying, "No one can be certain that the successes will be overwhelming, but given the attitudes—the tough-minded idealism of the Manhattan Country School staff—the odds seem to be in the school's favor. That alone makes the place worth watching and worth supporting."

I wrote Peter Schrag a letter of appreciation and told him of my phone call from *Time* magazine's education editor, who also wanted to do a piece on the school. "We were rather chagrined to learn of your school through Mr. Schrag's piece," he had said.

Time magazine's story about MCS, published on April 5, 1968, was captioned "Mixing Races in Manhattan." The article described MCS as unique among New York City private schools. "As urban public schools grow increasingly black, private schools are thriving as select enclaves for ever brighter whites. Many such schools are seeking more Negroes, but in New York City, for example, private school enrollment is still only about 3 percent black. Now one unusual school is showing others how to break the racial barriers." Grateful for *Time*'s recognition, I recall most of all my sense of despair in reading the article the day after Martin Luther King Jr.'s assassination. His terrible loss, which seemed to me to mark the death of the civil rights movement, juxtaposed with the increasing visibility of MCS, made our mission even more urgent.

In a second instance of tragic irony, a *Life* magazine story on the school appeared in the June 14, 1968, issue, the week following the assassination of presidential hopeful Robert F. Kennedy. A three-page feature accompanied by seven photographs, the story was entitled "Making Prejudice Impossible." Referring to our location on East Ninety-sixth Street, the reporter, Irene Neves, wrote, "The city location was not picked at random. The dividing line was deemed the perfect place to start New York's only realistically integrated private school."

The *Life* story included lengthy excerpts from my conversation with Neves, and concluded with the following quote: "As I read the newspapers, I get an increasing sense of the validity of what we are doing at Manhattan Country

School. At the time of Sputnik, we went into a panic about our educational excellence. Sputnik was a warning that our system was not adequate. The events following Dr. King's assassination, the Riot Commission Report, the unrest on college campuses—these things are as significant a warning to American education as Sputnik was. The worry is no longer the space race, but the human race." In the context of recent occurrences, my somewhat sententious comments reflected my personal panic over a national crisis of fearsome proportions.

The *Life* article brought one negative response from a John G. Floyd in Spartanburg, South Carolina. Mr. Floyd began by telling me my views were wishful thinking. "Black and white children have always played together," he wrote. "Close friendships have been made that last in life to old age, but each knows his race, respects each other, and does not participate socially together beyond puberty or the early teens." Then reproachfully, he added, "You are disallusioned [sic] because God made all men with a natural prejudice and you and nobody else can change that. However, it is a fact that people can be taught compassion and understanding of each other (regardless of color), and each can accept the other's right to live his own life without interference. In fact, the racial question will continue to worsen until its course is changed and directed to compassion and understanding of each other." Keep going, I thought, and soon we may be on the same side.

Floyd ended on an unexpectedly friendly note. "I admire people who do things. No doubt you are quite capable of any goal you set for yourself. Keep up the good work, but get on the right track. Discrimination is God-given but understanding and compassion can be developed by man to offset discrimination." Floyd's transparent confusion and innate goodwill, cloaked under his racism, led me to reply in as kind a manner as possible. "Of course, I cannot agree with all your opinions as stated," I wrote him, "although I suspect that if we were to have a chance to converse at length we would not find ourselves so separate in our points of view. Undoubtedly we share a deep compassion for the betterment of all the human race."

The only other "hate" mail that I am aware the school ever received came from someone with the initials GK, who was responding to a listing we had posted announcing our Martin Luther King Jr. Commemorative Walk. "Why are you honoring this man?" he began and then spewed out: "Don't you realize the world would be better without niggers? Let alone those who hate whites. I don't understand why whites love those fucking jungle-bunnies. Is it political correctness or something? Send all the niggers back to Africa where they came from—that would stop them from overstepping their mark." GK's message was sent to MCS by E-mail on December 29, 1999. Mr. Floyd, I wish we could talk now, thirty-one years later. I think we would each be deeply saddened.

ALTHOUGH I WAS only a novice on the topic, *Life* magazine's article made me an instant authority on race relations. Two months later, I was in Minnesota to speak on "The Nature of Prejudice" and to conduct two days of workshops at a preservice training program for teachers new to the Minneapolis public schools. Title IV of the Civil Rights Act of 1964 was at work funding such programs across the country, and my consultant's fee and expenses were to be paid by Uncle Sam.

In September 1968, Negro students would be bussed across the railroad tracks which divided Minneapolis's North and South sides to enroll in the city's first integrated school, Lincoln Junior High. A riot near the school had destroyed a movie theater the week before I arrived. The school board, which had one black member, had three weeks to prepare.

Having decided to speak without a written text, I worried that I would not be able to fill my allotted time. Other presenters who were listed in the printed program had impressive titles and advanced academic degrees. Upon entering the auditorium for the plenary session, I flinched upon seeing a huge blown-up picture of myself taken from the *Life* article. Indeed, my only qualification for being there seemed to be that *Life* magazine had said I was doing something to "make prejudice impossible."

Lacking the expertise of my colleagues, I relied on the credentials of McGeorge Bundy as a source for my remarks. As president of the Ford Foundation, he had just published a powerful address entitled "The Corrosiveness of Prejudice" in the foundation's annual report for 1967. He stated that the "struggle for Negro equality" was "the first of the nation's social problems," and alleged that "the most deep-seated and destructive of all the causes of the Negro problem is still the prejudice of the white man." Bundy could not have been more emphatic about the subject on which I was there to speak. "Prejudice is a subtle and insidious vice," he said. "It can consume those who think themselves immune to it. It can masquerade as kindness, sympathy, and even support. The cause of the American Negro has nourished the self-righteousness of generations of white men who never troubled to understand how destructive it can be to make the uplifting of others the means of one's own self-esteem."

Sharing Bundy's remarks with the white and black teachers and administrators who would enter Minneapolis's newly-integrated school system that fall, I asserted that no single school or governing board could make prejudice impossible. However, I did agree that until prejudice among whites was acknowledged and overcome, true racial integration could not be fully obtained. With this as my underlying theme, I proceeded to talk of my own background and to tell the story of MCS.

At lunch afterward with the superintendent of schools, I asked why he had selected me to be one of his speakers. "Because you are white from the white establishment," he said, "and you are doing something about bridging the racial divide."

"But I'm only thirty-four, I've never taken courses in education, and I'm just a beginner at this," I protested.

"That has nothing to do with it," he answered. "You're a symbol. Once you started to tell us what you were doing, the people this morning knew they were hearing from an activist, not an academician. Our program is filled with scholarly presentations. I asked you because I knew you wouldn't preach theory. Your talk was about practice, and the fact that it came from someone young, someone just starting out, and someone white makes it all the more meaningful. These teachers are brand new to the classroom and none of us has ever taught blacks and whites together. That's why I wanted you here, so they could have someone to identify with next month when they go into their classrooms."

Taking my cue from the superintendent's candid comments, I began the first of my workshops by talking about Paul Bickers, a sixteen-year-old high school student from Leawood, Kansas, whose letter I had received the day before going to Minneapolis. In his letter, Paul explained that there was one black student in his high school. "Ernie," he said, "that's his name. He's our school Negro." According to Paul, Ernie had more friends than he did, but most of his friends were "secretly using him to show how liberal they are." Paul continued, "I always end up yelling when people say things like 'I think Negroes are just fine' because I know they don't mean it in the right way. It's like saying 'I like blue-jays or cats.' They don't even realize that they are talking about human beings who live and breathe and feel the very same that I do."

None of the new teachers in my group expressed surprise at Paul's story. Black participants identified with Ernie; whites with Paul, not his schoolmates. Then I read Paul's last paragraph which caught the white participants off guard. The young man had written: "One of the things that really bugs me is that when I see a Negro anywhere, my mind chalks up 'Negro,' but when I see a Caucasian on the street the word in my mind is 'person.' I'm searching for ways to make 'person' come up both times."

Hearing Paul's unexpected admission, the black participants waited for the whites to respond, and when they did there was an uncomfortable acknowledgement by whites that Paul's experience was also their own. They knew that blacks and whites were equal, but not one white person present had ever known a black person personally. Eight out of the eleven whites in the group could not recall ever having shaken hands with a black person, meaning they had never even touched one. Blacks in the group had had closer contact, many as caregivers for white children, but most said that they could not remember a time when a white adult had looked them in the eyes.

"Next month," I said, "there will be at least one Ernie in each of your classrooms. He will be among the first of his race to join an all-white school, and for many of you, he will also be the first black child you have ever taught. In thinking about what you can do for Ernie, I suggest you focus your attention on his white classmates and help them to see him as he is, as a person, an individual like all of his schoolmates, not simply 'the class Negro.'

"Hopefully," I continued, "there will also be some Pauls in your class who can help you, and whom you can help in their search to overcome prejudice."

We then talked about prejudice. Having learned from Kenneth Clark about his approach in promoting the reduction of prejudice, I asked people to respond to the question "Where am I prejudiced?" Clark had said, "Don't ask people *if* they are prejudiced. That just puts them on the defensive, and in most cases they will deny it." Clark's method levels the playing field, giving people, black as well as white, permission to share their biases without fear of reprisal.

Some years later, Bill Webber of the East Harlem Protestant Parish suggested a similar approach to discussing racism with whites. Bill maintains that all white people are "at best recovering racists." If accepted, his definition, which is more hopeful than accusatory, allows white people to join cooperatively in analyzing their own family history and the evolution of their racial attitudes without having to be bogged down by their resistance to feeling guilty. Once they are given the prognosis of recovery, most white people are able to talk more freely about racism.

From my two days of workshops in Minneapolis, talking with a racially mixed group, I came to recognize that effective integrated education would require much more than the classroom experience that a school could offer. We had had discussions among the staff at MCS like those I conducted in Minneapolis, and our teachers were accustomed to talking with children about racial identity and their perceptions of one another. But I left Minneapolis convinced that for the school to reach a deeper level of understanding about race, we needed to extend our work to include not just teachers and staff, but also the children's parents and school's trustees.

Gus Trowbridge in the second grade classroom of 1967-68,
with teacher Marge Trimble, who later became lower school director.

CHAPTER 9

A Disappointing Courtship

IN THE FOUR years from June 1965 through June 1969, MCS raised almost half a million dollars in contributions, a good sum of money in those days, especially for a newcomer. However, given a deficit in our operating budget of nearly 50 percent, the funds we raised were spent as fast as we received them. We met our goal each year, never closing in the red, but like the bear who went over the mountain, every goal that we surmounted meant another trek in the wilderness where, each day, I would anxiously open the mail to see what I could see. Our payroll was monthly, which offered some relief from a weekly one. In the middle of each month, I would pace on the corner of Madison Avenue, waiting to greet the postman. Then I'd hasten five blocks away to deposit the checks. Except for weekends and national holidays, five hundred dollars a day in contributions was what we required to make ends meet. An occasional gift of $5,000 or $10,000 eased my nerves somewhat, but only for a week or two.

Eighty percent of the funds we raised in these four years came from thirty-six foundations. Excluding the Kettering Foundation gift of $60,500 in 1966, which had helped us to purchase our school building, our average foundation grant was $5,000. These were primarily from family foundations associated with MCS sponsors, friends of my parents, or friends of friends. Overall, our track record with foundations was much better than Peggy

Douglas had predicted. Our ratio of rejections to acceptances was more like ten to one instead of twice that, and taking Peggy's advice to heart, I doggedly pursued those who declined us and ultimately won some of them over.

The first of these was the Alfred P. Sloan Foundation. It helped that the president, Everett Case, was a classmate of my father's and a fellow trout fisherman. At the end of my second meeting with him, he told me that he admired and favored what I was doing, but that I was "fishing in the wrong pool."

"Excuse me," I replied, "there's a very big fish in your pool, and as my father taught me, I'm prepared to keep casting until it strikes."

After months of further meetings and correspondence, the foundation struck with a $10,000 check and letter of commendation, citing MCS for "extraordinary leadership in establishing a school which, in the course of a little over a year, is already demonstrating the values of a truly integrated educational program." The hitch, however, was that the gift was nonrenewable. In making an exception to the foundation's general policy, Case was generously lending his encouragement, yet making certain that my fishing rights would not be extended. In essence, Sloan's support came in the form of a "recognition grant," accompanied by an endorsement that lent credibility to our work. My only future success in fishing in posted waters was to persuade a few other foundations to make such one-time gifts.

Surviving principally on small renewable grants from several family foundations and a rare couple of one-time recognition grants was a fateful means of existence, which caused me continuous fear that if we failed, no one outside the school would give our demise a second thought. We urgently needed one or two major gifts, sizeable enough to establish an endowment or to underwrite our scholarship program over a prolonged period.

Hoping for a favorable outcome, I returned to the Kettering Foundation in 1968, remembering that their vice president, Ed Vause, had written me two years before. In his letter, he had expressed his confidence that MCS "would rapidly become a real lighthouse school." I was optimistic that, having since gained some national recognition, we would be a source of pride to them and warrant renewed support. I had also become friendly with their staff, with whom I had kept close contact. Charles Kettering himself had said, "Call me Chuck," and when he visited the school shortly after we opened, I felt comfortable enough to tell him my nightmare of the prior night: I dreamed that on the day of his appointed inspection of MCS, every black student was absent.

Kettering strung me out for nearly two years and then said no. When I asked Chuck what I had done wrong, he said, "Nothing. The committee considered their initial gift as seed money and concluded that it was up to New York funding sources to pick up the ball." I replied, "I thought you folks from Ohio were farmers and knew enough to not just plant seeds. They need cultivating." My remark prompted a chuckle, but that was the end of it. Apparently the foundation had forgotten its hope that MCS would be a beacon, whose influence would spread beyond Ninety-sixth Street.

While I was dispirited by Chuck's rejection and many similar ones from other promising sources, the effect was always to get my dander up, urging me to take a more activist stand. MCS was not simply another private school. Nor was it only an integrated school. It was a partner of the civil rights movement, and its mission was to convince the establishment there was a need for change.

My belief that MCS could be an agent for change had been bolstered by President Johnson's U.S. commissioner of education, Harold Howe II, who delivered the keynote address at the annual conference of the National Association of Independent Schools on March 4, 1967. Howe exhorted private schools to undertake a public mission. Gently scolding an audience that included the headmasters and headmistresses of nearly every private school in the country, the commissioner said, "In view of our national concerns about the availability of first-rate education for all children, I think independent schools have some obligations which they have not assumed . . . . First, it seems to me the independent schools must avoid thinking of themselves solely as servants of their somewhat specialized clientele and start considering themselves as a community resource with a distinctive contribution to make toward solving local, state, and national educational problems."

After speaking of the need for private schools to open their enrollments to "disadvantaged" students, Howe turned the discussion around, saying, "The term 'culturally deprived' applies as surely to the majority of your students as it does to the young prisoners of the squalid ghetto life. The boy who spends his early years in the green reaches of suburbia and his teenage years in a private boarding school can be one of our really underprivileged youngsters . . . . Bring into his life a classmate from the inner-city slums and I think you begin an educational process that transcends textbooks and classroom instruction."

Howe never spoke directly of racial integration. He took a leap beyond that and advocated radical change within the establishment itself. "Our battles of tomorrow—economic, social, political—will be waged by the most able among our students today, regardless of which side of the tracks they live on. It is to our benefit as a nation and to theirs as individuals to prevent unconstructive attitudes learned as youth from dividing them into mutually hostile adult cliques. We have enough folly of this sort today; perhaps we are mature enough and intelligent enough to rescue our young from the social prejudices which have hampered their elders in our search for a just and decent society."

I don't know how the commissioner's speech was taken by the heads of the nation's leading blue-chip schools, but I went home armed with ammunition and buoyed with optimism. The highest educational official in the land was banging at the doors of the establishment, urging them to "get out in front."

My encounter not long after with the Carnegie Foundation proved to me just how necessary Harold Howe's challenge to the establishment really was. Hoping to secure major funding, I had gone directly to the largest foundation of them all, the lead player among the country's educational philanthropies. To my encouragement, they had agreed to review my proposal for a five-year grant of $300,000. The officer who subsequently met with me said that the committee had liked my presentation. "They found your objective innovative and worthy," he said. Leaving me no time to respond, he added, "Unfortunately, as one of the oldest foundations in America, the Carnegie Corporation can only afford to invest in blue chips." I was stunned and yearned for Harold Howe to be at my side. To no avail, I pleaded my case. "I understand your point of view and admire your purpose," the officer responded. "If you were the headmaster of Andover or Exeter with the same radical propositions, I believe we would be able to do something for you."

I left the Carnegie Corporation with the sad realization that though I was welcome personally to mingle with the establishment and to earn their admiration for our ideals, the lead players were not going to play ball outside the major league. To me, the Carnegie officer's defense was transparent. He knew he would never be visited by Exeter or Andover in 1966 to enroll 30 percent students of color, half of them on full scholarship. And he had determined that the best way to maintain the status quo was to keep the establishment a closed circle. It was becoming clear that my hope for MCS could not properly rely on "the oldest and largest foundations in America."

Nevertheless, I wooed one more lead player, the Danforth Foundation in St. Louis, Missouri. Here, too, one of its trustees, a member of the Danforth family, was an acquaintance of my father. While my entree was warmly received, my first approach in February 1966 was summarily rejected on the grounds that the foundation "did not ordinarily support programs involving elementary and preschool education." The qualifier "ordinarily" was my cue to find a point of reentry. As Peggy Douglas had taught me, I wrote back that I appreciated their consideration and understood their position. I then left them alone until I learned that the foundation was exploring ways to determine the future role of the independent school.

In September 1967, the Danforth Foundation had given the National Association of Independent Schools $170,000 to conduct "A Study of the American Independent School," directed by Dr. Otto F. Kraushaar, retired president of Goucher College, and a blue-ribbon advisory committee, which included at least two members who were advocates of MCS: John Coburn, dean of Episcopal Theological School, and Fred. M. Hechinger, education editor of the *New York Times*.

As I had hoped, the wrenching national struggle of the civil rights movement, and mounting evidence of the need for the North as well as the South to improve education for blacks, beginning at an early age, had apparently caused the Danforth Foundation to take another look at its priorities. I embarked, therefore, on a parallel course of intense correspondence with both Gene L. Schwilck, vice president of Danforth, and Otto Kraushaar. Over the next two years, MCS was included as one of the sixty schools nationally that were visited by Kraushaar and extensively consulted as part of his study of independent schools. Though he did not write checks, Kraushaar was Danforth's quarterback, and in eagerly taking part in his study, I hoped that Danforth would return the favor generously.

I was to be sorely disappointed. My correspondence file with Gene Schwilck is stacked with responses to his repeated rejections, letters that convey not only my frustration, but also rightful anger. March 26, 1968: "If I sound cynical and angry, it's because I feel that the needs of education today are far too urgent for them to deserve the sort of sluggish responses they are receiving at this time." December 2, 1968: "Where does a new school such as ours turn at this point, after continuing to bat zero with Danforth, Field, Ford, and Carnegie?"

I never saw the final report from the "Study of the American Independent School," despite my request that I be sent it. However, a letter we received from Otto Kraushaar in September 1969 gave me a sense of what he may have been thinking. He suggested that independent schools in New York City extend their support to Harlem Prep School, recommending joint extracurricular programs and tutoring services. "Taking into account the touchy relations between blacks and whites in New York City," he noted, "the thing would have to be approached with great care." While Harlem Prep School had good reasons to be an all-black school and warranted all the help it could get, Kraushaar's position told me that he had lost sight of the need for independent schools to be racially integrated.

My final disillusionment with the Danforth Foundation came from two letters I received in August 1969, one from George A. Sample from St. Louis, Missouri; the other from Stephen Fisher in Oakland, California. Both had written me on the recommendation of Gene Schwilck, seeking my advice about raising money for their efforts to start private, parent-community controlled schools for inner-city children. In my reply to these inquiries, I commended their objectives. At the same time I needed to set the record straight. "We have never received any support from the Danforth Foundation, and I find it ironic that they should steer you our way," I said to Stephen Fisher. To George Sample I wrote: "Like myself, you seem to be the victim of the buck-passing game that foundations have perfected. Your goals are great. The problem is whether or not one's appetite, which soon becomes hunger, will lead to starvation while one is chasing around following the carrot that foundations dangle before you."

I never answered the last letter from Gene Schwilck in my Danforth file, dated March 28, 1972. Its message concerned George Sample's school: "You will be pleased to know that the New City School continues to thrive in St. Louis. In many respects, they've modeled their operation after yours." I was very pleased for George Sample. Fortunately, his hunger had been nourished. But my own experience with the lead players, Danforth and Carnegie especially, taught me an unwelcome lesson. And yet, it may have been all for the better. MCS was not Exeter or Andover, nor should it ever be. Our purpose was to change the establishment, not to join it.

MCS student Matthew Schwartz, circa 1968.

His sign reads, "Don't knock that Empire State Building down."

CHAPTER 10

Growing Pains

BY THE FALL of 1968, with 124 students enrolled, we had achieved some visibility, and judging from the enormous number of visitors—more than six hundred a year—and the flood of applications, MCS was coming of age. Our faculty was cohesive and articulate about the school's goals, and our growing parent body was active and beginning to work together as a community seeking its own voice in realizing the school's mission.

Sensing the school's readiness to function more interactively and spurred on by the burning defeats of the movement, I wrote my fall 1968 progress report deliberately inviting the school community to engage in defining and sharing its common interests. In part, the report read: "The tragic national events of the last two years—the summers of riot, the brutality of assassinations—have bitterly demonstrated the extent to which racism corrodes our social and political life. To arrest our nation's progressive steps toward what the Kerner Commission calls 'two societies: one black, one white, separate and unequal,' we must devote more energy than ever in combating ignorance and injustice. Black Power has assumed what, for many, is a new and significant credibility, compelling us all to reevaluate our concepts of and responsibilities toward social progress in an honest and objective way. For us at the school, this includes providing an open forum through which the aims of integration may be redefined and made increasingly relevant to our entire school community."

The forum we chose, a series of racial-awareness seminars, took place in the early spring. Berlin Kelly, a black parent who had been president of the parent association the prior year, and I wrote a proposal to the Sarah T. Winthrop Memorial Foundation, which was accepted. We designed the project to include seminar sessions of twenty participants each, as well as lectures offered to the entire school, including one on Afro-American history by the noted historian John Henrik Clarke.

The seminars were scheduled weekly and conducted by trained professionals led by James Wiley, an MCS teacher, and David Helper from the Scholarship, Education and Defense Fund for Racial Equality (SEDFRE), an organization with experience in running encounter groups on racial issues. These sessions were attended by nearly one hundred parents and staff, with a few parents dropping out when the going got rough. For nearly all participants, the seminars provided their first experience in cross-racial conversation, and it was no surprise that those who had worked together without expressed conflict to build the school, would encounter a new level of relationship, charged with both yelling and yearning.

Parental opinions of the seminars, expressed in evaluations at the conclusion, varied greatly, although the majority of parents answered "yes" to the question of whether they would recommend resuming the seminars at another time. The following comments from a random sample of evaluations were reported in the parents' association newsletter: "Each week was a moving experience, and I found myself thinking about the seminars outside, all the time." "Often uncomfortable things came up. No matter how well we thought we had eradicated prejudice, we suddenly heard the strangest things coming out of our own mouths." "For whites, the unfriendly feelings of blacks were suddenly in full force. One found one had no idea of their despair, though one was always sure one had." "No attacks—a lot of truths—and I'm meeting blacks for the first time in the role of teachers and equals." "The white people didn't learn anything new, but became more aware. There wasn't anything in it for the black parents." "The blacks were voicing their experience, sort of in a teaching fashion. I noticed a difference in some of the white parents' attitudes afterward."

Jane Southern, a white charter parent of two students and an MCS staff member who later became my assistant director, recalled her participation in the racial-awareness seminars sixteen years later in a characteristically lighthearted manner. "I can remember finally being absolutely infuriated by a black parent who provoked me by saying he didn't think white women could dance. In the end we danced together at the final party. It was the kind of exchange where you could be funny and argue and be angry and come back and work again."

But Beekman Winthrop, whose family foundation had sponsored the seminars, was not at all sanguine about the way they had unfolded. He attended one session and promptly wrote me a negative critique: "The blacks were hustling the whites for all the guilt they had, and the whites were loving it and hating it at the same time." He then offered this broader assessment of MCS in general: "I think your school has charm and good will and many other things, including compassion and patience, but it also has sentimentality, which I think it should fight like a disease. Holding hands and saying how much you love one another or hate one another is only an expression of ignorance, flattery or spite. I don't consider it a very good investment of my money to promote that sort of education."

In future years, Beekman's assessment mellowed, and the seminars, viewed retrospectively, proved to be a more productive process than some people felt at the time. After following the school's progress with continuing interest, Beekman wrote me again in 1976: "Looking back, I wince at my letter eight years ago . . . . Since then, even as the government has grown more indifferent to the interests of the poor, ironically I see improvement in U.S. race relations. Your students, I'm sure, will build on that progress, remembering what MCS taught them and in the strength and soundness of your belief in the importance of racial integration in education and in life after school."

I shared this correspondence with my neighbor Bob Carey, who was a parent of two children at MCS and an old friend of Beekman's. Bob had written Beekman in hopes of regaining his support for the school, and in reflecting on the seminars and subsequent discussions on race, he brought a fresh perspective to what was a murky and difficult period for all of us. He wrote: "I think your concern and anger at the ease with which people played out assigned roles of professional victim and professional guilt-bearer are very much on target. It is the last sure refuge of racism. The bleak historical record of race relations becomes, too easily, a morality play which, whatever its charm as a form of medieval drama, loses on the side of human complexity. All of this it seems to me was at the heart of your critique and very much to the point.

"It was prescient, looking at the date of the letter, because it identified an issue at the school which I think is now well on its way to being resolved. It came to a head for Patte and myself when she found, along with some other black parents who had white spouses, that she was not thereby a black parent. This presenting issue led to a vigorous debate, laying to rest insupportable allegations concerning staffing patterns and educational service. It resulted in people finding that they could divide on an issue without choosing up racial teams."

The circumstance to which Carey referred had occurred a week prior to the racial-awareness seminars. That week, everyone in the school had received a letter, along with a proposed new constitution and set of bylaws for the school, from Bob Nichol, whose wife Marcia was president of the parent association. Bob and Marcia, both white, lived in East Harlem, where Bob was actively involved in the East Harlem Coalition for Community Control of Schools. He was also a member of the governing board of IS 201, one of the city's experimental schools aimed at decentralizing the public-school system by handing jurisdiction over to a local board governed by parents.

Bob's covering letter stated his "belief that if MCS is to develop into a truly multiracial, multicultural school, it must provide the opportunity for significant and decisive input into the school's operation from nonwhite members of the school community." While favoring the "stated objectives and goals of MCS," he referred to the school as "a pedestrian operation, which is really not significantly different than the myriad of other private schools in the city." He added that "at present, the school is operated by its administrative staff. The board is little more than a rubber stamp."

Bob's proposed constitution called for a board of trustees of twenty-four members, including twelve parents, three members of staff, the director, and nine members at large, who also could be parents. Half of the parent representatives would be nominated and elected by the nonwhite members of the parent association. The board's authority, Bob proposed, would include direct responsibility for all school operations, including hiring, appointing top administrative personnel, admissions, and overseeing curriculum. The director, who would be responsible for executing board policy and decisions, was required to furnish the board with copies "of all communications and directives sent from the Director's Office."

My first reaction to Bob's communication was bewilderment. I had no idea where such a proposition was really coming from. Who was behind it? Was it a unilateral move of his part? If so, what made him think he had the right to use the school's mailing list to promote his own wild scheme? Then I was enraged. It was the terrible thing that I had long worried about, an attempted *coup d'etat!*

Marty and I had received Bob's mailing when we returned from work, and I had no time to do anything about it as I was due back at school an hour later for a meeting. Later that evening, Marty told me Preston Wilcox had called. He, too, was taken aback. He said he would call Bob, whom he knew very well, and set things straight. "Ask Gus to call me when he gets home," he told Marty, "and tell him not to get upset about this." When I reached Preston around midnight, he said he'd talked with Bob. "He's really out of bounds, Gus, and I told him so," Preston told me. "That constitution of his is IS 201's. He just retyped it, substituting MCS and adding a section about the farm. Whatever you do, stay cool and don't act defensively." Coming from the person who had once suggested that MCS be called "Gus's Schoolhouse," Preston's call eased my mind.

In fact, Bob Nichol's proposal never got very far, but it generated schoolwide discussion, and ultimately aroused open controversy between the parent body and the board of trustees. At the April meeting of the board, Carl Flemister acknowledged the circulation of Bob Nichol's proposal and said he would write the parents, many of whom had already called him offering objections, and invite them to be in touch with him about their response. He would also advise parents that Bob's action was unilateral and not solicited by the trustees. Ten days later, when the parents met to discuss the matter, most people strongly opposed the recommended constitution. There was support, however, for increased parental involvement in decision-making, which resulted in a request to add a third parent representative to the board.

Board members were undivided in maintaining the school's governance as it was. The founding charter had given careful consideration to the school's governance and concluded that, except for two representatives each from the parent body and the staff, members of the board should be elected solely by the board itself. Control of the school would not be subject to any of its constituencies. While an undemocratic design, the choice for an autonomous board rested on the belief that preserving the diversity of the school was paramount, and that the potential for political factions in a representative form of governance could threaten the school's founding principles. A study of the alternative-school movement in the 1960s proved this to be the case. Most of these neighborhood schools, which had been started by parents, suffered from just this sort of political turmoil and collapsed.

The board met the following October and voted unanimously against a third parent representative. Given the absence of any action within the parent association on the proposed new constitution, they chose to ignore it altogether.

In the midst of our tumult over governance, a calming influence was the presence of the developmental psychologist Erik Erikson in the school. In December 1968 he and his wife, Joan, and Peggy Penn, an MCS parent, began a three-year study of children's play at MCS. The same study was also conducted at a nursery school in Stockbridge, Massachusetts, at a Navaho school in New Mexico, and at a Crow Indian reservation in Montana. Erikson believed that by observing young children from different environments playing, without external intervention, with toys such as dolls, animals, vehicles, and blocks, one could gain insight into children's means of defining and mastering life's predicaments.

During his periodic visits over three years, Erikson met with our staff to share his observations. In his letter to me at the study's conclusion, he wrote: "I would like to testify that in the play constructions done at your school, some messages came through with extraordinary force: the messages of being at ease with each other and with the staff; of wishing to express themselves freely; and of wanting at the same time to do a good job at whatever they were doing. I have also had the opportunity to discuss a few constructions with your staff, and their responses were equally natural and immediately helpful."

Erikson's closing remarks lifted our spirits. To me, they will always remain our highest tribute: "For me, the days at your school have always been a fountain of encouragement. I know that a few may argue that you are working under relatively favorable conditions with a more realistically willing group of parents, so that your accomplishments and experiences may not be representative enough to provide universal insights. I very much disagree with that. If we cannot demonstrate at least in some model situations the necessary conditions for the full development of the communal sense and the personal self-expression of a well integrated variety of children, we would not know what to aim for when we attempt to apply our findings to the wider scene."

Coming from one so highly regarded in education and other fields of human study, Erikson's assessment of MCS clearly supported our efforts to gain visibility and secure financial backing. To skeptics outside the school, it was strongly persuasive. To us inside the school, who struggled to work through our growing pains and find common ground, Erikson's blessings offered their own "fountain of encouragement.".

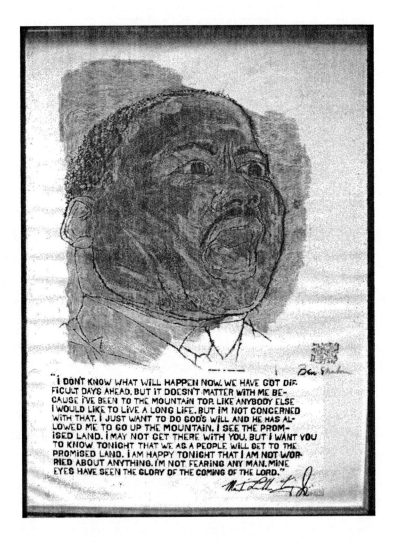

"I DON'T KNOW WHAT WILL HAPPEN NOW. WE HAVE GOT DIF-
FICULT DAYS AHEAD. BUT IT DOESN'T MATTER WITH ME BE-
CAUSE I'VE BEEN TO THE MOUNTAIN TOP. LIKE ANYBODY ELSE
I WOULD LIKE TO LIVE A LONG LIFE. BUT I'M NOT CONCERNED
WITH THAT. I JUST WANT TO DO GOD'S WILL AND HE HAS AL-
LOWED ME TO GO UP THE MOUNTAIN. I SEE THE PROM-
ISED LAND. I MAY NOT GET THERE WITH YOU. BUT I WANT YOU
TO KNOW TONIGHT THAT WE AS A PEOPLE WILL GET TO THE
PROMISED LAND. I AM HAPPY TONIGHT THAT I AM NOT WOR-
RIED ABOUT ANYTHING. I'M NOT FEARING ANY MAN. MINE
EYES HAVE SEEN THE GLORY OF THE COMING OF THE LORD."

Ben Shahn's portrait of Dr. Martin Luther King Jr.

has hung in the living room of MCS since 1969.

CHAPTER 11

Delving Deeper into Race and Class

THE RACIAL-AWARENESS seminars held during the fall of 1968 gave rise to two parallel developments: the formation of a Black Caucus, and a revamping of the school's tuition system, subsequently called Tuition Reform. The Black Caucus was a natural extension of black families' desire to explore their common interests and to develop a collective voice in defining their relationship with the school, while Tuition Reform was principally the invention of white parents, who in the course of the seminars had come to recognize a connection between classism and racism.

During the seminars, it had become clear that to many white parents "black" automatically meant "scholarship," despite the fact that there were many black and Spanish-speaking families paying full tuition and many white families on scholarship. In addition, many parents of color felt that their reduced rate of tuition meant they had less influence in the school community than parents who were paying more. Our tuition system had, in effect, divided the school between "haves" and "have-nots," fueling the polarization that the seminars sought to overcome.

A series of parent meetings the next fall, called "Integration to Pluralism," elicited stormy discussion between blacks and whites, with black participation more strongly represented than white. For the first time, the larger parent body learned of the existence of the Black Caucus, and it heard MCS

characterized once again as "a middle-class school inviting black children in."
In a letter to parents after the meeting, the president of the parent association,
Paul Trachtman, whose child was biracial, asked people to consider why the
discussion had been so polarized. "It is not enough to simply dismiss each
other as wrong-headed or racist or irascible," he wrote. "Some of us may be
all of these things, but in choosing this school, we have all made a commitment
that affects each other's lives."

Bob DeLeon, a Puerto Rican father, expressed Paul's sentiments more
caustically. Referring to the racial crossfire now prevalent in the school, Bob
wrote: "I see the 'white liberal mentality' chasing after the 'awakened black
identity' yelling, 'Come closer, come closer, yes, yes. I am guilty, but come
closer, I want to make up.' Suddenly the situation reverses itself and it is the
'awakened black identity' that is doing the chasing, going after whites yelling
'Honky! You've been doing me wrong . . . . ' Ridiculous? So is being hung up
on skin color, whatever the pigmentation."

On December 10, 1969, on the heels of the heated exchanges that arose
from the meeting on "Integration to Pluralism," the parent association met to
consider flaws in the school's tuition system. The germ of this discussion had
come to me one day when I was returning from a meeting with a foundation
director, frustrated by my failure to enlist support for our scholarship program.
"Why should I be raising money for Bobby R.?" I said to myself. Bobby's
parents, like all other full-tuition families in the school, were paying a fee that
was actually less than the cost of his education. It didn't make sense, although
this was common practice for most private schools, which simply set their
tuition schedules at what the market would bear. The difference wasn't
enormous; in our case, it was only a few hundred dollars. But the fact that a
wealthy family's child was effectively on scholarship was untenable, at least
for our school.

Full-tuition families typically think of themselves, compared to scholarship
families, as not only paying their own way, but also carrying a portion of the
load for those less fortunate. The implicit injustice in this circumstance was
completely contrary to our belief in equality. With no disagreement voiced

among parents that night, nor among trustees at their subsequent meeting on January 21, 1970, the school immediately adopted the policy that thereafter tuition would always be set at the actual cost-per-child. This decision, which was far more radical than the unanimity of its adoption suggested, led MCS directly into a prolonged process of revising its system based on the principle that every family's financial commitment to the school should be *proportionally equal.* But that goal was still two years and many heated late-night discussions away.

THE BLACK CAUCUS, founded soon after the racial-awareness seminars, was similar to groups elsewhere in the country that, according to Dr. Alvin F. Poussaint of Harvard University, demonstrated "a growing sense of black unity and solidarity as more and more Afro-Americans come to feel that their survival depends more upon group strength than upon individual strength." The Black Caucus at MCS corresponded to the national expression of black impatience exemplified by the Black Power Movement. "Now Black Power is legitimate and we can begin to challenge white institutions," the movement's leader, Stokely Carmichael had declared in a May 15, 1967, article in *Newsweek,* entitled "Which Way For The Negro?"

Indeed, by 1970, in the wake of the assassination of Martin Luther King Jr., the course of the civil rights movement had shifted abruptly. For blacks, the course moved from protest to the politics of power. With Richard Nixon as President, national policy on race relations threatened a turn of 180 degrees. A story leaked by the *Boston Globe* that year reported a White House memorandum sent to the President by his aide, Patrick Buchanan, which stated, "The ship of integration is going down. It is not our ship. It belongs to national liberalism and we cannot salvage it. We ought not to be aboard."

The audacity of Buchanan's warning to Nixon was given unexpected credibility by advice from New York Senator Daniel Patrick Moynihan. In an article in the *New York Times* magazine section, entitled "The Sound of One

Hand Clapping," Roger Wilkins reported that Moynihan "urged that less attention be paid to 'hysterics, paranoids and boodlers on all sides,' that the administration pay close attention to black progress, and that it court the 'silent black majority.'" According to Wilkins, "Dr. Moynihan also asserted that 'the Negro is making extraordinary progress,' citing census income figures to make his case. Later, in his paper, he suggested that 'the time may have come when the issue of race could benefit from a period of 'benign neglect.' Whatever Dr. Moynihan may have meant," Wilkins continued, "blacks read this as a suggestion that the momentum of the sixties had generated such a powerful force that the American government could safely lay its black burden down."

In light of such a disturbing reversal in national priorities, it was not surprising that the Black Caucus felt compelled to share its agenda with the school. On February 2, 1970, the Black Caucus issued schoolwide a set of ten "demands," which they had agreed upon at a meeting on December 1. They called for a response by February 15.

The demands themselves covered six areas of school policy. They called for: 1) the implementation of a comprehensive black and Puerto Rican curriculum; 2) the inclusion of black personnel in the admissions process; 3) an increase in racial diversity among the staff, with a goal of 50 percent; 4) the appointment of standing committees in the parent association, which would be consultative and advisory; 5) a larger number of black and Puerto Rican members on the board; and, 6) workshops, seminars, and sensitivity training for all professional staff to promote more effective teaching and learning in a pluralistic school.

Feeling shaken by the racial antagonisms of recent weeks, white parents protested the use of the term "demands" by the Black Caucus. White people weren't accustomed to being told what to do. Upon receiving the Black Caucus's resolutions, accompanied by imposed deadlines, many felt threatened and responded offensively. The demands, however, were in no way contrary to the school's goals, and the context, putting aside the rhetoric, was not unfriendly.

Our first task was to deflate the anger over the caucus's choice of language. To one white parent I wrote the following: "Black-white relations must be open and honest. But the more I find myself caught up in the process of racial confrontation, the more I realize that it is the obligation of whites to pass judgment on themselves, not others. I, too, was angered and sad to have their expression voiced as demands, but I realize that the plight of black America forbids 'asking,' precludes requests, petitions, or pleas. My greatest satisfaction comes from the fact that we are all talking . . . . In the first year or so of the school there was a 'togetherness' which in fact was probably less mutually trusting than we thought at the time. Now, perhaps, the real dialogue is beginning to open up."

Before the parent association meeting scheduled to discuss the demands of the Black Caucus, Paul Trachtman issued a letter sharing his own thoughts, which also addressed the use of the term "demands." "My initial reaction to the demands of the Black Caucus," he wrote, "was to regret the use of the word 'demands.' It is, after all, the language of political confrontation and crisis. On thinking it over, however, I welcome the word. Black people have been asking for things for so long that the very thought of blacks asking for anything now seems abhorrent. The presenting of the demands is a part of the pluralism we are all seeking. If we don't respect diversity of expression, how can we respect the diversity of people."

Paul went on to explain that a "caucus, by definition, is not a separation from the whole, but a working group within the whole." Indeed, in their relationship with the administration, the board and the parent association, the caucus proved that their primary concern was for "the healthy growth and success of MCS."

To assure parents of this, the Black Caucus's chairman, Bob King, read a statement at the opening of the March parent meeting in which he said, "In view of some past discussions that unfortunately became antagonistic, the Black Caucus would like to convey our concern and willingness to work, as in the past, with the entire parent body to achieve essential goals for the school, and by doing so possibly prevent the disintegration of this meeting into one of arguing and bickering."

Coming from the offspring of the abolitionist William Lloyd Garrison, Lloyd and Sarah Garrison's letter to the Black Caucus published in the parents' newsletter was especially helpful in dispelling some of the fears among white parents. "I suspect that there may have been an initial adverse reaction on the part of some white parents to your couching your proposals as demands," they wrote. "Whatever your reasons for this, it struck us that the overall effect of your memorandum was to produce an atmosphere of quiet confrontation, obliging us all, black and white alike, to take a long second look at the whole question of pluralism at MCS. Your memo was calmly as well as concisely composed—if anything, a model of moderation inviting further communication and involvement from all sides."

The views of these parents, together with the stated intentions of the Black Caucus, were strongly substantiated in an article by Homer A. Jack entitled, "The Dynamics of a Black Caucus." "A Black Caucus," he wrote, "is an attempt by blacks to find a power base within an organization to which they nominally belong . . . . The development of a Black Caucus is also a compliment because one usually reflects hope, in the hearts of the black members, that they respect the group or at least that they have enough faith in its past and future to want to spend time reshaping it."

The response of the white parents of MCS to the caucus also confirms Homer Jack's analysis. "Whites," he says, "whether vicariously or through direct experience, have two initial reactions to Black Caucuses. A few immediately see their value and go along, often enthusiastically. Most whites resist. Then some whites comply emotionally, but still resist intellectually. Other whites continue to resist both emotionally and intellectually. The latter feel outraged, violated, isolated, even discriminated against . . . . Very often those whites most hostile are those who have previously been active in race relations. They feel that they should be exempt from the abrasive action of the blacks."

In my personal seven-page written response to the Black Caucus, which I distributed to the community at large on February 23, 1970, I addressed each of their demands in the affirmative. The board's response and that of the parent association also expressed agreement with the objectives of the caucus, and in the course of the next year, the school took deliberate actions to help meet these objectives.

For 1970-71, staff salaries were raised by 20 percent. A part-time black social worker was added to the school's all-white administration. The scholarship program was increased to 35 percent of budget, allowing us to compose an entering nursery class that was 50 percent white and 50 percent students of color. By the following year, of the ten head teachers in the school, half were white and half were of color, and the director of the lower school, Marge Trimble, was black. The overall student enrollment became 59 percent white and 41 percent of color.

Statistics from the National Association of Independent Schools for that year reported the total enrollment of students of color at 5.5 percent, with 10 percent of all students on scholarship. Of approximately twenty-five thousand teachers working in the Association's 762 member schools, 1.2 percent were black. By the early 1990s, the figure for teachers of color in independent schools was 5.1 percent. As MCS strove to expand its commitment to diversity on all fronts, private education in America showed little signs of change.

The only demand about which I expressed a qualified objection was the caucus's stated preference for a separate course in Black and Puerto Rican Studies. "We are now concerned with the 'how,' not the 'why' and 'when' of such a curriculum," I stated. I wanted such a program to be a visible and sequential part of the school's overall curriculum. It and other studies of the struggle for equality should be designed "to prevent the closing of minds and the unthinking acceptance of the racist and nationalist viewpoints which dominate our society today, and to implant in every child the seed of a rational anger at the present state of world affairs."

Despite the fact that we developed and distributed an extensive, grade-by-grade syllabus of the school's curriculum in Black and Latin studies, the caucus and, later on, the Committee of Concerned Black Parents, continued to call for a separate required course of study, which ultimately became the one demand on which the school would not yield. Although the official stance of the spokespeople for black parents in the school never changed on this matter, a number of families of color eventually accepted the school's position. In one of many quarrelsome discussions, the controversy notably lessened when the chairman of the caucus and I had the following exchange:

"Are you saying that you want black studies listed in the weekly schedule just like math or lunch or music?" I asked.

"Yes," he replied.

"Is that because by writing it into the schedule you would take that as a guarantee that it's in the curriculum?" I pressed.

Again, he answered, "Yes."

"What if we didn't put it in the schedule, but we did guarantee it was in the program? Would that make a difference?"

The chairman held his ground, but others in the room seemed partially persuaded.

My broader disagreements with the caucus, which grew stronger over this two-year period as their attention focused more probingly on the school's curriculum and managerial style, were with what I considered the subtext of their demands. To me, the educational views of the caucus were out of sorts with the school's progressive, child-centered pedagogy. The caucus seemed to want a more prescriptive approach to teaching and learning, and underlying their unrestrained assertions, I sensed a measure of formality which favored a more vertical order of authority.

I had always believed that values were better learned by practice than by preaching. Equality, the central value of the school, had to be experienced not only by the children themselves, but by the example of the adults who taught them. Thus, in the preamble to my letter to the caucus, I spoke about my conviction that it was the first obligation of the school to nurture free growth and autonomy within a climate imbued with "unshakable mutual respect among individuals and groups."

"Perhaps it is idealistic to envision a social structure in which no part of the whole wields power over another," I went on to say. "A vertical or authoritarian order is simpler, clearly more efficient and, what is most comforting about it, predictable. Direction, once initiated, can be rapidly implemented down through the structure.

"I resist this structure as it operates among adults as much as I do when I see it at work in the classroom. One of my favorite questions when taking visitors through our school is to ask whether they can identify the head teacher, the assistant teacher and the student teacher. Invariably, the external distinctions are undetectable. The superintendent of an urban school system in the Midwest commented after viewing our classrooms that she would give anything to have her teachers witness the cooperative roles played by the staff of our school.

"This kind of communal interchange has existed not only within the classrooms but also throughout our entire building. Older children work with and help younger ones; parents who spend a great deal of time in the school are viewed by the children as an integral part of our community. I know the absence of stratification within our school can be confusing to those who are accustomed to a more corporate environment. A foundation director spending the day in our school last year was visibly discomfited at lunch to find that while talking with the 'headmaster' (a loathsome title), he was also seated next to the 'janitor' (another loathsome one)."

DESPITE OUR ONGOING discussions with the Black Caucus, the internal life of MCS during that period seemed peaceful compared to the escalating violence in America and overseas. In May 1970, a year that had begun with 250,000 people demonstrating in Washington against the Vietnam War, schools throughout the city took their stand in protest. On May 7, together with fifteen other heads of private schools, I signed a letter to President Nixon. Composed by Coit Johnson of Little Red/Elisabeth Irwin Schools, the letter stated:

"We are appalled at the expansion of the war into Cambodia. We are appalled by the killing of students at Kent State University. And we are appalled at the statements made from the White House in your name in recent days.

"As educators, we teach democratic ideals, traditions and procedures. We teach peace, not war. We teach reverence for life, not brutality. We teach the values of constitutional government and the reasonable settlement of disputes.

"Now we see these values assaulted by the government of our own country and we fear for the future of democratic government.

"We urge you to reconsider your policies in Southeast Asia and at home in light of their devastating effects on the youth of our nation."

A number of private schools closed their doors the following day. After consulting with the faculty, MCS chose a different course—to stay open, but to spend the day in the park together, engaged in activities that both adults and children would find meaningful to the occasion. Announcing our decision, we sent home the following "Declaration of Peace."

"The Manhattan Country School hereby declares Friday, May 8, 1970, a day in celebration of life and peace. In face of persistent and apparently deliberate national efforts to pervert and pollute the human spirit, the Manhattan Country School calls upon its entire community to join together in reaffirming its unshakable commitment toward the inviolability of life, the preservation of peace, and the interdependence of all mankind. The Kent killings and the escalation of war in Southeast Asia are proof of the corrosive forces shaping America and represent an immediate threat to the founding principles of this school community and those for which our country must always stand.

"We cannot be still, and we insist upon the unquestionable rights of our youth to a fair future and an uncorrupted environment. We will not permit education to be a process of dehumanization or alienation. We support the outcries of our youth and ask you to share in their insistence that peace prevail."

The day included the painting of a giant peace mural a hundred yards long and the singing of freedom songs. Parents attended in large numbers, especially during their lunch breaks. Children distributed peace buttons and collected signatures petitioning for the Hatfield-McGovern amendment, which called for halting funds for military operations in Vietnam, Laos, and Cambodia. In reporting the day's event, the parent newsletter wrote: "There were two days from our first discussions to Peace Day. One theme stayed through the ad hoc meetings and telephone calls between, stressed by staff and parents again and again: that we should not close school and send the children home, but demonstrate with them. One child, who had fully enjoyed the peace mural and the singing, said afterwards, 'Well, it's not an ordinary way of demonstrating, but it's friendly.'"

Two weeks later, on May 22, 1970, the New York City public schools closed in honor of several young black people who had been shot and killed in Augusta, Georgia, and at Jackson State College. Again, MCS chose to respond in a more activist manner. The faculty and some of the parents had met two days earlier and decided to keep the school open, wanting "to engage our youngsters in a deeper understanding of the national scene and to provide them with appropriate means for effective action."

The staff also unanimously adopted the following three-part resolution: "1) To keep ourselves continually informed of developments in the struggle of black people for freedom, justice, and equality, and to follow with close attention the course of the opposition to the war in Indochina; 2) To consider and develop a positive strategy within the Manhattan Country School for carrying ourselves and our school family beyond the temptation to hopelessness and cynicism that besets us when we look at the state of our world; and, 3) To set aside a portion of our salaries on May 22, 1970—a day when we will pause again as a school to consider the effects of war abroad and racial killings at home—as a contribution to those who are on the front lines waging the struggle of opposition."

That Friday, MCS upper school students wrote letters and messages of support to children at a school in Georgia participating in a march against repression. "I hope your march will be successful and safe and that you will pick up more people on your way. Just keep going right on! If you have got confidence you've made it." "I feel with you completely and wish I could be with you. I hope you are successful in your fight to end oppression. I cannot find words to express the way I feel about unlawful killings of people black and white." "I am a black student at Manhattan Country School. I think that it's a very good idea that you are walking to Atlanta to talk to the Governor of Georgia. I feel bad because the Governor wouldn't send in the National Guard to protect you. I wish you good luck."

For their part, the staff conducted a telephone campaign to all parents, requesting that they send telegrams to local and state authorities in Georgia demanding that fair protection be extended to those marching to Atlanta. Later on, we sent a check for $520 from the day's wages to the Albany Georgia Nursery School.

Despite the sad circumstances of these two May occasions, they were the first of many instances in which the school collectively asserted its common principles by means of affirmative public action. Parents, who had experienced disagreements among themselves, were in full accord with the school, taking its stand. Teachers, who worked daily in the classrooms to give children a sense of hope in a climate of despair, greeted positively the solidarity of the school's activist stance. But it was the children who benefited most. Staying home, they would have had little to learn. Instead, they were able to practice what we preached in the company of their parents and teachers. For us all, those two days were a welcome expression of the school's underlying unity of purpose.

Taken in the sixth grade classroom, this photo appeared in the NAACP's *Crisis* magazine in 1989. The accompanying article cited MCS as New York's "only realistically integrated private elementary school."

CHAPTER 12

The Storms Within

BY OUR FIFTH year, like the children in our first class, our innocence was showing the signs of budding adolescence. Growing older was often hard, and at times it seemed the promise of our dream was being deferred more by forces within than by those beyond our doors.

One frustration was that the eight children of the class of 1971 were refusing to graduate. They did not insist on remaining in MCS, but they would take no part in a graduation ceremony. Though annoyed with their obstinacy, I understood their emotions. They had been at MCS for only five years; they weren't sure where they were going, if they were prepared to go, or if they would be welcomed elsewhere. I did an end run, and at the closing assembly, which the children were required to attend, I gave my speech, conferred diplomas, and in the presence of the entire school, acknowledged their role as pioneers, describing the occasion as a "moment in the history of the school which would never be repeated or matched in the future."

My graduation speech to the children of the class of 1971 was secretly also addressed to the adults of MCS who were struggling to find their way. "You have been the oldest from the beginning, and I know that this has been a mixed blessing," I told all those gathered at the assembly. "You are like the firstborn of any large family; you have suffered and enjoyed that position.

You have had the pride and the pleasure of knowing that your place here has been unprecedented and unrivaled, that the path you have traveled has been over fresh ground, yet you have suffered from having no one ahead of you, no one older to lead the way, no one to take the blame or to warn you of the good places and the hard places that you have had to travel."

For these young pioneers, who had entrusted themselves to a brand-new school with no record of success, the excitement of founding a school had fueled a feeling of liberation that touched all of us. At the same time, the absence of any prescribed course to follow sometimes clouded and confused our common sense of direction. We were like a ship sailing by dead reckoning, fairly certain of the distance we had come, but without the aid of a charted destination. It would be many more years before the uncertainty of this condition and periods of being off course would diminish, giving way to the stability required of any lasting institution.

The school year of 1970-71 had been another of unrest. After he resigned as parent representative to the board in January, 1970 due to an apparent conflict of interest with his position as chair of the Black Caucus, Bob King became chair of the parent association's newly appointed curriculum committee. This committee, while more representative of the parent body as a whole, became the principal forum for parental involvement, including grievances, and for continued effort on behalf of the Black Caucus to force implementation of their demands. Lacking the specific focus of one racial viewpoint, the committee's monthly deliberations during 1970-71 produced two distinct results: the controversy between black and white parents diminished, but communications between parents and the school's administration hardened as the committee's agenda invited open season on any or all educational matters.

Even so, many of the parent inquiries about the curriculum and the academic performance of students were warranted. During its first years, the priority for the school had been to address its central mission of making racial integration work. Our primary attention was therefore focused on social relationships. To turn now to an in-depth examination of curriculum and methodology was perhaps a sign that the MCS community was ready to address its long-term educational goals.

The work of the administration and faculty with the curriculum committee, requiring extensive preparation of reports and sharing of information, was time-consuming, and on frequent occasions, discouraging. Many parents in the school favored a more traditional academic approach to schooling. On the other hand, the faculty acknowledged the school's need to attend to more strictly academic interests and did not feel defensive when the merits of programs were questioned. They had all been trained in progressive education and were in a strong position to explain the school's educational practices.

We would soon be faced with explaining the school's tuition practices as well. Shortly after graduation, MCS broke new ground when we learned on June 22, 1971, that the Ford Foundation had approved a grant of $30,295 "for the exploration of a new tuition system based on 'ability to pay.'" Prior to receiving this grant, we had been working for nearly two years to develop just such a system. We began with private conversations with some of the full-tuition parents, initiated and conducted by the finance committee. Next came open discussions at parent-association meetings, and formal consideration by the trustees of a plan prepared by Hugh Southern, then chair of the board, and Frank Roosevelt, father of three MCS students and also a trustee, who chaired the subcommittee on tuition reform. Their plan, called the Southern-Roosevelt Proposal, had been offered to the board in October, 1970.

At our follow-up parents' meeting, which was devoted to the concept of tuition reform, I introduced the subject, using the analogy of a group of people going out to dinner together. "Pretend MCS is a group of twenty people sitting down to dinner in a restaurant which charges $5.00 a head. The total bill will be $100." The question I then raised was, "How does the group pick up the tab?" I proposed the following solutions:

1. The guest list could be arranged so that only those able to pay the $5.00 were invited. This solution, which applied to some private schools, obviously did not suit MCS.

2. Charge $7.50 for the meal and let those who can't afford it pay less. This solution was a tempting one and was used by some private schools to underwrite their scholarship programs. It's flaw was that once those paying less learned what was going on they felt beholden to the others.

3. Vary the menu according to the price you pay. No private school would entertain such a plan, yet ironically public education in America is funded precisely on this basis.

4. Offer a cheaper meal to everyone, providing fewer services. As a school whose budget already included no luxuries, this solution was punitive to all.

5. Charge less to those who can't pay their $5.00 and if the total collected is not $100, then find someone who will cough up the difference. Most private schools that provided scholarships, including ours, chose this solution.

6. Don't charge people on a one-meal-equals-one-payment basis. The meal is a collective undertaking requiring that twenty people produce $100. Serve the same menu to all and charge each guest a sum that is proportionally equal to their level of income. Applied to MCS, this solution was the basis of tuition reform.

To date, MCS had chosen solution number 5 above. It was true that we offered a higher percentage of scholarships than any other private school, but beyond that, our system was working against our purposes. Both our procedure for determining who would be a scholarship family and our vocabulary were patronizing, and we were driving a harder bargain with our less well-off families than with those who could pay full fare and make additional contributions as well. Although based solely on need, scholarships were "awarded" and contracts cited a "grant-in-aid," reminding parents that they were "beneficiaries." I wrote thank-you notes promptly to parents in the full-tuition bracket who gave additional donations, even though in many cases the combined tuitions and gifts of many of these families incurred less hardship than the adjusted fees of our scholarship families.

In the Southern-Roosevelt Proposal, Frank Roosevelt spelled out the rationale for tuition reform as follows: "Faced with the divisiveness, unfairness and inadequacy of the present system, a number of MCS parents have begun to search for a new way of financing the school. The new way would be based on the precept that the school is one community of individuals joined in the common task of educating children. In such a community there is no such thing as a cost of educating one child; rather, there is a total school operating budget, the burden of which must be shared among the parent body—and perhaps other individuals and groups—in an equitable manner. In such a community, therefore, the concept of 'tuition' becomes obsolete and is replaced by some kind of flexible fee; the 'scholarship' category also disappears. The important thing is that all parents would be treated alike: All would be expected to contribute amounts of money which would reflect the economic circumstances of each family."

I have never known anyone who did not believe, or at least claim to believe, in the basic tenants of tuition reform, even those parents at MCS who withdrew their children when our final plan was adopted for 1973-74. The principle of "from each according to his means," which underlies tuition reform, is after all in strict keeping with socialist ideology, the English religious tradition of tithing, and the American system of income taxation. But the devil was in the details, and it was in working out the plan itself that we encountered passionate controversy.

As a condition of their grant, the Ford Foundation stipulated that we needed a clear mandate from the parent body before the board could adopt our proposed new system. While the Southern-Roosevelt Proposal was persuasive in arguing the case for tuition reform, its authors underestimated how long and how difficult it would be to satisfy the Ford Foundation mandate. The proposal assumed that its adoption could be swiftly achieved by gathering all MCS parents together to discuss the plan. If given general approval, parents would then anonymously submit their after-tax income so that the school would know the degree of collective support, which Southern and Roosevelt hoped would be nearly 100 percent of the budget. Finally, parents would be provided with a financial worksheet on which to calculate their commitment. Using an honor system, they would then simply notify the school of what they were able to pay. If indicated, they would also contribute beyond tuition. Paul Moore, the Episcopal bishop of New York, who was one MCS parent to whom this applied, always referred to his donation as "my overage."

In fact, it would take a hundred hours of parent meetings before the mandate finally came to a vote on April 12, 1973. The mandate passed, forty-eight to six. The board of trustees also had their own say on the matter, and by the time the final plan was submitted, trustees were sorely divided over the issue of disclosure. Their final vote cast on May 15, 1973, passed only by a narrow margin of nine to seven.

The school year 1971-72 reminds me of Edward R. Murrow's legendary 1939 radio newscast reporting on the Battle of Britain, in which he closed with the words, "The lights will burn late in the Admiralty tonight." More meetings took place that school year than ever before in MCS's history, and quite possibly ever since. They included ongoing meetings with the curriculum committee and a series of eight "Economic Awareness Seminars" about tuition reform. Additional meetings were held in response to new concerns raised by the Black Caucus. Then there were the meetings about unexpected issues that simply cropped up. MCS, it seemed, was conducting a night school, with the lights, some evenings, still on after midnight.

SHORTLY AFTER THE opening session of the economic-awareness seminars on October 20, 1971, a racial tempest swept over the school. It would become known as the "Kiosko Affair," or by some as the "Kiosko Fiasco." A group of Latina mothers had planned to feature a Kiosko as part of the school's farm festival, our October street fair. But on the posters prepared for the festival, mention of the Kiosko had been omitted. Hispanic parents withdrew from participating in the festival, accusing whites of discrimination.

Paul Mayer, the new president of the parent association, Hugh Southern, who had just succeeded Carl Flemister as chair of the board, and I, responded immediately to the incident, expressing regret for the offenses given and acknowledging that "the major responsibility for such injuries lies with the school's prevailing majority—its white component." We stated further: "We recognize the validity and importance of the feelings of those who throughout the life of the school have borne the burden of our individual and institutional racism."

Our letter was a red flag to those white parents in the school who had been harboring frustrations and resentments over the racial crossfire they had encountered with black parents. One such parent was Vic Cantor, who first objected to our "attitude of appeasement and overbalance" and then protested that we had no authority to speak for the "white component." Vic proceeded to tell his story of attending a meeting at MCS at which "a black parent stood up, refused to yield the floor, shouted and threatened to tie up that and any meeting until 'they' got what they deserved. When I answered, I was called 'Charlie,' poked at with a finger and shouted at. I wonder what would happen had a white parent done this, using terms such as 'blackie' or other derogatory words?"

Hugh Southern chose to reply to Vic almost as one would to a younger brother, reproachfully but with the intent to gain a convert. "Your feeling of being threatened by the expression of some black rage is understandable," Hugh acknowledged. "However, the expression of anger is not in itself destructive; it can also be regarded as a sign of a healthy community, where such hostility is ventilated and permitted to subside. The outburst you refer to was not directed at you personally; we are all 'Charlie.'"

Hugh concluded his letter by addressing Vic's complaint that he and other white parents weren't consulted about the contents of our letter. "Our letter spoke for ourselves, in our respective positions to be sure, but not as representatives of consensus," Hugh explained. "We felt it essential to respond immediately to the Latin parents who withdrew from participation in the Farm Festival, and we agreed on the content of the letter. As we saw it, we were simply stating a fact, that there is racism in the school, in us, in everyone, and that the time had come to deal with it before passing it on to the next event, the next potential offense, the next sweeping-under-the-rug of issues that divide our community.

"If you believe that this position constitutes appeasement, then I must say that in my opinion you have construed the entire matter precisely upside down. If there had been appeasement, it has been that offered over a period of years by minority parents to the white majority, years in which racist attitudes and insensitivities inflicted on them have been swallowed, forgiven and endured without protest, while white parents excused all of it by declaring that their intentions were noble and good, and that the 'errors' as you term them were, after all, not 'major issues.'"

Following the Kiosko affair, the Hispanic parents formed a Latin Caucus, which later merged with the Black Caucus. At my bidding, the officers of the parent association called for a White Caucus. The purpose was to create a steering committee, representative of each group, which would bring recommendations for resolving racial conflicts in the school to the parents' meeting to be held on December 7. In announcing this plan, the three parent-association officers, one of whom was black, wrote: "Many people may be initially saddened by the realization that the school has been brought to the point where there are now three recognizable 'caucuses' whereas five years ago we prided ourselves on being blind to racial differences and saw instead only a single, ideal, 'integrated community.' However, times have changed, and it is now apparent that in the attempt to merge into a single community we have ridden rough-shod over old wounds, both individual and cultural, so that it is now time to retract into smaller groups to examine the sore spots and begin the difficult process of healing."

The White Caucus met once. The meeting was attended by approximately forty parents, most of whom gathered in protest. Tempers rose as I closed the doors to the room and the chair began to define our purpose. "I didn't feel good when Gus shut the doors," one parent interrupted. Her remark excited others to voice their unrest. "I know what white people do when they meet alone behind closed doors. I don't like this." Then someone said, "We're not the KKK and we shouldn't feel ashamed. We're not here to talk of 'them'; we've come to talk about 'us.'" As the discussion moved forward, voices like Hugh Southern's led the way. Parents who had come feeling uncomfortable with accusations of racism by blacks, felt less threatened when confronted by other whites.

The evening ended with all parents wanting to meet again. The following week, the staff and I met with the Latin Caucus, and in the few days before vacation, small groups of white parents met informally, including "the front desk mothers," a group of white volunteers covering the school's reception desk, some of whom had been openly criticized for racial insensitivity.

The White Caucus never met again, nor did the three-caucus steering committee. But over the December vacation, the Black and Latin Caucus, whose new chair was Raymond League with Bob King as vice chair, issued a second set of "demands," now termed "Recommendations." These recommendations, incorporating broader concerns that had emerged in the curriculum committee, extended the scope of the caucus's inquiries far beyond their original areas of concern. Also, in contrast to the first demands, the phrasing and content of their memorandum reflected rigidity and a lack of educational understanding. The caucus asked, for instance, "What kinds of assignments are being given to make free time worthwhile?"

In all, thirteen recommendations were offered by the caucus. In summary, these requested: 1) A more probing evaluation of prospective staff; 2) A more probing evaluation of personnel presently employed to include concrete methods to determine efficiency; 3) A more structured training and supervisory program for teachers; 4) A more effective initial teaching of reading; 5) A reevaluation of the independent study time allowed students; 6) A clearer definition of the academic standards of the school; 7) More regular written reports on student performance; 8) Implementation of a separate Black-Latin studies program; 9) A schoolwide consideration of whether MCS was giving students "respect, humanity, warmth, challenge, learning, and individual consideration"; 10) A report explaining how MCS dealt with troubled children; 11) Urgent attention to the admissions procedures for screening parents in-depth to evaluate them as humanists and racists; 12) More black and Latin educators in administrative positions; and, 13) Serious consideration given to what kinds of secondary schools and colleges MCS students were being prepared to enter.

My response to the caucus, dated January 24, 1972, was a fourteen-page detailed accounting of school policies and practices pertaining to each topic. This report was prepared over a four-week period with all appropriate administrators and faculty participating. We kept its content strictly informational, reserving our judgment until a meeting of staff and trustees scheduled for February 10. In discussions among ourselves, however, staff were decidedly disgruntled with most of the recommendations and particularly their implied bureaucratic solutions, which we viewed as antithetical to the school's founding principles.

While many trustees felt the same, the board as a whole took positive steps in support of the caucus, which were unexpectedly rebuffed. In reply to the board's invitation for the caucus to attend the February 10 meeting with staff, caucus president Raymond League answered, "We view the purpose of meeting as an evasion of responsibility and basically a stalling tactic." The caucus would not attend. On learning of this breakdown in communications, on February 2 the trustees reversed their earlier decision against a third parent representative and invited the caucus "to nominate an individual to serve on the board of trustees as a full member with all voting rights and privileges for as long as the Black and Latin Caucus finds it necessary to exist."

The February 10 meeting took place as scheduled with extensive discussion that led the board to two conclusions: first, it needed to convey unequivocal assurance to the Black and Latin Caucus that the school valued their participation and would continue to act in their interest; second, the negative responses to the caucus from the staff and many trustees indicated that relations would continue to deteriorate unless the board directly took over responsibility for future dialogue. As a result, on March 7, 1972, the board established a policy-review committee, which promised that the concerns of the caucus would remain paramount. At the same time, the staff would no longer be on the front lines.

The response of the caucus was to decline the opportunity to nominate a representative to the board, and shortly thereafter, to disband membership. Not being privy to the caucus's own discussions, I never learned their principal reason for this decision. Whether out of overriding satisfaction with the board's assurances or whether because of internal politics, the caucus elected closure, and for the next six years there was no visible presence in the school of an ad hoc committee of black and Latin parents.

Frank Roosevelt, MCS trustee, parent and grandparent,
and a coarchitect of tuition reform.

CHAPTER 13

"Don't Ask Me to Talk About My Money"

THROUGHOUT 1971-72, WHILE WE were was still deeply immersed in matters of race, which many viewed as reaching the level of crisis, the school was also hard at work crafting its tuition reform plan. Though never directly connected in discussion, the two issues were closely akin, as Frank Roosevelt explained in his summary presentation to parents at the end of the economic-awareness seminars held that fall: "To set up a school like this, which crosses so many huge gaps and barriers and dividing lines in our society, the only way we can possibly succeed is if we have no dividing lines within the walls of this school. So the basic idea . . . has been to work towards equal treatment of all families when it comes to money."

The economic-awareness seminars proved that for many affluent people, talking about money was as hard as it was for white people to talk about race. As one father explained, "Asking me to talk about my money is like asking me to talk about my pecker." In the racial-awareness seminars three years earlier, no one had disagreed about the wrongs of racism or segregation. Similarly, although some thought tuition reform was unworkable, no one objected to its goals or defended the double standards of our existing system. The difficulty rested principally in two areas: the topic of money itself and the association of wealth with elitism; and the proposal that for a uniform system to exist, financial disclosure would be required of all parents. A third area of concern, which aroused less heated debate, was over the question of the effect of tuition reform on the school's economic profile. Both sides worried about this. Those in favor of tuition reform asked, "Will the rich folks buy it?" Those opposed declared, "The rich guys will never buy it. You'll lose them all." These three subjects dominated the course of our deliberations over two years.

Sixty-eight parents signed on for the economic-awareness seminars, which met in five groups every week. Fifty-two were white, sixteen were black or Hispanic, and forty-four were full-tuition parents. Each group was led by a professional facilitator from SEDFRE, the same organization for which David Helper worked when he assisted in our racial-awareness seminars. All sessions were taped, and transcriptions were made of selected meetings. Jane Southern, the wife of board chair Hugh Southern, served as the official historian. After listening to nearly one hundred hours of tape, she wrote a masterful sixty-four-page report analyzing the project for the Ford Foundation.

As the seminars progressed, a new set of dynamics emerged from within the MCS community. While nearly a third of those attending were parents of color, their participation was more that of audience than actor. The chief protagonists were white, and when division arose, it was the white people who quarreled with one another. One black participant, who had identified himself as a scholarship parent, was asked by Frank Roosevelt if it irked him that he was paying 10 to 15 percent of his income to the school while he, Roosevelt, might be paying two percent. The parent responded, "That should make you feel bad, not me."

Another black parent, after listening to a long and confused discussion on the problems of getting "poor people" to meetings, finally said, "I think you need not be so concerned about getting those people who have babysitting problems here to meetings; they are not here for a reason. I think the people who are here—I mean the full-tuition paying people— should do their work by themselves. We're not talking about blacks; we're talking about economics."

One parent, who was not happy contemplating making a substantial donation each year, asked if the school had sufficiently explored all possible outside sources of support. A second parent quickly responded, "I do not think that we have the right to go hat in hand to sources outside the school and ask them for money until we have done our damnedest to find out how much we can really support ourselves. If we can't do it alone, then fine, but let's find out."

Unless parents had privately shared or publicly stated that they paid full tuition or that their children were on scholarship, participants in the seminars did not know one another's precise financial circumstances. However, they made their assumptions, which were frequently off the mark. White parents believed that most parents of color in the group were scholarship parents, whereas the turnout among parents of color was mostly middle-class, including full-tuition families. Black parents, for their part, assumed that most of the white participants were full-tuition.

One recurrent question was, "Why aren't all the rich parents here?" Opponents to the plan answered, "Because they want no part of it." Proponents argued, "They're not here because they are already convinced." Knowing who was who, I took secret comfort in seeing the four or five richest parents sitting in the room, all of whom had personally pledged their support. Though itching to speak out, I kept silent.

In general, it was from the middle-class parents in the school that the opposition to tuition reform emanated, not those with substantial, inherited wealth but those who were rich enough to pay full fare and a little more. For these parents, a contribution to MCS would result in a sacrifice of sorts, if only in how they would spend their disposable incomes. Some parents in this circumstance asserted falsely that the increase in the maximum compulsory fee, or full tuition, was due to the school's enrolling more "scholarship" students. In fact, the cost-per-child, which was in line with tuition charged at other private schools, had no bearing on the extent of the school's scholarship program. It was simply the school's budget divided by the total number of students enrolled—meaning that if the school had no scholarship students at all its tuition schedule would be the same.

On one occasion when a parent submitted his worksheet indicating a $5,000 increase in his family financial commitment, he complained that MCS was raising tuition too much. In response, after looking at his worksheet which showed a $50,000 increase in income, I congratulated him on a very good year.

Another parent wrote me, saying, "I find somewhat disingenuous, or naive at best, a statement in a recent communication from the trustees to the effect that the effort to enroll 50 percent black and Puerto Rican students is not causing the sharp upward rise in tuition costs. To use a term often applied with derision by some of the less enlightening literature emanating from your school, I am just a middle class family man with middle class problems. I am also self-employed and unlike most people today, I am not sure where the next dollar is coming from. I would regret it very much if the school's missionary zeal led to the exclusion of the middle class, and to its appearance as a place for Roosevelts and Rockefellers and the poor." In reply, I assured him that should his income diminish, so would his school fee. This parent was no Rockefeller, but nor was he poor, and I believe he knew that as a lawyer with his own practice, he was not likely to be a candidate for tuition assistance in any private school.

THE FACT THAT the concept of tuition reform grew out of discussions within the finance committee, which originated to help with fund-raising, produced a mixed message. Was tuition reform designed chiefly to secure more financial support from parents, or was it a means to distribute financial responsibility evenly among rich and poor? In truth, it was both, but opinion was divided over which goal was considered more important.

In our first and second years, income from parents represented 49 and 60 percent of our operating costs. Our third and fourth years were better, and in our fifth year, parents contributed almost $60,000, bringing total income from parents to 80 percent of our operating costs. These impressive results, which were naturally encouraging to the finance committee, caused those who were designing tuition reform to have high hopes for the outcome of the economic-awareness seminars.

The first three sessions of the seminars each focused on a separate question: 1) How do you feel about the present system? 2) What are your opinions on requiring disclosure of all parents? 3) Will tuition reform produce enough money? After the third session there was a two-week hiatus, during which the school distributed a confidential questionnaire to parents in order to ascertain the financial profile of the parent body.

The questionnaire produced the results we had hoped for: 75 percent of full-tuition parents responded, and projections based on all returns indicated that the financial resources of the total parent body were sufficient to cover between 70 and 80 percent of our budget. On the other hand, the experience of going over the worksheet confirmed the opposition of full-tuition parents to financial disclosure. It also aroused new objections concerning the inclusion of assets, and raised questions about how income would be evaluated for parents with more than one child in the school, or those supporting two households.

Our next two meetings contended with these issues. We determined that a strong majority of parents favored tuition reform, but there was too little time to resolve remaining differences about certain details of the plan before the January reenrollment deadline, when trustees would have to notify parents of tuition decisions for the following year. Given the time constraint, the parents decided to form a task force of eight volunteers, chaired by Frank Roosevelt and charged with developing an interim tuition reform plan by January 1972.

Five days before the deadline, the parents held their last meeting to consider the task force's proposed interim plan, which called for full-tuition families to assess their financial commitments on a voluntary basis. Specifically, the plan permitted full-tuition parents to choose to return their worksheets, or to pay full fare without disclosing their income. Although everyone acknowledged the compromise, the intent of the plan was to institutionalize the principles of tuition reform and to allow more time to resolve the remaining issues. Six parents voted against the interim plan; forty-eight favored it.

When the board met on January 10, the trustees received the proposed interim plan with a sense of relief. There was important business awaiting them at their next meeting, which would be devoted to the concerns of the Black Caucus, and the interim plan was regarded a partial victory, even to those opposed.

Frank Roosevelt had brought an independent CPA to the meeting, who attested to the validity of financial projections made by the task force and commended the progress made to date. "You could sit here forever and come up with five hundred projections and never stop," he said. "Frankly, I feel that what has been done is reasonable. You've got a remarkable start and a basis for deciding whether you want to pursue it any further. If you've got something that is workable now, then take it and run."

Two trustees were not ready to take it and run. One, who had chosen not to attend the seminars, went so far as to say parent opinion was of little value to him. He wanted a "full bedrock, basic discussion" of the principles of tuition reform then and there before moving on. Sensing the board's exasperation, and feeling myself at wit's end, I played every trump card in my hand.

"The fact that last year parents provided 80 percent of the year's budget has proved to me that this school can raise just as much as Roosevelt's slide rule says it can raise," I argued. "But it is raising money while perpetuating a dual citizenship and perpetuating the notion that the rich must pay for the poor. We are not asking the rich to pay for the poor; we are simply asking for the rich to pay a just proportion of their means, and on that one principle alone I ask for tuition reform.

"I think that one of the unfortunate things that has happened in the whole discussion of tuition reform is that somewhere into the discussion has come the question of 'Is it going to work?' rather than, 'Is it right?' Though I know it was necessary to take a financial profile, I think that perhaps was one of our mistakes. The system of tuition reform is equitable and right. So I dismiss workability as a point of argument. We may be financially in no worse shape a year from now, but we will be in better shape because we will have advanced the position which this school first took on the color question with a much stronger and more powerful statement consistent with our commitment to pluralism." In the end, the two trustees who had held the board at bay, voted for the interim plan in the only unanimous decision made by the board during its tuition reform deliberations.

By June, the results of the interim plan were known. Seventy-five percent of the school population had opted for tuition reform. The number of families qualifying for reduced tuition had risen from 46 percent in 1971-72 to 64 percent in 1972-73. This was because tuition had been raised from its former scale—ranging from $1,200 to $2,200—to a flat rate of $2,400. Even so, total tuition income for the upcoming year was modestly up. The audits for the years 1971-72 and 1972-73 did not confirm the views of those who doubted the workability of tuition reform. In each year, parent support equaled 73 percent of the school's operating costs, and voluntary giving was approximately $70,000, nearly ten times what it had been three years before.

While the trustees adopted the interim tuition reform plan without amendments, it was a source of mounting frustration that the final conflict over disclosure could occupy another full year of indecision and heated debate. Opponents of mandatory disclosure based their objection on the grounds that it was a violation of privacy. However, they failed, or more likely declined, to acknowledge the school's well-known policy that the reporting of a family's financial circumstances was based entirely on an honor system with no supporting documentation required. Also, MCS policy assured parents that information provided on the family financial worksheet was to be kept confidential, and any resulting contribution made by a parent would be voluntary. In fact, a family whose financial means indicated they would pay full tuition (otherwise called the "Maximum Compulsory Fee") could opt to maintain their privacy by submitting a worksheet declaring their commitment to the school to be no greater than the maximum fee.

As the debate ensued, it became clear to the majority of the board that opposition to uniform disclosure was a last-ditch effort on the part of a minority who were against tuition reform from the beginning. Consequently, by April 1973, with sentiment among MCS parents overwhelmingly behind uniform disclosure, the trustees expressed the opinion that the debate had gone on too long. The wealthiest families in the school had already submitted worksheets and declared their support, and Frank Roosevelt and I had estimated that perhaps only a few families would leave if required to disclose.

At a board meeting called to discuss the issue, Peter Ribicoff, a parent trustee who had been committed to tuition reform from the outset, proposed that by the end of the following school year, 1974-75, the board would resolve its differences and enact a final uniform tuition plan. "I feel a special responsibility to deal with this," Ribicoff said. "I don't want to pass the buck from one year to another. The board should take a stand for once and for all."

Not all trustees agreed, and the two opposing members played down and dirty, claiming that the motion was out of order, and offering a motion for adjournment, which was then defeated by one vote. Whereupon the two trustees left the meeting, and the remaining board members approved the Ribicoff motion and instructed the committee on tuition reform to draft a plan to implement his resolution.

As expected, the committee opted for uniform compulsory disclosure for all families. However, to protect those families who might be forced to withdraw their children from MCS, the resolution provided a two-year exemption available to parents who had enrolled their children prior to the introduction of tuition reform. The committee's proposal aroused objections from both sides of the aisle, with a flurry of defeated amendments. In the end, the board voted for the resolution by a margin of one.

While the board lacked the solidarity that Southern, Roosevelt, and I had hoped for in adopting tuition reform, the parent body was all but unanimous, giving the school the mandate that the Ford Foundation was looking for. "Scholarship" families expressed relief that the long process was over and that finally the school had eliminated a dual standard that separated the "haves" from the "have-nots." Wealthy families pitched in, contributing over $80,000 in each of the two years following the climactic adoption of the plan. On the down side, five families withdrew from the school and two trustees resigned.

After this initial fallout, the board never quarreled again about the school's unique and radical tuition policy. In 1974, we obtained a second, smaller grant from the Ford Foundation that was used to underwrite our 1981 publication of "Tuition Reform for Private Schools: The Manhattan Country School Plan," coauthored by Frank Roosevelt and Thomas Vitullo-Martin, an independent consultant on private-school finance. The book, which was distributed to several hundred independent schools nationally, sparked a favorable response and an article in *Time* magazine, but only a handful of schools undertook to consider our plan, and none that we knew of adopted it.

Within MCS, however, the positive effect of tuition reform was so strong that teachers elected to apply its principles to their own compensation. Until then, the board had annually determined the percentage for salary increases, which were then distributed equally to all staff. At the staff's request, the board allowed the faculty to recommend how the overall allotment would be distributed, which resulted in preferential treatment to categories that the staff considered to be undercompensated. For 1974-75, for example, teachers adopted a policy of providing a dependency allowance to staff with children, which was doubled for single-parent employees. The cost of this provision and others adopted in future years was borne by a reduction in increases for staff who did not fall into the category in question. In their own way, the school's staff, like the parents, were setting policies designed to offset inequalities among themselves.

In November 1974, a few days after President Gerald Ford had pardoned Richard Nixon for his involvement in the Watergate scandal, Frank Roosevelt and I were returning to school in a taxi from an appointment at the Ford Foundation, where we had reported on the first year of tuition reform. I said to Frank, "If Ford can forgive Nixon, perhaps we should do the same for those parents at MCS whom we had compelled to disclose their income or withdraw their children by 1976." Frank agreed, and by unanimous consent the board ruled not to enforce disclosure for any family whose fee was at the maximum level, on the condition that such families would thereafter be held to the maximum fee.

The board recognized this compromise. Knowing that they could not legislate compliance, and determined not to prolong its indecision, the trustees elected to institute the new plan regardless of those who declined disclosure. Thereafter, our system was renamed the "Family Financial Plan" and nowhere in the school's literature did we ever again use the terms of "scholarship" and "full tuition." In eliminating the divisive language and patronizing attitudes associated with these classifications, MCS became the first independent school in the country to ask all families to conform to the principle of tithing.

Kenneth Clark, Ira Glasser, and Nathaniel Jones at a
Center for Integrated Education conference in 1973.

CHAPTER 14

Carrying the Message Forward

IN OCTOBER 1972, I was the keynote speaker at a conference in Pittsburgh, entitled "What It's Like To Be Me. What It's Like To Be You," sponsored by the city's board of public schools. The title assigned to my talk was "Examining My Attitudes toward My Own Racial Identity." Although still far from an expert on the subject, I was better prepared than when I had gone to Minneapolis four years earlier. From my exposure to race relations since then, I was beginning to understand better what it was like to be me; that is, to be white.

In my opening remarks, I spoke about the need for "a new consciousness among whites, a consciousness without which white America could not begin to be humanized, and pluralism in society could not be obtained." Drawing almost verbatim upon my conversation with the White Caucus at MCS the year before, I said that in my effort to create an integrated school I had grown less concerned with what whites could do for blacks and more concerned with what whites must do for themselves in order to gain a sense of their own positive identity.

"The fate of black America still rests upon whites," I argued. "Just as the so-called Negro problem has been the deliberate result of the institutional racism of white America, the liberation of blacks and other oppressed minorities is tied to the emancipation of whites. To enable blacks to gain their self-worth, we must force ourselves to shed the historical privilege of our whiteness."

My audience of two or three hundred educators and school administrators, like that in Minneapolis, was racially mixed, though principally white. The goal of the conference was to help facilitate the integration of Pittsburgh's school system. Knowing the resistance of the city's white population, I therefore told the story of MCS, emphasizing the effect of integration on our white parents and students.

The comments of those who came to my discussion group afterward revealed opposite reactions from white and black participants. Unexpectedly, blacks in my group outnumbered whites. I asked them why this was so. "Because we've heard enough about the problems of bringing Negroes into the better schools," one person said. "And we're tired of hearing about what opportunities white people want to give our children. I came here because you turned the discussion in the other direction, and I want to learn more about how our schools can generate racial awareness among white parents."

White participants nodded in agreement but did not choose to help answer this question. They were more anxious to talk about Black Power, expressing their fear that militant blacks were working against integration, forcing whites to be on the defensive. "What more can we do?" they said. "Whenever we reach out, we're shouted down."

In answer, I quoted from an essay titled "The Honor of Being White" by *Saturday Review of Literature* writer Peter Schrag. The date of Schrag's writing is lost to me, but his words remain in a faded clip that I've kept since: "What scares liberal intellectuals most," Schrag had written, "is the real possibility that Black Power has begun to steal their virulence and their courage. They are supposed to be the initiators, the critics, the cranks. The blacks are forcing them into that most revolting position: defense of the Establishment."

Returning to MCS after the conference, I thought about how we and those in Pittsburgh and in thousands of public schools in America were traversing the same ground. Our "Experiment on Ninety-sixth Street" had a more pressing purpose, and I thought it was time for MCS to reach out and grapple with its determination to serve a public mission. Internal discussions about race and the school's prolonged debate over tuition reform had taught us a great deal, but we were running the risk of being too self-absorbed.

In my talk to parents that year, I expressed these feelings, saying, "We must approach our work with a fresh outlook and more determined passion. In our six years, we have secured a measure of the establishment's recognition and regard. Now, therefore, is the time to shout louder and to use our institutional credibility to aid the advocates of racial integration whose cause we share."

DESPITE THE VICTORIES of the civil rights movement in the 1960s, racial isolation in northern city schools was at its highest levels in the 1970s. While the Brown decision of 1954 desegregated Southern public schools, every year thereafter fewer and fewer black and white children were going to school together in New York City. In 1955, the population of Manhattan was 75 percent white and 25 percent "minority." By 1966, the year we started MCS, the ratio was one to one. Nearly a decade later, the white population had dropped to 32 percent in New York City. (In our nation's capital, it was only 2 percent.) The demographics of New York City, affected by a vast influx of people of color and by a corresponding "white flight," made racial integration for millions of school children almost impossible.

The problem in the North was de facto segregation, which was neither unlawful nor subject to forced intervention. In 1973, with city school districts confined to racially isolated neighborhoods, only 15 percent of New York's children of color attended nonsegregated public schools, and in the private, nonparochial schools, the percentage was 3 percent. In contrast, in Little Rock, Arkansas, where the struggle for equal opportunity had begun, four times as many black children attended desegregated schools than in New York. In fact, according to Dr. Kenneth Clark, half the population of black children in the seventeen Southern states were attending nonsegregated schools by 1973.

Clearly the playing field for the advancement of integrated education was no farther than our front door. When I first met with Dr. Clark to share my desire to use MCS as a model for interracial schooling, it was nearly twenty years after he and Thurgood Marshall, then head of the NAACP's legal-defense fund, had worked together to convince the Supreme Court to outlaw segregation. Dr. Clark, though encouraging, expressed remorse that we should still be having to talk about institutional racism in our school systems. "It is a personal and collective embarrassment that we are required to still consider this question," he said. He then told me of a conversation he'd had with Marshall on a train ride from New York to Washington, where the *Brown v. Board of Education* case was before the U.S. Supreme Court. On the train, Dr. Clark noticed that his esteemed colleague had begun to cry. When he asked what was wrong, Marshall replied, "I'm terribly tired; I'm tired of trying to save the white man's soul." As he recounted the story, Dr. Clark himself was on the verge of tears. "I, too, weep for my nation," he said to me. "I weep because of the moral schizophrenia at the heart of the American people. Nothing in our present educational system is preparing children for the realities of racial equality." Deeply moved by Dr. Clark's candor, I was more determined than ever to do my part to help bring about a change, at least in the realm of education.

With Dr. Clark's endorsement and his promise to lend assistance, we designed the Center for the Advancement of Integrated Education, an organization to be sponsored by MCS and Dr. Clark's firm, Metropolitan Applied Research Center (MARC). The organization would be administered by a steering committee that would be one-third white, one-third black and one-third Hispanic. Half its members were from MCS, and half were community people from Yorkville and East Harlem. To gain visibility and attract funding, we assembled an advisory committee of integration advocates such as Julian Bond, then head of Southern Poverty Law Center; Robert Coles, the child psychiatrist from Harvard; Jack Greenberg from NAACP Legal Defense Fund; Theodore Hesburgh, president of Notre Dame; and Eleanor Holmes Norton, from the

Commission on Human Rights. Of the thirty or so people we invited, none turned us down.

Our funding efforts were not as successful, despite the fact that our projected costs were modest, as staff support was assigned from MCS and MARC, and speakers at our conferences waived their fees, charging only for transportation. Our annual budget was never more than $5,000, which MCS and MARC donated for the first year of the center. Thereafter, we determined that the organization should be self-supporting. The Grant Foundation then gave us $5,000, but the following year, upon reapplication, we were told that the trustees had lost interest in school integration.

During the four years that the center was active, its major work was to hold public meetings addressing the need to reduce racial isolation in New York schools and promoting the means by which schools could move from desegregation to integration. The first of these meetings, held at MCS in spring of 1973, offered a lecture by John Henrik Clarke, editor of *Freedomways* magazine and a professor at Hunter College. It was followed a few weeks later by another lecture from Thomas Pettigrew, Harvard professor of social psychology.

In May 1974, we honored the twentieth anniversary of the Brown decision with a gathering at PS 198, attended by three hundred people. Our guest speakers were Kenneth Clark and Thomas Pettigrew, whose talks fortified my confidence in the potential of MCS to serve as a model for integration, and eased my discouragement at the recent racial conflict within the school. Following the event, the *New York Times* printed Dr. Clark's speech in its entirety, and the National Association of Independent Schools, which helped pay for our transcription of the evening's presentation, distributed our report to its membership.

In his talk, Pettigrew called himself a Southern liberal. "There are only about thirty of us, and my wife says we all know each other," he joked. He then spoke about the need for a careful distinction between "desegregation" and "integration," something that had occupied much of my own thinking when founding MCS. "Mere desegregation is the end of segregation," he said. "You have children of different races together in the same building. Now Ken Clark and I have been accused of saying that all you have to do is put children together from different groups and they'll love one another, and there will be peace and harmony and a wonderful America from then on. I don't remember us ever saying anything like that. What we did say was that segregated education was not only morally reprehensible but educationally defeating for all children.

"I am happy that this Center is being established, calling for the advancement of integrated education—not desegregated education. I'm not a desegregationist; I'm an integrationist, and by integration I obviously mean not just having children together in the same building, but rather something about the quality of the contact that goes between them. I'm talking about racial acceptance and friendship and equality. I'm not talking about assimilation, as some people seem to define integration.

"The question comes: How do you go from 'desegregated' to 'integrated institutions?'" Pettigrew acknowledged he had no answer as yet, stating there were not enough examples of integrated schools, and commenting that "we're fumbling our way in learning how to integrate institutions; we have no experience in the United States, and we have to learn it and do it as it unfolds."

Pettigrew then made a pointed reference to MCS: "As you here know better than most people, and particularly from the last eight years' experience of Manhattan Country School, integration is not an easy process. We know how to make desegregation fail better than we know how to make it succeed, for all of us, black and white, are products of a society that did not prepare us for integration. Indeed, it prepared us for quite the opposite. To succeed, we must overcome our training. This is the critical task for this school and others like it."

The opportunity for successful integration, according to Pettigrew, resided in the primary grades, an assertion any teacher in elementary education would have applied to all learning, particularly when the process required "unlearning." He then cited the Kindergarten Plan of the 1950s in the South, which proposed incremental desegregation beginning with five-year-olds.

"The Klan and the Citizens Councils were really furious over this idea," Pettigrew recalled. "They went to the Federal Court and pleaded with the Federal Judge in Meridian, Mississippi, and I was present. 'Please, Judge,' they said, 'you can't start with the little kids because it wouldn't be right; it wouldn't be fair. Those children are simply too young to know any better.' And that's precisely the principle I'm putting forth. They are too young to know any better. They are too young to have picked up the full force of American racism, and so you're much more able to develop integration in the first grade than you are in the ninth."

As a member of the New York State Board of Regents, which governs public education, Kenneth Clark knew well the politics of race in New York, and in his talk he spared no words in pinning the blame for integration's downfall on those in the highest positions of power. "I will never forget the time," he said, "when John Theibold was superintendent of schools in New York, and John was a friend of mine when we were colleagues in college. One afternoon I went to talk with John about the problems we were having desegregating the schools. John said to me, 'Kenneth, you know, I've got to tell you something. Some of the very people who are on committees working with you for desegregation of the schools, who are on the commission on integration, they come to me, and they come into the office, and they say, "Look, John, you know that's our public posture. What we really believe is we don't want these schools changed."'"

Clark characterized Northern resistance to integration as more elusive than Southern resistance, asserting that Northern resistance was shielded by double-talk and hypocrisy. He devoted his speech to urging integrationists to take a more outspoken stand by using desegregation as "an educational opportunity to help young people overcome the deficits of past segregation." In answer to a young high school student who asked what could be done, Clark's reply underscored the rationale and future work for the center. Clark told the student to "confront his school administrators and teachers and demand that they set up opportunities for the young people to come to grips with the problems and the inevitable tensions which will come when a society or a segment of it is trying something which it had not previously tried."

In October 1974, we held a follow-up conference, again featuring Kenneth Clark, who was joined by Ramsey Clark, former U.S. Attorney General; Nathaniel Jones, NAACP general counsel; and as moderator, Ira Glasser, director of the New York Civil Liberties Union. Despite the distinguished lineup of panelists, attendance was low and the press declined coverage. The country was reeling in the wake of Watergate, and Congress, having defeated a busing bill, was successfully dismantling federal support for integration.

The Center remained active for two more years, less visible but more proactive, in keeping with Kenneth Clark's recommended approach. We published a newsletter called *Report Card on Integration*, designed to counter sensational media stories featuring resistance to desegregation in places such as Boston and Louisville, and we also provided small recognition grants of $500 to student-led organizations for exemplary work in promoting integration within New York City schools. When our funds ran out, the board of MCS properly declined to underwrite the Center, and it closed.

Despite its failure, the Center spurred MCS to begin to serve its public mission and to embark upon a deliberate effort of community outreach which would distinguish its future course as a model for educational reform.

The class of 2008.

CHAPTER 15

"We're Like a Family—We're Fighting Now, But That Doesn't Mean We Can't Stick Together"

IN THE SPRING of 1974, while disheartened by the demise of the Center for the Advancement of Integration, I was inspired by the attention civil rights activists had given MCS, and determined to advance our effort, setting more far-reaching goals for the school. In the eight years since opening MCS, as a result of both our own internal struggle and the national breakdown in the integration movement, my own language had changed radically, and so had the practices we preached. Compared to the school's founding year in which 30 percent of the students were of color, the racial composition of students in 1974-75 was 56 percent white and 44 percent of color, with our entering class of four- to five-year-olds holding constant at 50-50 for the past four years, consistent with our goal of a school with no racial majority. By then, our staff was 42 percent people of color, with an equal racial distribution of head teachers.

When the Black Caucus had rightly expressed objection to the school's all-white administration in 1970-71, I had appointed a back woman, Marge Trimble, one of our founding teachers, as director of the lower school. Two years later, I gave up directing the upper school myself and hired Jim Campbell, an educator from Bank Street College, who had come part-time to MCS the prior year to help us develop our African-American Studies program. Two of our top five administrators were now people of color. During the same time span, the school's curriculum became increasingly inclusive and activist. By 1974-75, we were teaching Spanish at all levels, beginning with four-year-olds. We also set the goal that all teachers would acquire a proficiency in Spanish at least at the level of the students they taught. Teachers were offered the necessary instruction, and later, when additional funds became available, teachers were granted the means for summer travel to study in Central America.

While we maintained the position that black studies would not be offered as a separate course, in revising our curriculum in 1970 we adopted the following educational platform: "That our school must provide continuous academic and social learning related to pluralism is indisputable. Healthy self-concepts, strong racial identity and awareness, knowledge of ethnic and cultural backgrounds, and a grasp of the horrendous personal, racial and institutional injustices of our past and present society—these objectives must assume paramount importance in our school's total curriculum. Among its principal, stated aims, the social studies program of our upper school is designed to prevent the closing of minds and the unthinking acceptance of the racist and nationalist viewpoints which dominate our society today, and to implant in every child the seed of a rational anger at the present state of world affairs."

The two years leading up to our tenth anniversary, and the two years after, were a coming of age for MCS—a period of constructive undertakings marked by a unity of spirit that the school had not felt since its pioneer years. In my report to the board at the opening of our ninth year, I reported that, "The year has gotten off to an excellent start, and there is a sense of excitement and peace in the school." Even John Hewitt, the chair of the Policy Review Committee, the board's "watchdog" for racial unrest, seemed to agree. At the committee's first meeting in January 1974, nearly two years after its establishment, John concluded that the school had "reached a plateau of sorts," and he saw no need to call a future meeting.

With the subsiding of racial conflict and the resolution of our prolonged debacle over tuition reform, the school was able to turn its attention to work it had neglected and to strengthening its precarious fiscal condition. Among our accomplishments was restructuring the governance of the farm. We dissolved the farm council, comprised of parents and friends of the school, and established a standing committee of trustees to oversee policy-making for the farm. Upon setting the objective that the farm should produce greater income, we started a summer session and set aside eight weeks a year for rentals to other schools. Other adjustments to our farm program included a house for our farm director. And, after the retirement of one of our cofounders, Ruth E. Cooke, we succeeded in raising funds in her honor to create separate and spacious facilities for a textile studio and a nature lab by renovating the old horse barn.

In addition, during this period of relative calm, we acquired our permanent charter from the New York State Board of Regents, set up an annuity program for senior staff, and eliminated our indebtedness on 7 East Ninety-sixth Street, applying $105,000 raised from our tenth anniversary capital campaign to burning our mortgage with the Bank of Tokyo.

Upon receipt of a $50,000 gift from the DeWitt Wallace Fund of Reader's Digest, we established an endowment fund, which ultimately became the principal source of our financial security. Mr. Wallace asked that we designate individual students as "DeWitt Wallace Scholars," requesting that they annually acknowledge his support. The board voted not to accept Wallace's gift unless this condition were dropped. To resolve the conflict in a manner that I hoped would satisfy Mr. Wallace, I took the problem to our sixth-graders, who understood the dilemma right away. They said, "Let us all write Mr. Wallace a thank-you letter, telling him that every student in MCS is benefiting from his generosity." I composed my official reply, explaining the nature of our school's tuition reform plan, stating that I had no objection to designating individual scholars, providing their identity was kept confidential, and enclosing twenty children's letters of appreciation. Mr. Wallace agreed and acknowledged every student!

IN 1976-77 THE BLACK Caucus was reactivated by a group of parents who renamed themselves the Committee of Concerned Black Parents (CBP). The relatively small group included some members who had been part of the original caucus, but the majority were relatively new to the school. From the outset, they made themselves known to the school administration, and we met frequently. In their initial approach, unlike the earlier caucus, the CBP posed no "demands," but rather, offered themselves as resources to the school in support of the curriculum.

The following fall, their offer led to the gift of a collection of West African art, donated anonymously in response to a request of the CBP. I appreciated the gift, and also the readiness of the CBP to assist in enhancing exposure to black culture in the library and classrooms. And I especially welcomed the group's expressed approval that black studies not be taught as a separate course of study.

In November, the parent representative to the board, Linda Sklaroff, who had met with the CBP, conveyed the message that the group, which she characterized as not being "hot-headed," asked to meet with the trustees. The board agreed, requesting that the CBP meet first with the faculty about whatever concerns they had with the curriculum, and that they provide the trustees with a written agenda in advance of their meeting, which was scheduled for May 17, 1978.

My confidence in working collaboratively with the CBP diminished when, soon after the November meeting, communication between the MCS administration and the group abruptly ceased despite my expressed desire that we continue to meet. Apparently, the CBP was meeting regularly with Preston Wilcox, who was still a member of the board, but rarely attended its meetings. Wilcox conveyed that the group's chief spokesperson, Judy Rollins, was opposed to any discussions with administration or staff prior to their May presentation to the board. The CBP, unlike the earlier Black Caucus, had no elected chair and never submitted consensual statements. Ultimately, a meeting with the school's faculty did take place without Rollins, and discussion points offered dealt only with enhancing the teaching of black culture. One particularly useful suggestion was that the school should "acknowledge the historical and contemporary role of black heroes other than Martin Luther King Jr." All in all, the meeting was constructive and relations were amiable with no indication of the tempestuous exchange that was to take place a week later with the board.

Of the four members of the CBP group who attended this ill-fated meeting, Judy Rollins took the lead and held the spotlight thereafter. She began by asserting that, concerning its "commitment to pluralism about which the school speaks so proudly, there was a gap between word and day-to-day action." Then she stated that members of the CBP had noticed that some teachers were "unprepared to build on cultural diversity in the classroom." Finally, she said that there was "a lack of support" felt by the CBP in admissions and high-school placement. Leila Snipes, a founding parent and the only member present who had also been on the Black Caucus, asked why "past promises had not been fulfilled," but offered a positive opinion concerning her children's preparation for high school. She then suggested that "new parents and staff do not have the same sensitivity to racism as the old," stressing the need for "an atmosphere where all elements—teachers, kids, parents—can interact freely so that the quality of relationships is known by all throughout the school." Bert Gibson raised the long-discussed issue of increased pluralism among the MCS staff. Gloria Brown, a founding parent and a member of staff as well, did not actively participate.

As discussion proceeded and other trustees and representatives of the staff responded and quarreled over points offered, Rollins extended her claim, stating that "the school is institutionally racist" and that "pluralism at MCS is an incredible hypocrisy." Preston Wilcox defended her and accused the board of being unable to listen "fully and openly" without resorting to hostility. Tempers flared and communication worsened despite fellow board member Bill Webber's attempt to give a measure of perspective. "White people," Bill said, "need to be in regular dialogue and under regular pressure by blacks to recognize and change their own racism that our society instills."

In the heat of debate, John Hewitt, the board's vice president, who was chairing the meeting, introduced a letter hand-delivered to him earlier in the evening. Coming from two black parents, Pat Carey and Marvin Hughes, both with white spouses, the letter alleged and protested that the CBP group had a policy of excluding parents in interracial marriages. For the most part, the board, including myself, had been completely unaware of this. "To the best of our knowledge," Pat and Marvin wrote, "the ad hoc black parents' group has taken upon itself the task of defining who is a black parent at Manhattan Country School . . . Two things can be said immediately. If some black parents are seen as true black parents, while others are not, the definition of blackness seems to have taken on a metaphysical quality that strains credulity and invites the charge of racism. Secondly, if by definition some black parents are excluded from significant participation in such a group, its representative quality as well as its moral legitimacy is open to question, if not dismissal."

The allegation that the CBP was an exclusionary group was never refuted. Instead, Judy Rollins, Bert Gibson, and Preston Wilcox took immediate objection to the circulation of the letter, and Judy attempted to justify the actions of the CBP on the grounds that they made no claim to represent all black parents in the school. As the board's secretary, Ken Erskine, wrote in the minutes: "There followed a very heated, emotional, name-calling, accusing-and-denying, crying-and-shouting period involving almost everyone."

Before the meeting ended, a motion was made by Hugh Southern to revive the Policy Review Committee (PRC) to discuss ways to deal with issues of pluralism that had been raised. The motion passed unanimously, and John Hewitt, who chaired the PRC, was no doubt relieved to adjourn the meeting and well aware of the hard times ahead of him.

Although overshadowed by brutal charges against the school and an unexpected division among black parents, the meeting of May 17, which led to a clutch of subsequent meetings over the next month and thereafter a year of unparalleled upheaval, opened the school to a new level of dialogue. For the first time, matters of race were no longer defined only by racial identity. To paraphrase Dr. King, it now seemed that perhaps we at MCS could begin to judge one another not by the color of our skin but by the content of our character. The fact that black people could openly disagree with one another not only about their assessment of white people but also about their own actions and views was, I hoped, the overture to a future unification based on human qualities rather than racial definition. It was sad that this state of relations arose at the cost of biracial families at MCS, but looking back, I believe that as harsh as matters would yet become, the boil which had burst that evening would eventually lead to healing.

But I was not so optimistic the next morning when I asked Gloria Brown to go for a walk with me in Central Park. Sitting together on a bench in the meadow, I spilled out my confusion and anger directed mainly at Judy Rollins. Gloria listened calmly. She neither defended Judy nor joined me in my frustration. "Gus," she said, "you need to hang in there; it's going to be all right. Believe me. Times are hard for us, and MCS is the only safe place we have. It's like family; we're fighting now, but that doesn't mean we can't stick together." I treasured Gloria's consoling words and her faith in the school's future.

In the remaining weeks before summer vacation, despite efforts to mend fences, the fighting ensued among all constituents of the school. On May 19, Lisa Petterson, the alumni representative to the board, wrote her fellow graduates inviting their help, saying that as former students they, more so than trustees, parents, or staff, knew better than anyone what was really happening at MCS. Four days later the staff met to hear a report on the board meeting from their representatives, Susan Morgan and Dick Dubow. Among their common reactions were a sense that the CBP had undermined the staff by not presenting their concerns at the faculty council meeting, and the observation that "the deliberations of the CBP are being reflected in the classrooms by racially divisive statements on the part of students."

On June 1, Nell Gibson, a parent who herself had been an active integrationist with Martin Luther King Jr. in the 1960s, answered Pat and

Marvin's letter with copies to the entire school. Her explanation for the exclusive nature of the CBP revealed that among its members there had been serious misgivings. "An issue which amazes me more and more," she wrote, "is the implication that we as a group set out in some cold and calculated way to hurt other blacks, your spouses and children by seeking to exclude you—and I am not in any way attempting to defend the position we took as a group. I would, however, like you to know that our decision to function as a black group was long (discussions of six months or more, centered around other group experiences with interracial couples) and extremely painful. To some of us it is still a painful and sensitive issue. (It was difficult for us as blacks to see many areas of concern in the same light as we bring such different experiences to the group.)"

Nell expressed her hope that Pat and Marvin, and by implication others in interracial marriages, would meet with the CBP group. She ended her letter by saying, "We have all been hurt by innuendos. This is an attempt to bring things out into the open. Hopefully some healing can take place borne out of the pain we have all suffered. This is my attempt to begin that process."

In response, Pat Carey welcomed Nell's overture and acknowledged that it remained for them as black parents, not for the board, to resolve their differences. Confirming one of the chief concerns of the teachers, she cautioned also that as parents they should be careful about what kinds of values they imparted to their children. "It is one thing to say that the school should do this or that, but if a child is hearing from his parents that blacks, or whites, or Hispanics, or other minorities, are no good, then the school has to do the repair work."

On June 2, the executive committee of the board met at 8:00 AM to organize the work of the Policy Review Committee, whose first open meeting was called for June 12. Given the importance of the meeting, the president of the parent association postponed its annual meeting of elections until September. In his invitation to parents, trustees, and staff, John Hewitt announced the composition of the PRC. There would be eleven members, five black and six white. Wary of increased turbulence in the school, the executive committee invited Carl Flemister to return to the board and resume as its chair, which he did after his unanimous election.

There was a fair turnout to the PRC's June 12, 1978, meeting, with fifty-five people present. But only six members of the PRC attended, Preston being conspicuously absent. The staff, which had met that afternoon in preparation, accounted for fourteen people present, and three alumni attended. Among the thirty-two parents at the meeting, nine were black, including Judy Rollins, who never spoke. Pat and Bob Carey, and Marvin and Monica Hughes were active participants, together with two other parents of biracial children.

I began the meeting by reading a statement in response to six topics of concern originally raised by the CBP. My comments were strictly informational on the first four matters: teachers' preparedness to build on cultural diversity; the racial profile of the staff; minority input in admissions and high school placement; and the Black and Latin studies program.

The last two topics, which had been raised for the first time at the contentious May 17 board meeting, required a more subjective response. Concerning the issue of separatism in the school and the exclusivity of the CBP group, I said, "While I am personally opposed to the denial of interracial parents in the CBP, I do not challenge the group's concerns. In the interests of all children, however, I am anxious that those of mixed racial parentage not be abandoned. Twenty-two percent of the minority enrollment in the school falls into this category. It would be a blatant injustice if MCS were to permit this group of youngsters to feel that their identities were inferior or in question. Pronounced and prolonged racial separation can only convey this message."

While I had hesitated to include the last of my comments, I could not refrain from going on record concerning the statement that pluralism at MCS was an incredible hypocrisy. I therefore ended saying, "I take great objection to this statement. I recognize that pluralism may not be what it should be within our school and that many of our ideals break down in their daily reality. It must be within this context that our future discussions take place."

The discussion that followed was lively but disjointed with occasional bursts of vindictiveness. Overall, participation was more positive than negative, and the underlying racial tension of the parents was diffused by conciliatory statements from some black parents, who did not share all the opinions of the CBP, and from sufficient numbers of white parents, who acknowledged that the school was not immune to racism, thereby averting a we-they racial showdown. To those whites who insisted that the CBP explain their allegations of racial insensitivity, a black parent who was also a staff member replied, "I can't list qualities of racism, but when I walk into a room, I can sense whether it's there or not."

The most extensive conversation of the meeting concerned the exclusionary stance of the CBP group, and though no agreement was reached, the mood of the gathering among most black and white parents favored an open forum for all. The one matter about which everyone seemed to agree was that the PRC had properly intervened in an effort to help resolve the school's problems.

Unfortunately, the faith expressed in the PRC was sorely shaken by me, at least, when we met on June 22. We began by considering John Hewitt's carefully prepared list of suggested topics for committee review the following year, and we generally concurred with his recommendations. Omitted from the list, however, was any mention of our need to address what to my mind were the two most flagrant issues at the heart of the matter: whether pluralism at MCS was a "hypocrisy" and the issue of the CBP's exclusionary nature. When Joe Renfield and I raised these subjects, Preston boldly reasserted Judy Rollins' charge of hypocrisy, and for the rest of the meeting he and I were at loggerheads. The extent of our acrimony was so intense that other trustees, except for Joe, could find no way to participate, much less ameliorate matters. Preston's final assault was to say that I had no idea what it was like "to be a nigger." The blow was meant to bring me to a halt, and I wish it had, but in my anger I retorted, "How do you think I feel every damn time I go downtown and kiss whitey's ass for money?" Ken Erskine then rose between us and stood in front of the living-room mirror, lowering his head and extending his arms horizontally with his hands drooping. Preston laughed; I was speechless, and John announced the meeting was adjourned.

I was sorry that Preston had lost faith in MCS, and I was hurt by his ill-feelings toward me. Most of all, I missed the integrationist in Preston. "Education must enable black students to comprehend their self-worth at a gut level," he had once said, "and it must enable white students to de-honkify themselves at a gut level." Further, he asserted that it is in the togetherness of their struggle that the races will achieve selfhood, and it is in the work of integrated schools that we "must convince both that their self-concepts are essentially intertwined and that their destinies are deeply interrelated. Students who know who they are will demand other students to find out who they are. Respect will be based on mutuality. Deference will not be demanded because of differences in skin color, religious background, or previous conditions of servitude."

So much of what I had learned had come from Preston!

Although disturbed by the turn in Preston's outlook, I understood where he was coming from. Once an integrationist, like Stokley Carmichael and so many of his contemporaries, Preston had become a militant separatist, convinced for many good reasons that white America had sold out on racial equality. The sixties were another time and another place. To make matters worse, the forthcoming Bakke decision, which would set the legal precedent that would effectively end affirmative action, would mark, in the words of Jesse Jackson, "the end of the Second Reconstruction."

Many at MCS, like Preston, could not set aside their disaffection with white power, nor could they tolerate blacks who had married across the color-line. Sadly, what was happening at MCS was a reenactment of the larger black/white experience in a still deeply divided country. "The decade which began with the elegiac 'We Shall Overcome' ended in angry shouts of 'Burn, Baby, Burn' and 'Black Power,'" wrote author and civil rights activist Julius Lester in his 1988 memoir, *Lovesong*. It should not have surprised any of us that in the course of the emergence of Black Power, the school was destined to suffer reprisals.

In an effort to quell my hurt and defensiveness over all that had transpired, John Hewitt wrote me two weeks later, urging that we not "make substantive issues either out of how the CBP choose to define themselves" or out of Preston's endorsement of the hypocrisy charge. "To try to put Preston off the board, as Joe [Renfield] seemed to suggest, or to try to legislate whom the CBP must open their membership to," he said, "would only generate more heat than there is now, and cut lines of communication that ought to be kept open and free-flowing." To my surprise John characterized Preston's inflammatory rhetoric "as merely his way of being intentionally provocative with you."

In my reply to John I assured him that I shared his desire to cease name-calling, that I agreed to let the matter of the CBP's membership be resolved by them, and that I hoped that in the fall the PRC would restrict its examination of the school to areas where there were specifically identified grievances. I concluded by commenting on a more overall concern of mine for the school. "You misunderstood my worries, John. I know the CBP group isn't going to abandon the school, but I fear that others may. Last month I had two meetings with an interracial couple whose child was told by other black children that she was not their friend because her mother was white. Her parents commented that it was enough to deal with white racism, but exclusion from both races was intolerable. I am fearful also that MCS may suffer white flight, if not from our own parents then from prospective parents who decline to apply. Integration is the keystone of the school's commitments, but regretfully it is no longer as popular a concept as it was in the sixties. I grieve about the social reversals of the last decade, and more and more I discover from sources from which I solicit support that racial integration is no longer a priority, hardly even a goal. We are running against the tide in a struggle which I can see as only becoming harder and harder, and under such conditions it is more important than ever to be assured that our experience with integration works, and works well. To this end I will continue to devote all my effort."

Bill Webber, MCS founding sponsor,

trustee, parent, and grandparent.

CHAPTER 16

Darkness Before Dawn

AFTER A WELCOMED summer of reflection, my opening talk to parents in September 1978 examined the nature of pluralism and its application to MCS. It was clear that the school community had been fractured by competing concerns and was near its breaking point. Yet somehow I believed that in revisiting the lessons we had learned, we could realize Gloria Brown's promise that we could weather our disagreements and stick together.

"Let me first measure where we stand among ourselves," I began my address that fall. "The issues raised last spring by a group of concerned black parents aroused conflict, confrontation, and some division within the school. The issues themselves are of real and ongoing importance, especially for a school aimed at combating racism . . . . MCS has and will continue to address those issues, and in helping to work through these questions, the Policy Review Committee of the board of trustees will devote its effort to evaluating how the school deals with racism.

"The question as I see it is not: Is there racism at MCS? Nor is the question: Is pluralism at MCS a hypocrisy? Years ago I learned from Kenneth Clark's writings on race that the question, 'Am I prejudiced?' must be rephrased to say, 'Where am I prejudiced?' So the proper question before us now, and probably for years to come, is 'How can we improve the means by which we cope correctively with racism?' Stated differently, the question is, 'How can we fully attain our pluralistic goals?' Pluralism as a concept is so deeply imbued with idealism and faith in the perfectibility of human beings that I'm afraid its achievement cannot be judged in absolute terms."

I went on to say that, because of the idealistic nature of pluralism, the task for MCS was very different from that of most other schools or social institutions. Most self-created communities are formed out of close and immediate bonds, and in general, are organized to promote or preserve likeness among their memberships. Integration may or may not be undertaken according to this objective. When it is, differences are usually sacrificed because the force of the total group is toward assimilation rather than diversity. In such instances the inevitable consequence is the subjugation of the minority to the majority.

"At MCS integration has always followed a different model, and we have called this model 'pluralism,'" I continued. "Literally, pluralism refers to a social organization designed to contain no majority, meaning a community having no superior parts. In contrast to conventional groupings in which there is persistent pressure to conform or to be homogenized, pluralism, applied fully, connotes a social structure in which all members function as a minority and wherein differences are mutually valued by all."

I pointed out that there are hazards to pluralism: "One hazard is that without a sense of community it may lead to dissolution and disintegration, whereby the numerous minorities tug against each other and harmony of the larger group is never achieved. To be effective, pluralism must attain a sense of community for all who are associated together. This means that every group must find ways to interact flexibly and in recurrent connection with one another. I know that cooperation and cohesive effort can exist in a pluralistic framework without the loss of individuality or group identity. For this to be so, however, there must be a high level of mutual trust among all which is rooted in respect for the underlying common needs and human rights of all people."

I ended my talk by tracing one development of the 'we-they' dichotomy that had marked the previous year's interactions at MCS. "For too long the white majority of America has stereotyped and treated minorities as inferior," I observed. "It is no wonder, therefore, that minorities have been forced to overcome their oppression by combating majority attitudes with an all-out united front . . . . Many whites under attack by those who have suffered racism are now caught in a stew which, though a product of their heritage, is not of their own personal making. They know not to respond with denial. Instead, they find themselves having to say 'Mea culpa' for fear that if they say otherwise they will be defending their historical guilt. And if they don't say or feel 'Mea culpa,' they retreat into a state of atrophy which can thwart if not paralyze their capacity to advance human rights. What I am trying to say is that while I recognize that the origins and perpetuation of racism are deliberate designs by whites, I do not believe that all whites need say 'I am guilty.' . . . In its best form, pluralism offers the chance at least for all people to transcend their natural and historical differences and to relate in new partnership.

"Put differently, this means that the protectors of pluralism ought not to be found only among the oppressed. Among those not oppressed, there are many and hopefully there will be more who also care about equality. At MCS, it is the privilege and obligation of all who share in this community to preserve and protect the values of pluralism."

By most accounts, my talk was well received, and I hoped it would set the tone for our work ahead. Just as the Policy Review Committee was getting underway, however, someone delivered a dirty blow to a community that was longing for reconciliation. On November 10, I received an anonymous letter, as did a presumably random number of other parents. To this day, no one except its author knows who wrote it, although it must have originated from someone within the school, most likely an adult and perhaps a parent who had listened to my talk. Entitled "A Letter to MCS Parents from the Gay Caucus," it read in part:

"As you know, the Manhattan Community Society is devoted to the ideal of pluralism. As such, we have 45 percent whites, 30 percent blacks, 5 percent Orientals, 10 percent Hispanics, 5 percent gays and 5 percent vegetables.

"The Gay Caucus, a happy bunch of narcissists, was formed to advance the views of a persecuted minority. In our efforts to put forth a united front, we have had to exclude all straights and all parents who have desecrated the gay ethos by habitating with the oppressor, namely heterosexuals. Therefore, if you are gay, but you are living with a straight, you will not be permitted into meetings of the gay caucus . . . ."

The letter concluded in a manner that clearly mocked the Concerned Black Parents: "We should like to establish our demands once and for all. 1) Four years of Gay History, with special emphasis on the Roman Emperor Augustus. And an entire term should be devoted to the uncivil war started by boorish abolitionists on Christopher Street. 2) Gay Chorus: There are many songs, especially those by Cole Porter as sung by Bobby Short, that have never been heard at MCS. 3) Gay English: We're tired of the monotonous drone of street English. Instead, we want courses devoted to Oscar Wilde, Ronald Firbank, the speeches of Ed Koch, and Kit Marlowe. Oh, yes, let's not forget Walt Whitman (or Whitey as he was known by his pals), Gert Stein, and Jimmy Baldwin. 4) How about some gay math? Really, math is so dull that the only way our kids will ever learn it is if it's gay. Otherwise, it's the pits. 5) We need Gay Pride Week, where certain teachers (you know who you are) and their favorite pupils romp about the living room, so that rich gay broads will donate even more money to the school. 6) Gay Sports: Why aren't boys chosen to cheer for the Dallas Cowboys? And ballet should be compulsory for all boys. Girls, of course, should be taught not to shop at Bergdorf's . . . . What's wrong with a local Army and Navy Store?" The letter then concluded: "We look forward to a gay, if not happy, year, if we all beat our flat stomachs and shout: Mea Culpa."

I was furious. It was hard enough holding the school together as it was. Many who shared with me their negative reactions to the letter said they didn't think it deserved a response. I wished it could be ignored, but I wasn't willing to let this wiseacre go unscolded. My reply cited six points of injury: "It is a mockery of the school's most serious purpose, its commitment to pluralism. It is an insult to the Concerned Black Parents. It makes fun of the school's responsiveness to this group. It debunks my Talk to Parents in which I attempted to set the standards of behavior and social interaction for all at MCS. It chooses to disgrace the cause of Gay liberation. It is a gross abuse of the school's mailing list and an invasion of the right of privacy of our parents."

I ended saying, "Like a teacher exasperated with the excessive ill behavior of one or two children in a class, I feel like saying, 'I've had it.' I am embarrassed to think that the important endeavors we have undertaken should be so demeaned. I am annoyed that one or some should indulge themselves at the expense of others, and I am furious by the damage that this letter may cause to the reputation of our school. MCS is a school for children. It is not a hang-out for self-serving adults!'"

My outrage, together with the repugnant nature of the letter itself, ended the matter with one positive outcome: A member of the Concerned Black Parents called me to say that the group wanted to express their thanks for the stand I'd taken.

SOON AFTER, THE work of the Policy Review Committee got underway. The committee called for eight areas of review with one trustee assigned to each: admissions (Bill Webber), staff racial profile (Ken Erskine), eighth-grade math tracking (John Hewitt), racism in the classrooms (Ruth Cooke), parent-school communications (Walter Christmas), student evaluation (Estelle Meadoff), high school placement (Preston Wilcox), and competition v. cooperation (Joe Renfield).

From the outset, the board chairman's determination that the PRC complete its examination by June was hindered by two circumstances: first, the topics selected for review exceeded those originally identified by the CBP, and second, the committee's decision to hold open meetings severely slowed its progress. A further hindrance, which ultimately led to a total deterioration of the committee's effectiveness, was the fact that three black members of the committee (Christmas, Hewitt, and Wilcox) continued to attend meetings of the CBP. This circumstance, rather than helping to resolve the concerns of the group, instead encouraged additional grievances and prompted the three trustees to want to extend the committee's purview.

The most problematic area was in our eighth-grade math classes, where tracking had resulted in de facto racial segregation, a condition that was known to the staff and considered a provisional means of remedying a serious gap between the achievement test scores of black and white students.

In his report, John Hewitt cited this circumstance as "a clear violation of the MCS policy on racially integrated classes." He also acknowledged, however, that there was no evidence of similar racial isolation elsewhere in the school, and stated, "The Committee recognizes that there may be exceptional circumstances under which a temporary departure from established policy may be permitted, and the administration and staff are committed to remedying this situation so that pluralism in math can be restored in the not too distant future."

By February, faculty members, who had already felt the strain of coping with the CBP group, were feeling doubly burdened by their experience with the PRC. The effect of eight trustees separately visiting classrooms, interviewing teachers, sharing alleged charges passed along from unidentified parents, some of which alluded to their colleagues, had taken its toll. I was keenly aware of the lowered morale of the teachers and wanted to take their concerns directly to the board. But the teachers wanted to convey their responses themselves, in part, I am sure, to protect me from having to put myself in an adversarial position with the PRC. Three elected representatives made their case to the board, saying that among the MCS teaching staff there was a pervasive sense of "wariness and weariness." They stated further that while they recognized national changes over the last decade that had eroded support for the communal goals of the school, they believed that the "climate of anxiety" currently felt by the staff was due to the investigations of the PRC, with the coinciding rampant rumors causing job insecurity.

A month later, when the PRC received its report on parent-school communications from trustee Walter Christmas, the concerns of the faculty seemed duly warranted. Walter called for reconciling opposing points of view and preventing further strife, but his analysis slighted faculty opinion, accusing teachers of being defensive, and it gave credence to causes for parental distrust, such as the assertion that "wealthier parents have a disproportionate influence on school policy."

Following Walter's report, Bill Webber wrote John Hewitt, calling for the PRC's closure and expressing his dissatisfaction with the committee's direction. "Our task, as I understood it," he said, "was to pinpoint areas where we need to work harder in dealing with the inherited racism of our society, where more attention needs to be given to overcoming misunderstanding that is seen in racial terms. But we must not be seen as some kind of watchdog committee of the trustees, ferreting out as our constant assignment anything that to some of us smacks of racism . . . . We do not intend any such thing, but by now we do seem to have sown considerable distrust among the staff, to have undercut the normal administrative procedures, and in general drifted into being part of the problem. We seem at times to be a gripe committee to which every problem, whether racist in origin or not, gets directed. This does not, I confess, seem to me to be the business of the trustees in a community where we seek mutual trust and collegiality."

Bill ended his letter with these words of commendation for the staff, which I read to them at their next meeting: "I end with one clear judgment on my part: that the administration and faculty of MCS are deeply committed to authentic integration and to fighting in every way possible the terrible institutional racism of American society. They need our confidence, support, encouragement in their never ending battle. We must convey to them no other message."

Bill's declaration might have concluded matters, had it been addressed to the entire board. Instead, it became the point of demarcation over which the principle players of the PRC mounted the most bitter political dispute in the school's history.

John Hewitt shared Bill's letter with the CBP group, causing them to write the PRC "to express our deepest regrets regarding moves to reexamine the validity of the Policy Review Committee," and to go on record that "it is imperative to a school like MCS that constant reexamination of certain issues takes place." To me, the implied scenario was daunting: a permanent committee of the board to review and dictate all school policy and practices with the primary source of its inquiries vested in a single group of parents who were self-appointed and exclusionary!

Only a month later did this scenario really appear to be in the offing when the PRC met to consider its year-end recommendations to the board. I had originally thought that I should not go to this meeting, knowing that should the committee's recommendations reflect or pass judgment upon my administration of the school, I should not be part of that process. However, believing that my absence might be interpreted as an unwillingness to cooperate, I decided to attend.

John Hewitt began the meeting by distributing two sets of recommendations, one from himself and the other from Walter Christmas. Walter's recommendation contained ten points, the last of which asserted that there had been "serious instances of racism" in the school and called for the PRC to be a standing committee, "established to monitor adherence to policy, make recommendations to the board and devise its own grievance process." John's recommendations fell short of Walter's, although in proposing a nine-point agenda for the PRC for 1979-80, he too favored the committee's continuing surveillance.

The first item discussed was Walter's following recommendation: "As a matter of policy, under no circumstance, should tracking be used as a method in any educational area at MCS." Under other circumstances I may not have reacted as I did, but having read Walter and John's full proposals, I knew there was a fight brewing in which I did not intend to participate. In contrast to John's report on tracking, which gave the school the benefit of its wisdom, Walter's was too heavy-handed for my liking, so I left the meeting.

I explained my decision to do so in a letter to John, written two days later after having breakfasted with him and our board chair Carl Flemister. Concluding that I could no longer work with the PRC, I said that I had come to perceive it as "a vigilante committee which has dangerously affected the morale and operations of the school, usurping the authority of the administration and setting the stage for a double executive."

After expounding on the history of the committee's conduct, I ended by saying, "All year long I have tried to maintain a belief that the committee would tend to its work in such a way that it would be 1) responsive to the legitimate concerns related to racism at MCS, and 2) restore confidence in the school. I do not know whether the committee has successfully served the first of these functions. On the second function, it is my belief that the committee has utterly failed. Furthermore, in attempting to define its future function as a grievance committee established permanently to monitor the implementation of policy, it has entirely lost sight of its original purpose and if empowered to so operate it will have assumed an adversarial relationship with the administration of MCS that I would find unmanageable."

As chairperson and peacemaker, Carl Flemister saw the damage imposed by the PRC. While it was no doubt painful for him to stand up against three fellow black trustees, he pressed for closure of the PRC, and he wanted a final report that exonerated the administration and staff of MCS. To accomplish this, he appointed Bill Webber to draft the committee's final report to be presented on June 19, 1979.

This left John Hewitt with no honorable way to proceed. In a letter to Carl Flemister on June 6, he offered his resignation, stating, "I welcome debate and honest disagreement on issues. But I would find it unnecessarily uncomfortable to try to deal any longer with the kind of paranoia that had resulted in hysterical rejection of new ideas and threats of resignation if the Committee offers any recommendations whatsoever." True to his role as eternal mediator, Carl persuaded John to stay on the board, which he did for many years to come. John also agreed to cosign the report, which he and Bill offered directly to the board without prior consideration by the PRC.

Their seven-page report contained five sections, beginning with a background statement, followed by a description of the committee's makeup and mission. Section three covered six of the eight areas reviewed (Joe

Renfield's and Preston Wilcox's reports were never completed.) In section four, the report explicitly acknowledged the failings of the committee, stating: "In all candor the process of the committee's work has become a serious problem in its own right, and brings into question the utility of our work." The report went on to suggest that this may have been due in part to the fact that members of the committee "were not clear about our mandate. Some understood our work to relate only to matters of pluralism, while others thought we were to surface any problems in the life of the community."

In advocating suspending the work of the PRC, Bill Webber echoed his letter of March 24 to John Hewitt: "It would seem obvious that some better mechanism than the present Policy Review process be found in the future. The school can only survive on one basic reality—that all parties are committed to pluralism and eager to ferret out any vestige of racism that appears."

The showdown took place when the nine white and eight black trustees present at the June 19 meeting took a vote on four resolutions outlined in the final section of the report. The first read: "That the trustees affirm in every way possible their faith in our present director, the administration and faculty. We are blessed with a truly dedicated group who are, without any doubt, totally committed to the basic principles of the school. Any question about their devotion, competence and loyalty must be set aside. We must find, as trustees, effective ways to communicate the reality of this recommendation."

In discussion that followed, Preston Wilcox and Walter Christmas said the motion was unnecessary. "It convicts us of distrust," said Preston. In the end, the fifteen other trustees voted in its favor and the motion passed.

Resolution two read: "That together, trustees, administration and faculty seek ways both new and old to deepen the commitment of parents and students to the urgency and importance of pluralism. The present committee has, in our judgment, completed its usefulness. But it is urgent that the trustees and director determine at an early date what will be the appropriate mechanism for maintaining the necessary sensitivity and vigilance to insure pluralism."

This resolution in no way foreclosed further institutional evaluation; it simply terminated the authority of the current PRC. After some soul-searching discussion about the need of the trustees to deal with problems of pluralism within the board itself, the motion carried, with Preston and Walter voting against it.

Resolution three, which dealt with the issue of tracking, prompted several attempted amendments, and its final version, which came close to Walter's previous recommendation, read: "Tracking that results in racial segregation of students is a violation of a founding principle of the school and therefore is not permissible at MCS. Racial segregation is not an acceptable solution to educational discrepancies. If the problem should present itself again, another solution will have to be found." trustees Mike Pope and Sara Wilford opposed the resolution; all others approved.

Resolution four, as finally amended by Carl Flemister, was adopted unanimously and set the stage for the year to come. It read: "That the trustees seek the aid of an outside consultant as a process person in assisting the trustees in being able to work with each other more effectively."

Before the meeting ended, Preston spoke despairingly as a trustee for the last time, calling the entire report "a calculated whitewash" and saying, "I'm ashamed to be part of this group." He never attended another trustee meeting.

No meeting like this one could ever be said to be a victory. It was more like bailing out before an impending crash. While I would not describe the report as calculated, it was surely crafted to salvage the school, and given John and Bill's joint authorship, together with the endorsement of six out of eight of the board's black trustees, it could not properly be regarded as a "whitewash." But Preston's loss of faith was painful all the same.

Abby Michael, class of 1975, consoles Jenny,

a 2,000-pound workhorse, after a blood test.

CHAPTER 17

Salvaging the School's Mission

THE FOLLOWING FALL, the trustees at their own expense engaged Carl A. Fields, director of African Technical Educational Consultant Service, to carry out resolution four. Between October and December, he visited the school, interviewed me and other key trustees, prepared a written appraisal of the problems facing us, met once with the executive committee, and then attended a board meeting to present his strategy for working with the trustees: three small-group sessions of three hours each over a five-day period, followed by a full eight-hour meeting on Sunday, February 3, 1980. Preliminary discussions with Fields must have assured him how much the trustees needed his assistance. Preston Wilcox was conspicuously absent, and Joe Renfield felt the process would be useless without him. Sadly, teacher Martha Norris also resigned, saying, "I cannot in good conscience pledge a single dollar to pay a consultant to help me define 'how we can play a more vital and creative role in the life of the school.'"

Nevertheless, having made our bed, we had no choice but to go through with the plan, and Fields turned out to be an excellent "process person." There were none of the "shouting matches" that Joe had feared, partly because Fields had constructed the small groups to separate some of the key oppositional players, and he was careful to enlist participation from trustees who were normally not outspoken. One of his questions was: "Would you

213

accept the position of chairperson of the board?" Its purpose was unclear to me at first, but responses brought out the best in people as they were obliged to consider themselves protagonists rather than adversaries.

The principal merit of Fields's consultation was in his written commentary on the state of the school and its recommended future course, which was more optimistic than any of us had anticipated. "Integration," he observed, "is not the problem. Expectations raised to levels which in part may be unrealistic are probably the cause of unrest." His belief was that "private schools, with their aura of respectability and educational excellence" offered an escape from inadequate public-school education to aspiring minority families, but when some of their children were less successful in academic achievement, parents became suspicious and hostile, which negated "whatever positive effects were built into the concept of an integrated school."

While I suspect that the more militant black parents at MCS would have disputed Fields's theory, it made sudden good sense to me, clarifying dim understanding of complaints I had heard all the way back to the first Black Caucus, which I had characterized as favoring a more traditional pedagogy. What I had apparently never comprehended was that many black and white parents had different primary objectives in choosing MCS. Those blacks parents who met Fields's definition came to the school first and foremost in search of an academic refuge, while perhaps the majority of white parents saw MCS as a place where their children would be inoculated against their own historical racism. If this formulation was correct, then the school would have to assume greater responsibility in equalizing the academic achievement of students along racial lines. We did not fully realize this at the time, but the seed of recognition was there, and in future years MCS tightened its standards, and to the regret of some of our teachers, admitted fewer minority students who were at risk academically.

In retrospect, the conclusion of Fields's report was the precursor of an expanded definition of the school's central goal. In the sixties, MCS proclaimed "Integration;" in the seventies, "Pluralism." Thereafter, we spoke of "Multiculturalism," and it was in this direction that Fields pointed us. Early in his report he had made this observation: "Changing social conditions and the emergence of new ethnic and racial groups available to the school make it essential that extraordinary efforts be made to include these new people in the entire life of the school. The absence of Hispanic or Asian members of the board is glaring."

It was to this concern that Fields addressed his final advice: "It is important for the board of trustees to understand and reaffirm the nature of the mission and purposes of MCS. Integration, in its primitive form in the 1960s, envisioned only one step in the process of an integrated society, i.e. putting people with similar aspirations, desires, and expectations in a physical setting where quality education, as a product, could be acquired. The assumption that the acceptance of the individual in a humane environment would enhance, release, or accelerate intellectual capacity and ability was an accepted premise. The experience of the 1970s affirms the premise. MCS is still the prototype of what a school should be and can produce from its principles and format. It is now faced with the experience and sophistication of the students and parents of the 1970s, and asked to be progenitor of the new school for the 1980s and possibly the 1990s. The question to be faced is what did MCS learn from the sixties and seventies that can determine what it will do in the eighties and nineties? This is a significant responsibility for the board of trustees. Basic premises and assumptions must co-exist with new understandings and expectations. The board cannot just maintain, but should expand its horizons for the school, its future students, and its adult participants."

I welcomed Carl Fields's analysis of our problem and immediately took steps to begin closing the racial academic gap. I was concerned, however, that we ran the risk of substituting competition for cooperation. Joe Renfield's report on this topic had never been received by the PRC, so in my 1980 opening talk to parents I dealt with this matter accordingly:

"The academic aims of MCS are not based on pure educational theory," I told parents. "They are an extension of our belief that one's success rests upon one's individual performance, not upon the relative lack of success of others. Traditional grading systems and normative testing scores rank students in such a way that the rating of one student determines the rating of another. While I realize that competition governs the academic world in most high schools and universities, I do not see that the logical preparation for the competitive life is competition itself. It may be an effective approach for the half of the children who score above the fiftieth percentile, but it makes no sense to follow a prescription for all which will fail for half your enrollment and which will instill values of false superiority in those who rank higher than the grade-point average.

"I am not saying that competition is wrong and that we ought never to recognize it in our system. I'm only saying that as we prepare students for competitive academic schooling, we do better by supporting them through noncompetitive means. Almost all our graduates attest to the fact that their adjustments to the scholastic demands of high school were not difficult. The number of students who leave MCS to enter highly competitive academic schools and colleges assures me that our approach works."

The best illustration of our approach to helping students achieve their highest potential was in our effort mark system, which we borrowed from the Putney School and used in our fifth through eighth grades. Every six weeks students were graded in each subject according to their effort as defined by several criteria, such as meeting deadlines and preparedness for class. Comments were added to those students' grades if there was a wide discrepancy between effort and achievement so that they and their parents would know, for example, if their performance fell below grade-level expectations.

Like Putney, which kept private records of a student's academic achievement to be used if required for college admissions, MCS administered annual scholastic achievement tests to all students beginning in second grade. Results were shared with parents if requested, not with students. So, while we did not employ a competitive grading system, we knew how our students were doing on the basis of national private school norms. When I was talking to parents about the school's choice to de-emphasize competition, my confidence was based largely on the knowledge that the average MCS student was performing two and a half years above grade level and that half our students ranked above the ninetieth percentile nationally in reading comprehension and arithmetic applications.

It was in 1980 that, as part of our academic tightening-up, we added Friday afternoon study hall for seventh and eighth grade students with poor effort marks. While the concept of detention may seem a contradiction to progressive school pedagogy, I saw it as a necessary practice consistent with the school's noncompetitive methods. When I was sent to study hall in grammar school it was because I had failed; I was punished for my "stupidity" and my bright classmates who were "goofing off" but still getting by were spared reproof. As I monitored study hall each week, I felt satisfaction in knowing that those sent to me, many of whom were among the brightest in the class, were simply and fairly facing the consequences of not putting forth their best effort. To me, the MCS form of study hall was a clear example of holding children accountable to themselves, not to their achievement relative to others.

Three members of the class of 1988: Aisha Christian,
Kate Washburn, and Jeaneen Colon. "What the children were learning
about human relations, their parents were having to unlearn."

CHAPTER 18

Encounters in the Classroom

THE CLASS OF 1986 were six-year-olds in 1978 when Ruth Cooke visited Yvette Bravo's kindergarten group to prepare her report for the Policy Review Committee on "Racism in the Classroom." Describing her visit, Ruth wrote, "Clearly, in this group there was every kind of combination of boys and girls, blacks, Hispanics, whites, grouping and regrouping with remarkable ease. There were moments of delight, and moments in which one could see children learning to handle conflict. There were surely other tensions which I couldn't see . . . . Yvette and I talked afterwards of some of these. She told me that her group was full of stereotypes about Puerto Ricans and how they cause all the trouble, such as vandalizing elevators in apartment houses. So Yvette said to the children: 'Well, I don't break up elevators and I am Puerto Rican.'"

Yvette also told Ruth of a black child named Kenny who sat in the lap of the white assistant teacher, hugging her, smiling, and saying, "I hate you because you are white." The teacher asked, "Have I done something to make you hate me?" The child then ran off to play, but came later to say, "I don't really hate you, I love you."

Though too young to be racists, these children had clearly heard a lot at home, in their neighborhoods and among their friends. The mother of the boy who said he hated his white teacher, for example, was one of the most outspoken members of the Concerned Black Parents' group. For these young children, the battle of the races was not taking place on foreign ground, and the teachers knew how badly they needed their guidance.

Four years later, I was called upon to help this same class when they were in Doris Finkel's fifth grade. My initial discussion with the group turned into a series of meetings in which we repeatedly touched on subjects identical to those that had come up in parent meetings. I kept a log of these sessions, the substance of which I have recreated here. Only the names of the students have been changed, and occasional parenthetical comments have been added.

MONDAY, JANUARY 31, 1983, 1:00 PM: Elise, the fifth grade assistant teacher, comes to the office with Jeremy, a white child, and Kenny, a black child. Jeremy has called Kenny a "nigger" in the park. I listen to the recounting of the incident and suggest a class meeting at 1:30. Jeremy has had problems with his temper before, and perhaps the time has come for him to face the music.

At the meeting, Jeremy is outraged and outrageous. He acts like a caged animal. He says he's hated "this fucking class" for three and a half years, and also "this fucking school." He says he hopes he'll be expelled, that he isn't prejudiced; he just knows "more black people who are creeps than whites." The group is shocked. One white child, Rosemary, cries and says she can't believe what Jeremy just said. Selma, a black child, says, "When we fought, I thought it was because we just bumped around a lot. I never imagined it was racial."

Eliza, another black child, says. "I don't think Jeremy is prejudiced."

"I think Jeremy said that because of the way he was brought up," someone else adds. "He told me once his father didn't like black people."

Jeremy bursts out, "My parents are good people; don't blame them."

Wesley, a black boy, says, "If you stop picking on our parents, we'll stop picking on yours."

I turn to Jeremy. "Wesley just offered you something," I say to him. "Was it a fair trade?"

Jeremy, still outraged, yells, "No!"

Changing course, I say, "Okay, enough about Jeremy. Let's talk about name-calling. Who are the four biggest name callers in the class? We know Jeremy is the first name on the list. Who else? Kenny, you must be second because the feud's between you and Jeremy." Earlier, Kenny had admitted calling Jeremy a "honky."

The class agrees that Jeremy and Kenny are the biggest offenders. The question then is who is the third. All hands go up to speak. Sheldon, a black child, blurts, "I am."

I say to the group, "Does Sheldon annoy you?"

Keisha, also black, admits, "Sheldon really bugs me." Others concur. I ask, "How do you feel about that, Sheldon?"

"I think maybe I annoy people because I have problems with my family," he says.

I address the group. "Do you feel any less annoyed at Sheldon having heard that?"

The children say that they do.

"Sheldon," I say, "you just said something that took a lot of courage. Thank you."

The kids want to know who's the fourth biggest name caller.

"You're all number 4," I tell them. "I'll see you tomorrow morning."

TUESDAY, FEBRUARY 1, 1983, 8:45 AM: I begin the morning's meeting by explaining to the kids why Jeremy isn't in school. He is on probation. He had known that if he lost his temper again he'd be suspended. Yesterday, he blew it on three counts: he fought with Kenny, he referred to "this fucking class" and "this fucking school" during our meeting, and he told me to "fuck off."

Picking up where we left off the day before, I say, "So, Jeremy's the number 1 name caller." I then write the word "nigger" on the blackboard. "And Kenny's the number 2 name caller." I write the word "honky" on the board. "Now, I want all the other names." Almost every hand goes up. For five minutes the kids offer words that I write on the blackboard: "slut," "prick," "motherfucker," "shit-head," "gay," "lezzy," "whitey," "bitch," "whore," "asshole." And a few more.

After a while, I stop writing. "Is 'nigger' the only word on the board that hurts?" I ask the children. This is a hard question for them to deal with. They tell me that when they use words like those on the board, they are not meant to hurt. "That's just the way we talk to each other," one child says.

"So no one's been hurt except when called a nigger?" I persist.

Keisha says, "Miles calls us 'wenches.'"

Miles, who is white, stands up, hands over head. "Oh no, don't tell!"

Keisha keeps going. "He says, 'Wench, I wouldn't have you in my harem.' We looked it up; it doesn't mean what he thinks it means. It means 'girl.'"

"Did he think it means 'slut?'" I ask.

"No, no!" Rosemary says. "He thinks it means 'prostitute.'"

"Okay," I say, "how many girls in this class don't feel treated equally by boys?" Every girl's hand goes up. Various girls cite examples.

"So, there are other words that hurt," I observe. "I'd like to know about some of these other words."

Heather, who is white, says, "At the farm, Kenny teased us for not being able to dance like black girls."

A biracial girl named Judith says, "I think there are people in the class beside Jeremy who are prejudiced. I mean, I know one person, I'm not saying who, but he picks on white people. I guess you know he's a boy and he's black. Anyway he says 'honky' all the time."

"I think everybody knows who Judith's talking about," I say. "What do you feel about what she said, Kenny?" No answer. "Judith was talking about you, wasn't she, Kenny?" After some protest, Kenny says that he guesses he "used that word once."

I take the opportunity to speak about racism. "I'm worried that you all are so scared about being racists that you can't talk together about the way you speak to each other," I tell the class. "I don't believe Jeremy is a racist and don't think he meant what he said. None of you is a racist; you're too young to be racist. People aren't born racists; they become them. Don't be afraid to speak about the subject. Acknowledge things that you've said that hurt people. It's only when you don't acknowledge them and keep saying them that you become a racist. What I'm trying to say is that there's a lot more feeling about race than you're talking about in this class. Don't be scared to share your feelings, and above all, if you do say something to someone about their race, it doesn't mean you're a racist."

Various questions and comments follow. Finally, Ginger, a white child, says, "I don't think we should all have to talk about this."

"You don't have to," I tell her. "I just want you to think about it."

WEDNESDAY, FEBRUARY 2, 1983, AFTER SCHOOL: In a routine conference with Ginger's parents, her mother shares Ginger's reaction to our meetings. She tells me Ginger says white kids are called "honky" and "whitey" all the time. She feels that I don't care about that, but when Jeremy calls Kenny a "nigger" all hell breaks loose. She told her mother, "I don't know why we have to miss math class to talk about all these things."

THURSDAY, FEBRUARY 3, 1983, AFTERNOON: Rosemary's father calls to say she is very upset. He feels the school has been too lenient on Jeremy for his infraction; a one-day suspension is not enough. He says Rosemary was a witness to the incident in which Jeremy called Kenny "nigger" five times.

FRIDAY, FEBRUARY 4, 1983, 8:45 AM: Jeremy is absent for tutoring. At the morning meeting, I inform his class, "Jeremy and I spoke on Wednesday. He's sorry about the things he said. I told him he didn't have to apologize publicly, and he asked to speak to some of you privately. So that's where it stands with Jeremy." The group is silent.

After a moment, I continue, "I've thought about the meeting today and maybe the best way to get started is for you to respond to this: Some of you think I was too lenient on Jeremy. Some of you wonder why it is that there's so much attention given to what happened and no attention paid when white kids get called names.

Judith raises her hand. "When Jeremy came back he was really trying to be nice," she says. "I could see he was really upset for what he'd said."

Another child, Alexi, speaks up. "On the way to gym on Thursday I heard Kenny say to Sheldon, 'Come on with me and don't talk to Jeremy.'"

"Is that true, Kenny?" I ask.

He says, "No."

"Well, Sheldon's late, so we can't ask him yet."

A girl named Karen says, "Jeremy says a lot of mean things, but he doesn't mean them. Yesterday, he called my father gay; I don't think he meant it, but that's what he said."

"Did it hurt you?" I ask Karen. She nods.

At this point, Sheldon arrives and I ask him about yesterday going to gym. He says, "No one was being mean to Jeremy. I don't know what was going on, but Kenny said, 'Come on over,' so I left Jeremy."

I turn back to Karen. "So there are other words that hurt?"

Karen says thoughtfully, "Well, I call Rosemary names all the time, like 'stupid' or 'idiot,' but we're good friends and sometimes I apologize."

Norman chimes in. "Yeah, Miles and I call each other names all the time." Miles jumps up and dramatizes conversations with Norman wherein they joust in name-calling with one another.

I stay with Karen's comment. "How do you know that Rosemary's not hurt when you call her names?"

Karen shrugs. "I can tell by her face and the tone of her voice," she says.

"Using Karen's test, does Miles and Norman's name-calling mean anything?" I ask the class.

Someone says, "No, they were just fooling around."

Doris, the head teacher, comments, "So, it seems you have different standards for each other." The group concurs.

"How do you know what each person's limits are?" I challenge them.

Someone says, "We can tell."

"But does it always work? I mean, Karen, it didn't seem to work yesterday when Jeremy spoke to you about your father, did it?"

Karen frowns, but says, "I've already told you he didn't mean what he said."

Feeling the discussion is getting nowhere, I say, "Well, I think there are some of you who are hurt by things people say, but you're not saying so."

"Well, I'm not sure about this," Judith ventures, "but I think it really is worse to call someone a nigger than a honky."

"Let's think about that," I say, "and I want you to remember what you just said, because that's where I want to start when we talk next. I'll see you sometime next week."

FRIDAY, FEBRUARY 11, 1983: Doris is absent and I sub for her fifth grade class. At midmorning, Heather approaches me to say, "We want to talk with you." When I ask her what she wants to talk about, she is joined by Ginger and Judith. Judith opens. "We think Kenny puts Jeremy up for what he says." All three girls spew out incidents to illustrate Kenny's behavior.

"So does Kenny really control everything?" I ask them.

"No. He's powerful, but not popular," Judith clarifies. "Things are breaking up. I mean, Kenny doesn't have as many followers as he used to." Ginger adds, "I was with him once, and you can't not be with him because I'm scared of him not being my friend."

"Do you think things have changed in the last few days?"

Ginger says, "No."

"Are you willing to say this the next time we talk with the group?" I ask.

All three reply, "No."

"If we say what we feel, Eliza will defend Kenny, and she's the key," Judith explains. "I sat with her at lunch yesterday and she said she liked me. But if we said what we're telling you, she'd stick up for Kenny."

"So who's going to solve this problem, you or me?" I say.

Ginger says, "You are."

"How?" I ask her.

"I don't know." Ginger shrugs.

"I don't know either," I say, "but I don't think I'm going to solve it. In fact, I think it's up to you." Ginger looks disappointed.

"Do you think Kenny knows you're talking about him right now?" I ask the three girls. They glance around. "What about Eliza?" Eliza is within three feet of the girls, working on a project.

All three girls answer, "Yes."

"Next time we meet, I want you to say what you've said to me to the whole group because I'm not going to solve your problem. It's time for lunch set-up."

The kids bring out their Friday bag lunches and lunch time goes as usual, followed by free time until 1:45. A skirmish is observed in the bathroom. I overhear a flurry of statements: "She's ready to kiss him!" Sheldon runs to me and says, "Will you protect me?" with a big smile. "Absolutely," I tell him. Keisha runs out of the bathroom toward me and says, "There's going to be a wedding, and I'm the bride." I hug her and say, "Okay." Thereafter, the wild rumpus begins. The kids prepare for the wedding: Selma is the grandmother; Jeremy, the photographer; Karen, the bridesmaid. Norman says, "I'll be the jeweler, I'll make the ring." Kenny is the minister; Rosemary, the flower girl; Miles, the father-in-law. Suddenly, there's to be a double wedding with Eliza and Wesley also getting married. Wesley approaches me and declares, "No way!" Rosemary wants to marry Norman, but she can't do it because she's the flower girl in Sheldon's wedding. Leena, the science teacher, arrives to relieve me. Delighted and gratified by the children's laughing camaraderie, I nevertheless help Leena settle them on the balcony for a story. Afterward, she takes them all to the park, and the concerns of the morning apparently forgotten, they are "duly married."

OVER THE NEXT several weeks, discussion in the classroom periodically comes back to why the word "nigger" is worse than "whitey." The children understand that there are historical reasons for this. At one point, they want to know why the term "nigger" is acceptable when used among blacks. I tell the class about a problem the 4-5s' teacher saw with a grandfather greeting his grandchild, "Hi there, you little nigger." The black kids are very definite in their feeling that the 4-5s should be told that this is not a term to be used in the classroom. I then talk about names meaning different things in different contexts. I tell them, for example, that my sister calls me "Stink," a derogatory name which is used as an affectionate, familial nickname. All the kids associate this with examples of their own.

The fifth graders and I have one more meeting on the subject of name-calling on March 4, after the spring vacation. I begin with a long statement about the terms "whitey" and "honky" and how white people feel about them. I explain that just because "whitey" isn't as bad as "nigger" doesn't mean I like being called it. "Whitey" is a retaliatory term," I explain, "meant to get back at whites for what they've done. While I accept this analysis, it still upsets me to be made to feel guilty for what other white people have done, just because I'm white."

There follows some discussion of the fact that many black children in the class have been called "whitey" as an insult by neighborhood friends who feel that because they attend a private school, they're "acting white." "MCS is different from a lot of other private schools," I say, "but other kids don't know that. And that's why they give some of you black kids a hard time." We arrive at the conclusion that it is easier to call someone names when you don't know that person's story. "It's like this," I say, offering an example. "If I walked down 149th Street in Harlem—"

Kenny interrupts. "You'd get mugged," he laughs.

I keep going. "No, I wouldn't, because I've done it, and I'm here to tell you I wasn't mugged. What I was saying is, if I walked down 149th Street, someone is likely to say, 'Hey, there, whitey.' I'd be seen only as a white person. However, do you think Clint would call me 'honky'?" Clint Ingram, who is black, is the children's music teacher. The class is aghast at my suggestion, and someone says, jokingly, "No, because he'd get fired." But then Keisha says, "No. Clint knows you and knows you're not prejudiced."

"So let's get back to the words 'honky' and 'nigger,'" I continue. "They're like two weapons. You've got them in your pocket and you can pull them out whenever you want. Here's the problem that white people have: We know that 'nigger' is a worse weapon than 'honky' and we sure don't want to use it, but it makes us very upset if a black person starts using 'honky' and we know we've got a worse weapon in our pocket."

At this, Sheldon makes an astute observation: "'Nigger' is like a fifty-megaton bomb, and 'whitey' is just like a hand grenade."

It is almost time to end the meeting, but I want to touch on one more thing. "Eliza," I say, "the first time we ever talked about this subject, you made a comment, and I'd like to know if you could tell me more about it. You said you thought Jeremy wasn't prejudiced. What did you mean by that?"

"I meant that he wasn't prejudiced because I know Jeremy and he's never done anything that was prejudiced," she says,

"But Jeremy called Kenny a 'nigger.' Was that not being prejudiced?" I answer my own question. "I guess Jeremy wasn't being smart. He used the big bomb and said what he shouldn't have said, and I guess what Eliza's saying is that that's all he did. He isn't prejudiced, but he said the one thing he never should have said."

"Right," Eliza agrees.

"Okay," I say, "It's been forty-five minutes and we've got to stop. How many of you would like to talk again?" Most hands go up. Then Kenny says with some hesitation, "May I ask a question? Do we all have to talk again?"

"Are you saying you don't want to?" I ask him.

"No, I don't," Kenny responds.

"I don't understand," I say. "You've been one of the most important people in the discussion today. You've really helped us out."

"No, I mean, I'm sort of tired of it," Kenny says.

"Maybe we are talking about the subject too much," I concede. To the class I say, "I hope you will keep on with the discussion among yourselves, but maybe next time we'll just talk about the weather." Everyone laughs.

GOING TO MCS every day, I often felt I was attending two schools. During the day, MCS was a school for children; in the evenings, sometimes three or four times a week, and often in staff meetings or when I worked at my desk, it was a school for adults. The two schools, however, while sharing common physical space and at work on similar tasks, were not only generations apart, but also developmental opposites. What the children were learning about human relations, the parents were having to unlearn, and for those of us on the staff who were in the company of both the children and their parents, the challenges of our work sometimes tested our professional and personal limits.

I welcomed the meetings with Doris Finkel's fifth graders, and like any teacher, I took satisfaction in the children's capacity to resolve, even ever so gradually, some share of their problems. In my "evening classes" we adults were often like students without a teacher, behaving even more badly than Doris's name-calling ten-year-olds.

In the drama of MCS's creation and its formative years, the central characters were those who founded and fashioned the school: its staff, its trustees, and its parents, but it was from the children that I gained the reassurance that we were on course. "Make us laugh, and make us cry," the children said to me when I asked what they wanted me to say to them at their graduation. I followed their instructions every year, composing the funny section over Memorial Day weekend first, because that was the harder part. The teary part came easily because the children themselves never failed to provide me with the source of my script.

Graduations, which come only once to a student, ended my years at MCS twenty-six times. They were foremost an opportunity to celebrate the children, but also they were opportunities for the adults present to share and to affirm their faith in the school's teachings. Graduation night, in fact, was the one sure occasion each year that those from the "day school" and those from the "night school" came together.

June 9, 1977, was such a time. The children had selected Arthur Miller's *The Crucible* as their graduation play, and one of their parents, Sasha von Scherler, an accomplished actress and compassionate devotee of MCS, had volunteered to be their director. In compliance with orders, I began my speech with the funny part:

"About two months ago I received an ominous note, marked 'personal' from your play director, Sasha. She had just begun working with you on *The Crucible*, and it was the morning after a grueling session reading through the play with you. She had not assigned the parts yet and all of you were demanding leading roles.

"Graduates of MCS are not lacking in self-confidence. When I was in eighth grade, I was mortified at having to recite sixteen lines of A. E. Housman at a school assembly. I remember being prompted three times, once after the opening line: 'When I was one-and-twenty, I heard a young man say . . .' Suddenly blank! *Heard a young man say what, Trowbridge? What? Oh, my God, the headmaster's whispering to someone. He's getting up. He's going to take me away. Everyone's laughing at me. Thank goodness my parents didn't come. They had wanted to, but I'd told them it was another day.* Well, after a lifetime of agonizing starts and stammers with my English teacher mouthing line after line to me from the front row, I was finally two-and-twenty and I dissolved in embarrassment amidst my classmates.

"Not so with this eighth grade, Sasha! This self-assured, articulate gang no doubt attacked their director head-on. If the parts weren't big enough or good enough, then they'd choose another play; that's all there was to it! Furthermore, at MCS all productions are democratic. Sasha only had one vote; they had one-and-twenty, and she had no right to tell them to do anything they didn't want to do.

"It was considerate of Sasha, I thought, to have written me a note saying she was going to quit rather than storming into the office. I couldn't have faced Sasha's emotions directly or listened to the protesting of all those teenagers. I sat down to read her resignation.

"'Dear Gus,' her note began, 'Your liberated, free, bright, sharp, straight eighth graders . . . ' *Uh oh, here we go,* I thought. *They've really told her off. The William Kunstlers have argued her into a corner. They've reduced her to tears.* I read on. 'Your glorious eighth graders are having a terrible time learning how to be theologically grandiose, tyrannically snobbish, morally sexist and mean and afraid and manipulative! Being the wondrous people they are, they just don't know how to have the dark qualities of the spirit of the Puritans. As you know, I have never worked with children before. I need your help. These children are in need of some information they just don't have.'

"I was relieved, although I was somewhat disbelieving of Sasha's assumption of such complete innocence among our eighth graders. Even so, I was resolved to help her repress your goodness. Immediately we set out to instruct you in the ways of the Devil. Send them to Salem. Make them feel oppressed. Expose them to wickedness. 'Teach them original sin,' Sasha said. I reread Jonathan Edwards, Cotton Mather, Michael Wigglesworth, all the authorities on Hell and Damnation, and we put together a crash course to un-school you of your sense of justice, to destroy your trust in others, even to unsettle your self-confidence. Write a composition entitled, 'In Adam's Fall We Sinned All.' Look up the following words and memorize their definitions: torment, perdition, trepidation, persecution, malevolence, diabolical, delusion and doom.

"Judging from your impeccable performance tonight you have all passed our course with distinction and highest honors. However, I know you recognize that we did not remove all the sweetness and light from within you. We did not intend to transform your character.

"Only persons who have lived with love can know and can convincingly express the anguish of its absence. One of your assignments was to describe the absence of love. Your answers bear witness to the measure of love with which you are so generously imbued. The absence of love, you said, is 'a butterfly without wings.' 'It is someone alone in an empty room.' 'It is a tree with no leaves,' 'an abandoned child,' 'a dark and gloomy place,' 'a clay field of hate.' The absence of love is 'two people crying but not for each other.'

"As I stand here and gaze admiringly at the extraordinarily beautiful patchwork quilt that a group of you and your friends have made as a graduation present to this school, I feel the concentration and depth of love that you have shared with us who have known you during your lifetimes at MCS. The quilt is a stunning symbol of who you really are, individually and collectively, and as such a representation it is fittingly antithetical to the cheerless, demonic images of evil that have shrouded your production of *The Crucible*.

"For the sake of those here who do not know about this quilt, there are a few points of information worth special mention. A number of you began it in January. In total, your labors took hundreds of hours, occupying the bulk of your precious Saturday mornings throughout the winter and spring. Each of you sustained dozens of pin pricks, never allowing a drop of blood to soil your work. Counting the endless times you took apart your blocks in an effort to achieve perfection, the mistakes corrected as well as the quilting that was inadvertently thrown out with the garbage, you stitched enough stitches to make a pair of quilts.

"The form of your quilt is that of the traditional American 'Ohio Star,' a symmetrical pattern in which every square is identical in design yet different in detail. In this sense, I see your quilt as an emblem of the school to which you have presented it, a pictorial statement of unity within diversity, an ordered affirmation of the whole and of the uniqueness of its parts. And the means by which you have assembled this quilt demonstrates the power and purpose of this school within which you have been such a vital force since we began just over ten years ago. You have joined hands together to realize a dream. You have joined hands together to create a community which declines to accept the absence of love. No one of you could have made that quilt. No one of you could have made this school.

"Langston Hughes's poem, 'Freedom's Plough,' has special meaning to those of us here tonight. In this poem is a message which you have lived by and by which this school has been generously guided since we began, when you were three years old. It is summarized in these lines which I ask you to hear again:

> The hand seeks tools to cut the wood,
> To till the soil, and harness the power of the waters.
> Then the hand seeks other hands to help,
> A community of hands—
> Thus the dream becomes not one man's dream alone,
> But a community dream.
> Not my dream alone, but our dream.
> Not my world alone,
> But your world and my world,
> Belonging to all the hands who build.

"Thank you for your help in building this school. Thank you for joining hands with us. Though you graduate tonight, you will never lose touch with the dream, for dreams, like memories, last forever."

Celebration for South Africa, May 10, 1994.

Chapter 19

Capital Considerations

FOLLOWING THREE YEARS of absorbing self-scrutiny, culminating in the painful divisions that had marked the work of the Policy Review Committee, in 1980 MCS began a new decade with a determination to set its course in a proactive manner. Carl Flemister, who had fulfilled his promise to see the school through the deliberations of the PRC, stepped aside, and Sara Wilford, an early-childhood educator and former MCS parent, was elected chair of the board. That fall, indicating a shared sense of stewardship on the part of the board, one trustee volunteered, "This nagging feeling was growing that we . . . were just leaving everything to Gus, and were, in fact, failing to give the operational support and guidance that a school director has the right to expect from a board of trustees."

In assuming a more active role, the board chose to undertake two major tasks: to address the school's pressing financial needs, and to strengthen its public mission. The first of these required that the school build an endowment sufficient to underwrite in perpetuity the bulk of its built-in deficit, what had once been termed its "scholarship program." The second task dictated that we formulate a deliberate response to Carl Field's advice that the school broaden its commitment to diversity in the name of multiculturalism. To do the latter meant strengthening the school's public mission through outreach projects that would position MCS as a model for other schools, public and private. These two endeavors have remained the guiding goals of MCS to this day.

In founding MCS, we knew the school could not be self-supporting, but when its annual deficit in the late 1970s reached more than a quarter of a million dollars, or approximately 40 percent of the operating budget, the need to build a substantial endowment became clear. As chief fund-raiser, I knew our donor base intimately. Only a quarter of our parents were in positions to make contributions to the school, and unlike in the earlier days of the school, we had fewer parents of great wealth. Nor could we tap our alumni; our oldest graduates were barely out of college. Most significantly, those major donors who had helped found the school, while generous in providing continuing support, were now octogenarians.

Practically speaking, I could not see that MCS had the capability of raising more than $250,000 a year. Beginning with DeWitt Wallace's initial gift in 1975, our endowment in 1980 was only $150,000. Without an increase in the endowment, we projected that in six years' time the school's annual deficit would reach $330,000. Further projections forewarned either bankruptcy or the need to change the school's enrollment profile, thereby reneging on our founding principles. Given the prospects, the board instructed the finance committee to develop goals for a capital campaign for the endowment. The arithmetic was simple: To reduce the annual deficit to 20 percent of our budget, we would need an endowment of $1.25 million by 1986.

In earlier discussions about the need for an endowment, trustee Frank Roosevelt and I had devised a plan that set ours apart from all other institutional endowments. Frank, who was uncomfortable with the idea of amassing institutional wealth through endowments, objected to the common practice of applying only 2-4 percent of an endowment fund to annual expenses. The result of this conservative fiduciary policy in many institutions was that, given long-term positive market growth, their endowment funds outgrew their needs.

One didn't have to look far to find examples. When George Washington visited his nephews at Phillips Andover Academy in 1789, the school enrolled twenty-three boys. Nearly two hundred years later, the school was coeducational, enrolling 1,217 students, with an endowment of $95 million, which was sufficient to underwrite its entire scholarship program, assuming its proceeds were 3 percent of the endowment's value. Andover's endowment was the largest of any private school in the country. St. Paul's School had the second largest endowment, but measured on a per capita basis, it was twice the size of Andover's, equaling $156,000 per student versus Andover's $78,000. If one assumes that the endowment for St. Paul's yielded 3 percent, the school had an annual endowment income that was twice as large as its scholarship program.

St. Paul's case illustrated Frank's concern. While we did not know exactly how St. Paul's applied its endowment income, we did know that it was not to increase the number of students on scholarship. Like many schools, full-tuition levels at St. Paul's were below the cost-per-student, a practice MCS had rejected prior to adopting its tuition reform plan. Effectively, St. Paul's was using at least part of its "surplus" endowment income to help subsidize all its students. No doubt St. Paul's was also reinvesting a portion of its endowment yield, thereby increasing the principal.

In contrast, the sole purpose of the MCS endowment was to support the school's economic diversity; in other words, its "scholarship program," although we had abandoned this terminology. Though other endowed schools may have shared this ideal, MCS's commitment to economic diversity was roughly ten times greater than that of any other school in the country. The magnitude of our risk warranted drawing more heavily on our endowment than was commonly practiced.

The chief objective of any endowment is for long-term stability. At MCS we also needed to consider short-term security, indeed, our very survival. Accordingly, in May 1982 the board approved our recommendation for an 8 percent draw. With projected inflation and estimated market growth, this would allow our endowment to grow by 3-5 percent per year above and beyond our 8 percent draw, not counting additional gifts generated from our capital campaign.

We had our share of good fortune. On New Year's Eve 1985, I received a call from a former parent who told me that her lawyer had advised her that she would lose jurisdiction over one of her trust funds as of midnight. She had instructed that her funds be spent immediately and told me there was already a check in the mail to MCS for $100,000. Assisted by this unexpected windfall, we met our twentieth anniversary endowment goal of $1.25 million dollars a month later. Generous contributions from MCS friends new and old, including a few more six-digit gifts and bequests, along with a tireless bull market, pushed the MCS endowment to eight million dollars by the school's thirty-fifth anniversary in 2001. In addition to this extraordinary accomplishment, the actual performance of the endowment matched our 1982 projections. Not counting deposits or withdrawals, the annualized rate of growth for the MCS endowment for the period of 1989 to 2001 was more than 13 percent.

In 1988, when MCS underwent its evaluation for accreditation by the New York State Association of Independent Schools, the chair of the visiting committee, Gardner Dunnan, then head of Dalton, said to me, "Gus, you have a larger endowment than Dalton!" "Yes," I said, "and that's because we need it more than you do." To prove my point, I reminded him that MCS enrolled 50 percent students of color as compared to an average of 13 percent at the city's other independent schools. I added that 64 percent of our students received financial aid, compared to 15.5 percent at other independent schools. Further, financial aid represented 33 percent of our annual budget, while it made up only 12.5 percent of the annual budget of other independent schools in the city. Faced with these numbers, and in keeping with his friendly advocacy toward MCS, Gardner corroborated my assessment.

Although MCS had long ago declared its rationale for setting its tuition at cost-per-child, the fact that other private schools took the opposite approach was a moral thorn in my side. When our own children entered ninth grade at Riverdale Country School, the school's annual appeal to all families stressed that every Riverdale student was "on scholarship." While this was perhaps a persuasive point in soliciting voluntary giving among parents, many of whom were very wealthy, it only inflamed my discontent with the establishment and prompted me to argue openly that an endowment created by one millionaire should not be used to reduce the tuition of another millionaire's son or daughter.

My indignation failed to convince others in the education establishment. Five years after its adoption of tuition reform, MCS decided that it would publish a history of the plan, to be distributed to private schools nationally. The Ford Foundation ultimately gave us an additional grant for this purpose. But before approaching them, I had applied for funding from the NAIS's Independent Schools Grants Committee of the Commission on Educational Issues. The committee's director was Bill Berkeley, someone I had come to know and like in the early years of the school when he worked for A Better Chance, an organization dedicated to placing students of color in private schools. Bill and I were among those who attended annual conferences of the Leadership and World Society (LAWS) Foundation. As cograntees summoned to sing for our supper, we shared a strong interest in promoting educational opportunities for students of color. I believed, therefore, that Bill's committee might be a receptive source of funding.

My proposal to the committee listed six principles of tuition reform, the first being that the cost-per-child should dictate a school's tuition schedule. The proposal was rejected with a handwritten note from Bill, stating, "I'm not at all happy with having to write this letter, but for what it's worth, we felt that the essential element of your pricing scheme is not very transferable to other schools. You are so out in front of everyone else in terms of convincing people that they are buying into a very special group of people rather than paying for an individual child's tuition that I don't see the potential impact here, at least that has been our experience in using your material with other schools."

Recalling my anger at the Carnegie Foundation's rejection of MCS as not being a "blue chip," I wrote Bill a stinging reply, opening myself up to his return allegation of arrogance on my part. "To say that we are so 'out in front' that we lack potential impact on others is to write off the desirability of the significant social commitments out of which our school has developed its innovative programs," my letter stated. "I don't mind being characterized as unique if the intent of the designation is to give tribute to our exemplary role. My hackles rise, though, if uniqueness is a polite term for dismissing us as untouchables."

Bill's response, though upsetting to me at the time, revealed a central dilemma that MCS would face for many years to come: MCS, a private school principally committed to a public mission, was poised just outside the public sector and only partially inside the private one. How long could MCS sustain this solitary role?

Bill wrote: "Let me comment on your letter because I think it raises a number of interesting issues. I hope I don't have to convince you of my commitment to and admiration for what you have done at MCS. One of my greatest frustrations at A Better Chance was to have to say that, because we chose for legitimate reasons to work exclusively at the secondary level, we ended up providing moral and monetary support for a group of independent schools none of which had your personal and institutional commitment, yet we weren't able to help you. So I am an unabashed Gus Trowbridge and MCS fan. Yet, I think the basic premise of your letter is way off the mark.

"It seems to me you and MCS have always been quite vocal rebels with a cause. On occasion, you have taken great pains to thumb your nose at the independent school establishment. You don't belong to NAIS. You're not active in 'the club.' I've heard you dismiss the efforts of some pretty committed schools because their commitment didn't measure up to yours. You have on occasion exhibited that very special kind of hauteur which often characterizes people who know they are out in front, way out in front.

"If all of a sudden you begin spending any of your time looking over your shoulder worrying whether anyone is following, I think that will be the source of MCS's failure, not your perception that in some specific way MCS isn't being taken as a serious example by even the 'enlightened forces within the establishment.'

"I think MCS has had an enormous influence, particularly in the New York area," Bill continued. "The very public commitment you have made to minorities and scholarships has made it just that much more uncomfortable for your tonier New York fellows to live with their own performance, and their numbers and commitment have edged up as a result . . . .

"I get absolutely furious that schools like Andover and Exeter can use their non-profit status to solicit tax-deductible gifts which can be added to their endowments and used to discount their tuition to wealthy people. I wish the IRS would require schools to charge full-cost, then compute scholarships based on need to reduce the price from full-cost, not from an already discounted endowment-supported tuition. But lacking that sort of jolt from the IRS, the key elements of your plan will, I fear, remain ignored by the establishment and I don't think you should waste one minute of your time or one ounce of your anger worrying about it."

Reading over Bill's letter, as I have done many times, I am still confused by his assertion the I was "way off the mark." I believe his praise of me and the school was sincere, and I appreciate his advice that I should not be looking over my shoulder to see if others are following. I also acknowledge that in much of my rhetoric I have been offensive to the establishment. The line between anger and arrogance is a hard one not to cross, especially when fighting for one's welfare. In his scolding me for not joining the club, I cannot tell if he believed my doing so—joining the National Association of Independent Schools, for example—would have made a marked difference in the establishment's recognition and support of MCS.

Bill's final words are his most perplexing. On the one hand, he claims that the MCS plan has no bearing on other schools; on the other hand, he argues even more forcefully than I that the use of contributions to discount tuitions for the rich is an intolerable practice. If his latter insistence was heartfelt, then why did he decline giving MCS the small financial assistance it sought in order to promote views he claimed to share? Was it all because I hadn't joined the club?

With respect to the fiscal responsibility of private schools, in 1985 MCS joined another battle already in full swing: the divestment movement. At that time, sixteen states, thirty-five cities, and sixty-three colleges had taken action to limit or fully prohibit investing in companies engaged in business with South Africa's apartheid regime, but as yet no private schools had followed suit.

MCS had first registered its concern in the late 1960s to our bank, First National City Bank, now Citicorp. Their response that they had a policy of noninterference in the internal affairs of another country was one commonly cited by American banks. By the 1980s, however, the situation had changed, but not at Citicorp, which remained the largest U.S. lender to South Africa and the only American bank still operating branches there. Accordingly, we severed relations with Citicorp and took our business to Chemical Bank, which had ceased all its business in South Africa and announced that it would not resume connections until apartheid was ended.

As a logical extension of our decision not to sanction investments in South Africa, MCS resolved that it would also impose a higher standard of social responsibility on its endowment. But consistently screening the portfolio handled by our investment manager proved to be too difficult for us, so in 1988 we transferred our account to Walden Asset Management, a branch of the U. S. Trust Company of Boston, which had been committed to "Investing for Social Change" since its inception in 1975.

Walden requires the companies in which it invests to provide goods and services that are safe, to adhere to equal opportunity in hiring and promotion, to observe fair labor practices and pay living wages, to play a positive role in the community, and to treat the natural environment with respect. In addition to screening out companies that do not meet these standards, Walden also acts on behalf of its clients to exercise shareholder resolutions aimed at improving practices in companies that have passed the screen.

Like Walden, we wanted to go the extra mile to promote socially responsible investing. We decided to convene a conference of private secondary schools with existing endowments to encourage them to divest their holdings in corporations dealing with South Africa. Unlike colleges, which had taken a stand largely in response to protests by their students, secondary schools had been under no internal pressure to change.

Our conference, held on December 4, 1985, at St. James Church and funded by the New World Foundation, was the first time private schools had ever addressed the subject of apartheid in South Africa. Attended by the heads and trustees of sixteen independent schools, some with endowments the size held by small colleges, the day-long program was very favorably received. Assisted by a mailing from the National Association of Independent Schools urging their one thousand members to "declare their opposition to apartheid as part of their educational responsibility," MCS was clearly successful in launching the divestment movement among this lagging sector of educational institutions. After our conference, the headmistress of Chapin School, whose endowment was the largest of New York City's private schools, notified me that her board had voted "to divest the school of any stock of companies not adhering to the Sullivan principles," which were a set of carefully crafted antiapartheid standards.

Critics of socially responsible investment argued that the exclusion of certain large-cap corporations from their portfolios would diminish the performance of their investments. At least one MCS trustee shared this concern and voted against our decision to transfer our endowment portfolio to Walden. Even Walden's management in 1988 conceded that their performance might lag behind other market indexes by one or two per cent. But MCS felt that the school's commitment to social justice had to be put into practice in its fiscal policy as well, even given the possibility of modest adverse results.

Fortunately, these concerns have so far proved unfounded. The annualized rate of growth for equities in the MCS endowment from 1989 to 2001 was 15.7 percent compared to 15.5 percent for the Standard and Poor 500. Our fixed income investments have grown at 9.3 percent compared to 8.7 percent for the Lehman index. To everyone's satisfaction, especially Walden's, the record of MCS's socially responsible investments has so far proven to be without financial sacrifice.

May 10, 1994, was a day of jubilation throughout the world. On that date, Nelson Mandela was elected president of South Africa, officially ending apartheid. "Wasn't that a mighty day!" Marty later wrote in an article for the school newsletter. At MCS, in celebration of South African liberation, we cancelled classes and gathered for a morning assembly followed by a picnic and afternoon program in Central Park. Our procession to the East Meadow was led by an African drummer and a student bearing a dozen green, black, yellow, red, white, and blue balloons—the colors of the new South African flag. In the meadow, we formed a large, hand-over-hand circle, singing "Kum Ba Ya" and "Nkosi Sikelel'i Afrika" ("God Bless Africa," the national anthem, in Zulu). Our African dance teacher, Alala Dei, led her students in traditional African dances, and representatives from each class released the balloons, which rose high above the city, driven by strong westerly winds.

Everyone, including parents who joined us for lunch and even bystanders, signed a letter which Mayor David Dinkins would deliver personally to President Mandela on a forthcoming trip. "For hundreds of years, the struggle for racial equality has raged," it read. "Today, you have pushed past, set aside, and overcome old feelings of hatred and resistance to join together as a racially unified country. You, Mr. Mandela, are the embodiment of the struggle. Through your inspiration, you have given hope to the people, and all the world recognizes your accomplishments, and celebrates the day that all of South Africa voted together."

Later that afternoon, when we were leaving the meadow, the annular solar eclipse, in apparent celestial recognition of such an event, gradually darkened the sky. As the sun became obscured by the moon, images of light danced through the lacy leaves of the trees, permitting the eclipsing sun to create hundreds of delicate sun-crescent patterns on the pavement below.

Members of the class of 2004, outside the school.

CHAPTER 20

"After Grammar School It's Too Late"

IN 1981, I READ *Forty Years a Guinea Pig: A Black Man's View From the Top* written by E. Frederic Morrow, who coincidentally resided at the same building in East Harlem where our family had once lived. During the Eisenhower administration, Morrow had been executive assistant to the President, the first, and until then, the only black on the White House staff. Later, he became executive vice president of the Bank of America.

After reading his memoir, I was moved to contact Morrow. During our short introductory conversation, he agreed to meet me, and then later to visit MCS. After touring the school, he confessed to being "smitten" with our program, although he said he didn't approve of boys wearing hats in class. He shrugged this off when I told him, "I have to pick my battles and that's not one of them."

Morrow joined our board, serving for only a year due to declining health. In getting to know him during this post-Black Caucus period, I was fortified by the dual message of his experience: the need to stay alert to the continuing presence of racism in our society, and the need to empower young blacks with the means to achieve within the system.

Not that Morrow believed this approach would solve everything. He had once shared with me this story: When recently called to jury duty and asked his profession, he'd responded, "A banker." The lawyer questioning him said, "You're what?" Morrow repeated his profession. The lawyer pressed, "What were you before that?" When Morrow answered that he had been on the White House staff under President Eisenhower, the lawyer exclaimed, "Your Honor, let's cut out this foolishness," and the court recessed to check out Morrow's credentials.

"Gus," Morrow said, "Every day of my life I have to go through the same routine of being checked out. This is what happens when you try to do it the orthodox way, within the system. That's why there are thousands of blacks in this country today who are so thoroughly disgusted. You can't do it outside the system, but when you try to do it within the system, the sacrifices are fierce and the wounds are bloody."

When Morrow later spoke with our faculty, his message was unequivocal, resembling Preston Wilcox's early advice. He said, "The way out of the ghetto is with your head, not your feet. I envy your opportunity to set horizons for these youngsters. You teachers are the only ones who can turn it around. Attitudes for survival and achievement are formed at a very early age. After grammar school, it's too late. So keep the faith."

Some white parents in the early 1980s, perhaps still stung by the school's recent racial crossfire, complained that at MCS there was too much emphasis on teaching racial justice. Whites growing up in the days after desegregation may have been tempted to think that racial prejudice was a condition of the past, but Morrow's jury-duty story alone was enough to prove otherwise.

In answering these parents, I cited a recent conversation with a black MCS father whose daughter had just entered her senior year at college. "This June," he told me, "will mark the first college degree in my family's entire history, and that's three hundred years." Until black children are raised with the same educational opportunity as their white schoolmates—an educational opportunity that extends at least to the living generations of each child's family—we cannot assume equality among races.

With this in mind, I began to keep closer tabs on our high school placement record and I conducted three surveys of alumni academic progress over the ten-year period following the Policy Review Committee's deliberations, always with an eye to determining the relative performance of our graduates according to race. I was in a good position to keep track of our students' progress, because from the earliest years I had always devoted some time to teaching. My regular schedule included five periods a week teaching grammar to seventh and eighth graders, plus an additional session with the eighth grade, which I conducted with the administrator responsible for high school placement. I came to know well every student who graduated, and I was able to help guide them and their families through the complex and generally harrowing transition into secondary school.

While the pattern of secondary schools attended by our graduates fluctuates from year to year, with certain private high schools falling in and out of popularity, approximately half our graduates enter private high schools, with a small percentage going to boarding schools. Of the half entering public schools, nearly all seek admission to those with competitive entrance exams— Stuyvesant, Bronx Science, Brooklyn Tech—and to La Guardia High School of Music and Art and the Performing Arts, which has its own highly selective criteria. These schools are notably harder to get into than even the most sought-after private schools.

Despite the competitive nature of secondary school placement in the city, almost 80 percent of our students get into their first-choice school. This does not always mean they can attend. Unlike MCS, private schools traditionally separate their admissions decisions from financial aid considerations, the result being that frequently a student is admitted but not offered a sufficient scholarship. This factor has always weighed more heavily on MCS students of color needing substantial aid. In 1979, for example, nearly three-quarters of our eighth grade students of color required virtually full scholarships to attend private school. Nevertheless, I was pleased to learn from our alumni surveys that the overall record of our graduates is comparable to that of other private schools. Further, I was interested to discover that the small disparity in rates of college attendance between our white and nonwhite alumni is attributable almost entirely to economic circumstances.

These were the salient findings of our three alumni surveys conducted in the 1980s:

1. Seventy-eight percent of our eighth graders were admitted to schools of their first choice. In the class of 1987, five out of nine students who applied were admitted to Stuyvesant, perhaps the most sought-after school in the country, and 100 percent of those who applied qualified for La Guardia School of the Arts.

2. One hundred percent of our graduates completed high school.

3. Ninety-five percent of white MCS students graduating from high school entered college, compared to 91 percent for students of color.

That not a single MCS graduate dropped out of high school at a time when the drop-out rate in New York State was approaching 40 percent, revealed an outcome of our preparation, especially of minority students, that I might have overlooked had I not read Robert Sam Anson's 1987 book, *Best Intentions: The Education and Killing of Edmund Perry*. Anson's book tells the story of a promising black student attending Phillips Exeter Academy, who withdrew before graduation. Noting that their drop-out rate for black students was six times higher than for white students, and represented 30 percent of their total black enrollment, Exeter studied the possible causes and discovered that neither academic failure nor behavioral problems were a significant factor. The reason they cited was that the black students dropped out because they felt "psychologically crushed."

MCS's minority graduates on the other hand, seemed well prepared for survival within the system, which is not to diminish Frederic Morrow's warning that, even with such success, "the wounds are bloody." In interviews conducted with twelve MCS alumni who had graduated from college, we specifically asked about this aspect of their private secondary school experience. Our minority students agreed that the transition to predominantly white institutions had been difficult, and more than one white student said the lack of diversity in their "Ivy League" secondary schools had been a culture shock.

At the same time, all students confirmed that MCS had nurtured and supported their belief in themselves, and that their experience at MCS gave them an edge, an enhanced cultural awareness, political activism, and confidence. Referring to these qualities as his "internal ammunition," one black graduate stated, "The pain of racism I felt was eased by my memories of the good times I had with white friends at MCS." Four of the five white students interviewed felt they had left MCS with a uniquely informed position on race relations, which did not allow them to walk away from a racist incident without taking some action.

It was not the first time our students had guided my understanding of their experience at MCS and how it girded them for the world beyond our doors. A technique common to many school heads is to use the input of children when preparing a speech for their parents. A fifth grader once said to me that MCS was a "treasure box." Asked to explain, she replied, "By that I mean, I've collected things here that are treasures, things I want to keep." Her matter-of-fact words gave me the text to a full-blown talk to parents, and when I thanked her some days later, she was pleased but seemed perplexed that I had needed her help.

In fact, I would often turn to the children when I needed reassurance that MCS was practicing what it preached. On one such occasion, I asked the eighth grade class of 1994 to list everything about MCS that they valued most strongly, and then to choose and rank the most important items on their list. Their initial list contained eighteen items, ranging from "the absence of a dress code," to "the noncompetitive grading system," to "the school's racial diversity" and "the MLK Assembly."

In preparing to rank all their preferences, the students talked together in small groups and classified each item as "important," "quite important," and "vital." "Racial diversity" received their highest ranking. Next, scoring only a point below and within one point of each other, came "multiculturalism" and "the school's economic diversity." Fourth place was the "farm," followed by "the MLK Assembly" and "the curriculum's emphasis on justice and equality." "Coeducation" ranked in seventh place, causing one student to speculate, "If the school is not going to remain coed, then I would rank the farm much lower."

Several items I had predicted would be favorites received relatively low scores, such as the smallness of the school, no dress code, and calling teachers by their first names. In discussing these, I noted that the children of the nineties—unlike those of the sixties who would have gone to battle against competition, conformity, and bigness—were more deeply wedded to the philosophic underpinnings of the school than to the nontraditional practices of progressive education. "How come you gave a rank of 15 to addressing teachers by their first names?" I asked, recounting my own school days of "Yes, sir" and "No, sir." "But we're not treated as inferior as you say you were," responded one student. "What matters most is that teachers and students have a relationship of mutual respect." So often in conversations with the children, I was struck not only by their maturity, but also by the fact that MCS was getting its message across.

Before ending the "preferences" exercise, I returned to the MLK Assembly and asked why they had ranked it so high. "It's not the assembly itself," they said. "Martin Luther King Jr. personifies the school, and the assembly celebrates that personification." They, of course, had been to ten MLK assemblies and heard me and others repeatedly state that the birthday of Dr. King was the anniversary of MCS; that although Dr. King was not alive, it was up to us to complete the task which he had not been able to finish.

The image of Dr. King portrayed in these assemblies became so real that the younger children were inclined to think of him as a living presence. Once, when Carl Flemister spoke at our assembly, a five-year-old later told his parents that Dr. King had come to school that day. Another child, six-year-old Emily, went to a concert at Tanglewood where Yolanda King narrated Aaron Copland's "Lincoln Portrait." When later introduced to Yolanda, Emily proudly announced, "I go to your father's school." In a different sense, I share Emily's claim to have attended Dr. King's school. Dr. King's prophetic voice has always been our guide, the compass by which we steer our school.

In *The Moral and Spiritual Crisis in Education*, author David Purpel calls the prophetic voice a "voice of transformation." The prophets, he says, "urge, prod, dare and encourage us to change our ways and continue the struggle to create that vision; they moan and curse, but not with despair alone; their outrage moves us to act and change rather than to be defeated and resigned." In this sense, Dr. King was indeed our school's prophet.

Even his wife might agree. In a letter responding to my invitation that she join us for our twentieth anniversary, Coretta Scott King sent this message: "I am writing to applaud a continuing history of a vision and a sense of what we can be. You will remember I am sure the vision of society that Martin described so vividly in his speech at the Lincoln Memorial—a society where children can simply be and discover the joy of each other. To the extent that you and your students, parents, and teachers have remained true to that future not yet seen in society, you are bearers of a vision. I cannot be with you on what I know will be a joyous celebration, but please convey to all my sense of joy in your history, in your future, and in your celebration of a continuing sense of possibility."

Implicit in Mrs. King's message was the confirmation that so long as there are bearers of Dr. King's vision, his work would continue. The movement's dream, prodded by discontent, would continue to empower us with a "sense of what we can be."

Sara Wilford, MCS trustee and parent, with
daughter, Betsey, on graduation night 1977.
In 2000, Betsey and her husband, Tony Brown, founded an
elementary school in Tallahassee, Florida, modeled after MCS.

CHAPTER 21

A Minority of None

IN THE DECADE following 1988, MCS at last achieved its goal of a student enrollment with no racial majority. In a *New York Times* article dated April 14, 2002, writer Randal C. Archibold described our enrollment as "A Minority of None," stating, "At Manhattan Country School, diversity rules; no race can be in the majority."

We were encouraged to publicly promote our achievement by the results of our first New York State Association of Independent Schools (NYSAIS) accreditation report in 1988, which included this glowing commendation: "Today, Manhattan Country School offers an extraordinary program to a student body which reflects an economic and cultural diversity that is perhaps unique in this country. While our society has retreated from some of its best intentions of the sixties, MCS has remained true to those principles and has continued to evolve in the complexity and the application of those principles. Supporters of independent education usually cite their capacity for innovation and demonstration as a justification for the privileged existence of independent schools in our system; yet, all too often we fail to fulfill our potential for innovation. Manhattan Country School is a shining exception to this tragic generalization, and, for this reason, enhances all of independent education. The challenge for the future is to continue and solidify the excellence at Ninety-sixth Street and Roxbury [the Farm], and to disseminate the mission and mechanics of the school to others both public and private. Only through the extension of the principles of MCS will we move towards a more just school system and society."

NYSAIS went on to recommend that our school "make further efforts to disseminate its philosophy and objectives and to promote the emulation of these worthy goals in New York City and nationally." To the extent that NYSAIS represented the private school "club" of New York State, I welcomed their acknowledging that we were a model to other schools, and I was eager to share our experience in a more deliberate fashion.

Jo Levinson was among our strongest allies in this effort, and she was one of our wealthiest. A former MCS parent and thereafter a trustee, Jo came to see me to say that she had appointed herself a committee-of-one to aid the school's radical underpinnings. "Call me DIP," she said. "It means director of innovative programs." An activist by nature, Jo had offered to fund a Jewish Studies program in the 1970s. "How can I allow that when I've just refused to teach a separate course in Black Studies?" I asked. She had conceded, giving the school a hefty contribution anyway.

This time, her proposal that MCS become a bilingual school, teaching all classes in English and Spanish was again out of bounds and even contrary to the school's concept of pluralism. We settled on a Spanish Enrichment program, to which she made a five-year pledge to be used for three purposes. First, we would increase Spanish instruction for seventh and eighth graders to include the cultural and political life of Central American countries. Next, we would fund a teacher-exchange program with Brenda Cano School in Tipitapa, Nicaragua, our sister-city school with which we had established relations in 1986 just after the Sandanista revolution. Jo wanted our students to go to Nicaragua; instead, we sent Michèle Solá, our Spanish teacher, and three classroom teachers.

Finally, we established the objective of attaining over a five-year period a bilingual faculty. To do so, we offered three annual summer fellowships of intensive language training in Latin America and weekly Spanish classes throughout the academic year. All teachers were asked to acquire a working knowledge of Spanish at least sufficient to converse with the students they taught. MCS was already the only elementary school in New York City that offered instruction in a second language beginning with four-year-olds.

Our board chair, Sara Wilford was also a generous and devoted advocate of the public mission of MCS. She paved the way for us to solicit support from Greentree Foundation, which was controlled by her mother, Mrs. John Hay Whitney. Our proposal was to develop a Public School Outreach Program (PSO) to train teachers in multicultural education. Escorting me to her mother's house, where I was to meet with the foundation officers, Sara said, "Take a look at her stockings. If they are black lace, be prepared for an uphill battle. If they are white lace, you're in." We arrived a little early and were greeted by two trustees and George Patterson, the foundation's director. Fifteen minutes later, Mrs. Whitney descended the stairs, and before I saw her face, I glimpsed her white stockings. We got the grant, which has been renewed ever since.

Our first PSO program was a conference on multicultural education, entitled "Equity and Excellence," which was held at MCS on April 30, 1988. The conference was a success, enrolled to capacity and well attended by public and private school teachers from across the city. Evaluation forms submitted by participants revealed that most of these teachers felt a sense of isolation in their schools. The consensus was that MCS should conduct such conferences annually, and that through our PSO project we should develop a broad network of teachers committed to the pursuit of multicultural education.

"Multiculturalism" is a mouthful; the spell check in my computer doesn't even recognize the word. The concept of multiculturalism, however, is a direct descendent of the civil rights movement. Indeed, in the thirty-five-year period following the 1954 *Brown v. Board of Education* decision, the defining goals of the movement's dream can be traced through its evolving semantics.

In the fifties, the debate over segregation moved from "separate and unequal" to "desegregation." Then, in the sixties, debate arose over the essential purpose of integration. Was the creation of a racially heterogeneous group to achieve equality for all or to integrate the minority into the majority? Those in strong support of integration opposed the latter aim and argued against the concept of the "melting pot" and the process of "assimilation" on which it rested. A decade later, the popular term among integrationists was "pluralism," and the idea of the "melting pot" was replaced with terms such as "inclusion," "rainbow coalition," and "mosaic." For those in search of true racial equality, underlying their new rhetoric was the declaration that equality was not sameness, that no two parts of the whole should be seen as alike.

In the eighties, "multiculturalism" overtook "pluralism," but differences in the thinking behind the two terms were hard to find. Both rested on an emphatic affirmation of diversity and the belief that all students profit from being together. Despite this, the idea of "multiculturalism" provoked a prolonged and heated debate, particularly in New York State, where proponents of multiculturalism were seen as unpatriotic for embracing differences and challenging the notion of a common American culture.

One explanation for this conflict was the fact that thirty-five years of changing and presumably improving goals for equal opportunity had yielded too little progress. For black students in 1987, the school system of New York State was the third most segregated in the country, and for Hispanic students it ranked number one. By the turn of the twenty-first century, according to Harvard education professor Gary Orfield in a March 28, 2002, *New York Times* article, New York State operated the most segregated school system in the nation.

Frustrated by this record, racial minorities, aided by strong representation of blacks and Hispanics in the state legislature, used the rubric of multiculturalism to challenge the stagnant educational system. Their circumstance resembled that of a favorite political cartoon of mine by Jules Feiffer, published in 1965. It shows an aged man slumped over in a chair, saying, "I used to think I was poor. Then they told me I wasn't poor. I was needy. Then they told me it was self-defeating to think of myself as needy. I was deprived. Then they told me deprived was a bad image. I was underprivileged. Then they told me underprivileged was overused. I was disadvantaged. I still don't have a dime. But I have a great vocabulary." Like Feiffer's pauper, those awaiting the fulfillment of the American dream were feeling destitute.

Thomas Sobel, then the Commissioner of the New York State Department of Education, proposed to tackle the problem through curriculum reform. When his department presented the State Board of Regents with a new social studies syllabus entitled "A Curriculum of Inclusion," Sobel attached this memo: "To what extent, if any, should the children of New York State be taught a social studies curriculum which is more 'multicultural' than that now in existence?

"This question," he continued, "so seemingly ordinary in its pedagogical jargon, entails many deeper questions: Who are we, as a people and a nation? What is the truth of our history? What are the realities of our present? What binds us together and makes us one? What differences among us are worth understanding and respecting? How can our differences and unity best be harmonized? To what extent should ethnic and cultural differences be used as one lens through which to study the American experience? For what kind of society, in what kind of world, do we have a responsibility to prepare our children?" Sobel acknowledged that these were "heavy questions," sure to "provoke disagreement among reasonable people."

Another cause of the increasingly strident debate over multiculturalism in the eighties and nineties was the fact that, despite all the victories of the civil rights movement, racism in America still inflicted devastating wounds, and those who deplored it had ample cause to react in anger when told that their attempts to reform the system were un-American. A case in point: In the midst of his effort to gain consensus for the curriculum of inclusion, Sobel learned of a black teenager's murder by white residents of Bensonhurst, New York. In late August 1989, sixteen-year-old Yusef Hawkins had gone to a predominantly white, Italian neighborhood in Brooklyn, New York, to look at a car he was interested in buying. A gang of white teens, apparently mistaking him for a black youth they'd fought with earlier, pummeled him with baseball bats, then shot him to death.

The following day, Sobel wrote this impassioned instruction to all his school principals: "Our job is not only to impart academic skill and knowledge, but to help civilize the human race. Within the profession, reasonable people can disagree about pedagogical tasks, but in our democracy there can be no disagreement about the role of schools in rooting out prejudice. Racism is wrong. Cruelty is wrong. Ignorance is wrong. And it is our duty to dispel them."

Among white Americans in the late eighties, those wedded to the dream of racial equality were actually in the minority. In an NAACP survey comparing racial attitudes over three decades, pollster Louis Harris found that while prejudice and inequality had declined, they were far from extinguished. Twenty-three percent of whites interviewed admitted to racist attitudes, and 52 percent said that progress for blacks since the sixties had been "at about the right pace." *Time* magazine in July 1989 confirmed Harris' findings, stating that white resistance to equality was the main cause for the stalling of black progress.

That year, after seeing *Mississippi Burning*, a film about the murders of civil rights workers James Chaney, Andrew Goodman, and Mickey Schwerner in Mississippi in 1964, Marty and I overheard a man saying to his friend, "Yes, it's terrible, but people aren't like that anymore." Perhaps the 52 percent majority of white Americans who thought race relations had progressed "at about the right pace" would have agreed with our fellow moviegoer. However, recent events—the racial violence in Bensonhurst and a similar tragedy in the Queens, New York, neighborhood of Howard Beach, along with the burning of Torah scrolls the summer before in a Brooklyn synagogue, and the refusal of the City of Yonkers to integrate public housing—spoke volumes about the immediacy of racism. It was neither a thing of the past, nor did it reside only among fanatical groups remote from us.

Another sad example occurred on Mother's Day 1988, the day after our first conference on multicultural education. Paula Wehmiller had conducted one of our workshops entitled, "Identity, Self-esteem and Learning: What's the Connection?" Paula's first job had been at MCS in 1969, teaching six-year-olds. After MCS, she moved with her family to Swarthmore, Pennsylvania, where she directed a daycare center. In 1986, Paula was appointed principal of the lower school at Wilmington Friends, becoming the first black administrator in the school's 243-year history.

Before she took the job, Paula's father had called her with a note of caution about her moving to Delaware. He reminded her of when she was a child driving south with her parents, and the family had been unable to find a restaurant in Delaware that would seat them. He also recalled that when Martin Luther King Jr. was killed, violence between whites and blacks had erupted in Wilmington, forcing the governor to call in the National Guard for nine and a half months, the longest military occupation anywhere in the United States since the Civil War. Paula was aware that the school system in Delaware had been segregated until 1978, twenty years after Little Rock, Arkansas. But she did not realize that bylaws of suburban development associations in the neighborhood where Wilmington Friends was located included an "all-white, all-Christian code."

Paula awoke on the Monday morning following Mother's Day in May 1988 to a phone call from Dulany Bennett, the head of her school. In her 2002 book, *A Gathering of Gifts,* Paula recounts the substance of Bennett's phone call: "On Sunday evening, May 1, four students in the senior class met by prearrangement to paint the soccer kickboard, a flat rectangular structure, approximately 8 feet by 25 feet, standing in the midst of the Wilmington Friends School playing fields. They worked for approximately one hour under bright moonlight and then went home. What confronted students and staff the following morning, depicted on the kickboard, were racist and anti-Semitic slogans and, most disturbing of all, threats of violent assaults against one clearly identified member of the senior class. The slogans written on the kickboard included: 'Save the land, join the Klan,' and 'Down with Jews;' the drawings included at least twelve hooded Ku Klux Klansmen, Nazi swastikas, and a burning cross. The most frightening and disturbing depictions, however, were those that threatened violence against one of our senior black students. He was drawn, in cartoon figure, identified by his name and his initials, and by the name of his mother. Directly to the right of his head was a bullet, and farther to the right was a gun with its barrel directed toward the head. Next to the gun was a drawing of a burning cross under which was written 'Kill the Tar Baby.'"

The horror of Paula's story is both in its graphic ugliness and in the response it provoked. The boys responsible, who were immediately identified, expressed remorse but could not explain their actions, stating that it was not their intention to threaten violence. The boys were expelled, prompting a group of parents to protest, defending the incident as a "harmless prank."

Reflecting on this traumatic event in *A Gathering of Gifts,* Paula evokes the metaphor of a table. "Now the picture of the table would forever include one in which all the people of one color, one economic status, one class, one religion, one section of town are seated for an elegant meal. And all of the people of different colors and languages and backgrounds are standing, invisible, aside, silently waiting table. After they are done serving others, these people will eat dinner in the kitchen or just wait till they get back home.

"I felt then a kind of hunger that comes to me still when I am in a place where it doesn't feel safe to be myself, where I have to unremember who I am in order to survive. And though it is a painful feeling, it is food for fueling what would become my life's vocation—a vocation of breaking the Jim Crow rules about who gets to come to the table."

Despite Paula's story, many like the moviegoer leaving *Mississippi Burning* are still tempted to conclude that people "aren't like that anymore." James Baldwin knew better when he said that he was born two thousand years too early, implying that true racial understanding was still millennia away. Any black person who has stood on a street corner and tried to hail a cab as taxi after taxi passes them by experiences just what Baldwin means.

Paula Wehmiller, an MCS teacher from 1968 to 1971, is now an ordained minister. In a letter to Gus Trowbridge after revisiting the school in 1990, she wrote: "I wanted to know what keeps the original mission of the school current. The answer came in this refrain: The children sustain us. Yes, it is clear that the children sustain the teachers and the school . . . because they challenge the teachers to reinterpret the school's mission in their presence, in their time. They demand that the vision and the dream be theirs too."

CHAPTER 22

E Pluribus Unum

FOR MCS, 1988 WAS a seminal year. It not only marked the beginning of the school's recognition as a standard bearer for multicultural education. It was also when I planted a seed that would bear fruit within the next decade.

The night before the NYSAIS visiting committee began its three-day site evaluation of MCS, I met privately with the committee's chair, Gardner Dunnan. He wanted to know if I had any special goals for the work of his committee. "Yes," I said, "I'd like you to help the board prepare for my eventual retirement. It's been twenty-three years, and I'm thinking that thirty is the most I should do."

In our 116-page self-evaluation report I had deliberately not raised this matter, although the section prepared by the trustees included a passage that I urged Gardner to explore in-depth. This read: "As a board, we have had a special relationship with MCS's founder and director. In a sense, he selected and 'hired' us, rather than we, him. In many respects, he has been our guide, our helper and our inspiration. Our relationship is one of co-workers, rather than one of employers and employee . . . . We recognize that some day the board will be called upon to find and to hire a new director."

Although I had no intention of retiring fewer than six or eight years later, I told Gardner that I thought the board needed time to set its objectives and to develop its own leadership. Furthermore, I knew first-hand the task of selecting a successor to a founder posed enormous challenges. The successor to Charles Merrill who founded the Commonwealth School in Boston, for example, was a distinguished educator from Harvard, but he lasted only a short time. I was determined that this shouldn't happen to MCS. It was also my hope, although there were those who strongly felt otherwise, that after I retired I could maintain a productive working relationship with the new director.

The examples of two well-known schools in New York City, New Lincoln and Walden, both of which had folded since MCS began, made me worry that unlike old-guard traditional schools, progressive schools were generally more vulnerable in times of transition. Howard Levy, an MCS parent who was on the faculty of Walden during its final years, told me of Walden's bitter struggle involving a "faction new in the school that wanted to push Walden into a college preparatory mode, at the expense of the ethical education it had pioneered. The result was the loss of their ability to articulate a vision and of their whole reason for being."

The NYSAIS Committee addressed the issue of transition in their report to the school, saying a "major function of a board of trustees is the selection and supervision of the chief executive of the school. Prior boards have been spared this burden as the founding head has provided continuity of leadership and has insulated the board from this responsibility. The present board or a board in the near future will face this responsibility when the director elects to leave the school, and the board should begin immediately preparing for this by becoming more informed about the school and more active in its functioning as the policy making body for the school."

Claudia Grose became chair of the board in June, and from the start of her three-year term she made clear not only her dedication to the school, of which she and her husband, Peter, had been an active part for many years, but also her determination to meet the challenges identified by the NYSAIS evaluation. As with other parents, the Groses' commitment to MCS was not without some misgivings, which they had expressed openly in parent meetings. In 1978, when their older daughter was about to graduate and move on to

Horace Mann High School, and their younger daughter was in sixth grade (she would later become a Rhodes Scholar), I asked them a blunt question: "Would you do it again? I mean, when you came back from living abroad as foreign correspondents, you could have sent your children to an established and proven private school, but instead you took a leap of faith and enrolled them in MCS when we had no track record at all. If you could do it over, would you still send them to MCS?"

I knew Claudia and Peter well and respected them a great deal, so I was not surprised that they took my question to heart. After some family discussions they wrote me an extensive reply that, with their permission, I published in the school newsletter.

In part, their letter reads: "We have discussed your question, and each of us admitted some disappointments, but there is no doubt among all four of us that we would make the same decision now. We decided back then that a value system and sense of self-assurance had to be instilled from the earliest years if these are to have any endurance at all. If this was a 'leap of faith,' as you said, how has it worked out in retrospect?

"From our first community meetings, you remember how we raised our doubts about your commitment to the intellectual potential of all the kids at MCS. After all our arguments over the years some of our worries have been overcome while others remain. The curriculum is surely adequate and has been improved in recent years. But too often there seemed to be an ambivalence at MCS about setting standards. Slippery deadlines and indiscriminate pats on the head for any piece of work turned in made it very tempting just to slide through. A lack of coordination of content led sometimes to repetition or gaps from class to class. We didn't really care that our children might not learn about Napoleon in the fourth grade, but we were not expecting them to graduate with year after year of American History and no European or Asian history at all.

"Clearly, however, something good was going on anyway. Over the years both girls would burst in with provocative statements about apartheid or Nicaragua or the inadequacies of news reporting (a touchy subject in our household), and regularly our dinner table talk would be dominated by heated discussion of diverse topics brought home from school or the farm. In no uncertain terms we have seen how MCS teaches students to think for themselves, to assert and defend independent judgments. Both our girls rejoice in the sharing of learning experiences with their teachers, whom they regard as human beings and friends, not mere dispensers of rigid knowledge. And we have seen them with their classmates learning to cope with conflict and injustice, developing all the while an astute sensitivity and love for diversity in human contacts . . . . It is to MCS that full credit must be given for developing the sense of self that enabled these two students to evaluate and open themselves successfully to new experiences. Maybe there is more to elementary education than whatever happened to Napoleon.

"So, Gus, we would make the same decision to send our daughters to MCS if we were starting now. We would continue to argue that you don't have to relax the academic standards in order to achieve the other results; you would continue to deny that you are doing so—your presentations of the high school placement record certainly seem to bear you out. We would go on asking for clearer commitment and continuity in the curriculum as we have done over the years, and we would go on talking it out, each of us hoping to make a dent in the other's perceptions. Meanwhile MCS would go on giving our children what we firmly believe is the best possible preparation for life."

Eleven years later, when Claudia addressed the parents in the fall of 1989 as the new board chair, she voiced no lingering misgivings. Perhaps this was because she was no longer an MCS parent or because she herself was professionally aligned with progressive education or because the school, thanks in part to her own input, had raised its standards for continuity and excellence. Whatever the reason, Claudia was wholehearted in her support when she told parents, "I am convinced that MCS has filled out academically without losing its spontaneity, vitality, or its central concern for moral and social issues."

Our little school on Ninety-sixth Street had come of age in another way as well. One pleasing outcome of the NYSAIS evaluation was that the committee gave MCS an A+ on what Gardner Dunnan called "Administrivia." Our record-keeping, our fiscal accountability, and our degree of compliance with mandatory requirements were judged impeccable. Gardner told me that the committee members were surprised—pleasantly so. They had not expected a relatively new and small school with a familial style and a de-emphasis on formality to be so highly organized in its administrative management. "After all," he said, "even Dalton failed its fire drill on our last evaluation."

The credit for our performance goes mainly to Marty, whose job was to keep the school on course, managing the office. If she knew there was a needle in a haystack, she found it. My share of the credit rested on a long-held belief that those committed to social change must be as smart, as well-trained, and as determined and resourceful as those whose control they sought to overtake. Were I a revolutionary, I would favor the Jesuits, who knew how to get to the revolution on time.

Perhaps some progressive schools may be to blame for their poor reputations among those who accuse them of permissiveness. However, I learned a different lesson from going to Putney, where rules of conduct as they related to attendance, deadlines, and accountability for jobs assigned, were stricter than those practiced in more traditional schools. We were not allowed to miss a meal, to get up before 6 AM, to let our hair grow too long, or to leave the campus without permission. One detected slip-up and there was a note in our boxes from Mrs. Hinton, our director.

In my defense of progressive education I was, therefore, always on guard to disprove the widely held presumption of sloppiness in matters of administrivia. Our fire drills were conducted to the highest standards, and I smiled on those frequent occasions when visitors observing them would comment on our decorum. In overseeing the school's finances, I did not use a quill pen, but even after the introduction of computer technology, I used my own penciled accounts to corroborate the bookkeeper's printouts. I believe that the demise of some of those schools founded in the 1960s was due more to fiscal laxity than to loss of faith among their parents and supporters.

As burdening as our annual deficit has always been, MCS has never failed to meet payroll or to conclude a year without operating funds carried over.

My professional association with Gardner Dunnan continued for three more years while he was chair of the advisory board of a citywide program called Public-Private School Partnership (PPSP), which was initiated by Mayor Ed Koch to explore ways in which private and public schools could share resources, facilities, and professional expertise. Inspired by Chancellor Richard R. Green's desire for such educational collaborations, PPSP sought to build institutional alliances among the city's one thousand public schools and one hundred private schools.

PPSP's goals were laudable, and its initial support was promising. The Board of Education of New York City contributed $30,000 in its first year, and Gardner raised an additional $50,000 from two private foundations. By 1991, one hundred public and private schools were paired and linked by fax machines. The extent of their joint activities, however, was minimal—in some cases merely informational exchanges; in others, shared extracurricular programs. Fourth graders from PS 87 attended a Collegiate School chamber music concert. Students from PS 151 and the Spence School together published a literary magazine, and seventh graders from JHS 143 and Riverdale Country School communicated through computerized bulletin boards; at the semester's end, they met for the first time for a picnic.

With approximately $1,000 available for each participating school, limited funding prevented more meaningful contact. To be of real mutual assistance, schools needed to foster collaboration among teachers in curriculum development and pedagogy, which would have required extensive financial support. Without such support, it was questionable whether the city's private and public schools could find sufficient common ground. Indeed, at Brearley School, the tuition for students was higher than the median income for families in its partner public school in Chinatown.

PPSP was dissolved sometime after Mayor David Dinkins's election in 1990 and the appointment of the new chancellor of education, but thanks to our public-school outreach program, MCS's association with its partner, the Lab School, continued. The same year, using the Greentree grant and other restricted contributions, MCS added a half-time position to the school's administration, and Michèle Solá, the school's Spanish teacher, was appointed director of special projects.

MCS and the Lab School were ideally suited to one another, as was Michèle to her new post. Being bilingual and with a Puerto Rican and European background, she was naturally versed in muticulturalism. Her knowledge of MCS was also extensive as she had been on the faculty for eight years, during which time she had written her doctoral dissertation on the school's "evolving definition of diversity." Known to her colleagues for her outspoken devotion to social justice, she referred to herself as "MCS's radical rooster."

Officially called the New York City Lab School for Gifted Education, and located within the PS 198 building a few blocks east of MCS, the Lab School had opened in 1988 as a public-school model of educational reform. Its director, Celenia Chévere, was coincidentally an MCS parent. Unlike other PPSP partnerships, MCS and the Lab School shared common educational philosophies and similarly diverse enrollments. Michèle and Celenia worked closely together, organizing individual teacher exchanges, joint staff meetings, a panel of MCS parents who met with Lab School parents to discuss child-centered education, and a program for MCS sixth graders to assist in the Lab School's kindergarten.

Our major public-school outreach project for 1991 was a second conference on multicultural education, entitled "Models That Work." Cosponsored by the Lab School, with over three hundred participants, the conference opened with children from MCS and the Creative Learning Community in East Harlem presenting their hand-sewn "Gorgeous Mosaic of Children's Lives and Dreams" quilt to Mrs. Joyce Dinkins, wife of New York City's first African-American mayor. Following a presentation by the MCS student choral ensemble, the morning plenary session was devoted to a panel discussion of educators, entitled "Unity or Separatism in Multicultural Education?"

In the three years since our first conference, the national debate over multiculturalism had escalated, especially in New York State, although there was some progress in favor of reform. The state's proposed social studies curriculum, called "One Nation, Many Peoples: A Declaration of Cultural Independence," promised the inclusion of all groups who had taken part in the making of America, the elimination of "prejudice-laden language," and recognition of achievements by women and people of color. There were dissenters, some of them very high profile. Kenneth T. Jackson, professor of history at Columbia University, argued that "within any single country, one culture must be accepted as standard," and Albert Shanker, president of the American Federation of Teachers, in his Sunday *New York Times* column the week prior to our conference, took the position that focusing on ethnic, racial, and religious differences breeds strife. In an article in the *Village Voice*, Diane Ravitch, a conservative educational historian associated with Teachers College, who was hired by the State to review their proposed curriculum, declared, "History should not be used to teach self-esteem. It should not be used to pull scabs off the wounds and recreate hatred generation after generation. Nor should it be used to teach devotion and reverence."

Haywood Burns, dean of City University of New York Law School, and a participant in our conference, did not agree with any of them. He defined multiculturalism as "the whole truth and nothing but the truth, not somebody's history but everybody's history."

On one level, the two sides of the debate had nothing to quarrel about. All reasonable people cherished the diversity of America and advocated freedom of opinion and a respect for the rights of minorities. However, opponents of multiculturalism felt they had some cause for rejecting the language of the "curriculum of inclusion." Words such as "greed," "racism," "national egoism," "exploitation," and "dehumanization" are harsh ones to have used against you. There was also the worry that exposing conflict could promote factionalism and separatism. MCS had certainly experienced that outcome in the 1970s, and quite painfully so. Finally, some were concerned that in accepting the divergent beliefs, attitudes, and practices, we would become morally neutralized.

It was this last concern that most perturbed Albert Shanker. "We don't want students to be prejudiced, but is every value, belief and attitude as good as every other?" asked Shanker. Responding to his own question, Shanker then cited a series of indictable offenses, such as putting unwanted children to death in certain countries in Asia and Africa, and the Afrikaner values that undergirded apartheid. Shanker's final reference—"And must we look respectfully on Hitler's beliefs and actions?"—revealed how far he'd missed the mark.

No one advocating respect for cultural diversity had ever defended a neutral stance on all human conduct. A global view of society does not preclude expressions of disapproval, providing such disapproval is not determined solely by those in power. Injustice, meaning humanitarian injustice, may be determined only when we subscribe to the commonality of human values which transcend cultural differences.

Years later, when Michèle Solá and I worked with the Teaneck public-school system to help redesign its social studies curriculum, we again confronted this paradox. The curriculum as it existed centered on two themes, "Food" and "Harmony," assigned to the first and fourth grades respectively. The Teaneck teachers recognized that the lesson plans for these topics took a fairly superficial approach to multiculturalism. Agreeing that ethnic cookery was a bland recipe for teaching diversity, I pointed out that in teaching about inclusion one needed also to teach about exclusion. "To teach about food, you need to teach also about famine," I stated. "To teach about harmony, you must teach about disharmony as well."

To resolve the debate over multiculturalism, we need to understand and embrace the paradoxical notion of unity within diversity contained in the most precious Latin motto associated with the American dream: E Pluribus Unum—From many, one. Unless there is more inclusiveness, the oneness of our society will remain deferred for groups who have been historically excluded. The crux of the matter is not "How much 'pluribus' and how much 'unum.'" Neither is to be marginalized. The issue is the ownership of America by *all* its citizens.

The American Dream invites all people to the Welcome Table. The failure of its realization has been that those controlling society have assumed America is *their* table. Like George Orwell's pigs in the classic *Animal Farm*, who say, "All pigs are equal, but some are more equal than others," the establishment has never set the Welcome Table with sufficient places. The deeper irony is that opponents of multiculturalism are not afraid of fragmentation so much as they are afraid of losing control.

THE WEEKEND OF our "Models That Work" conference, America was on the brink of the first Gulf War. The day before the conference I had spoken to the seventh grade committee in charge of the upcoming Martin Luther King Assembly, only a week away. They told me they were scared, and didn't know what to say. "How can we talk about peace when we're going to war?" they asked me. I could tell that they were angry too. For them, the "MLK model" wasn't working as they had been led to believe it would.

I suggested that they interview their schoolmates to find out how they felt. They took some comfort in sharing their own feelings with others, and the following Friday they presented a choral reading in the form of a diary of the preceding week, with student reflections on the juxtaposition of war and peace. Some of their entries were as follows:

"Today is January 14, right before the U.N. deadline. I have mixed feelings. I am scared, worried and depressed. I can't face the fact that there might be a war."

"My favorite picture was a huge, blown-up one of King in the hall, addressing a crowd at the March on Washington. We may end up having a war soon. I wish that Martin Luther King, Jr. was still alive to help."

"January 15, 1991. Happy Birthday, Dr. King! All I feel is anger that he is gone. But in some ways I also feel hope for the human race because maybe his death will make people more aware of how grateful we should be."

"I don't know how they could mix war and peace together. It's King's birthday, a day of peace. How could they put a war deadline on this wonderful man's birthday?"

"Dear Mr. Bush, How are you? We are only seven, but we think that the war is not necessary. We think that the money should be used for homes for the homeless. Please, we are scared. You may not listen, but give it a thought."

"The war has begun. We invaded first, but why? Do we have any business being there?"

"I don't want war. My cousin is over there; he's only twenty years old."

"I feel helpless. I give support to the soldiers but not the war."

"It is two hours before the Martin Luther King, Jr. assembly. We have done this Assembly for twenty-two years, but something makes this year different."

"This year is different because there is a war going on, as we all now know. It is hard to talk about peace during war."

"I hope that there is peace in the world soon. I think we lost the war the moment we gave up on a peaceful resolution."

"Martin Luther King, Jr. had many powerful opinions that he expressed. I wish he were here today; maybe he could have made a huge difference, and maybe the spirit of peace would live on and on."

When I went to thank the seventh graders for their presentation, one of them said to me, "Every year we sing 'We Shall Overcome Some Day.' When will we be able to sing, 'We *Have* Overcome'?"

Eighth grade girls in 1976. *From top:*

Stacia Ross, Amanda Rotardier, Patience Moore, Katell Pleven.

Chapter 23

Gender Equity—the Interplay of "Isms"

AT OUR YEAR-END parent-teacher conference in June 1990, Peter Thom, whose older daughter was in our sixth grade, said to me, "Gus, if a white student in this school called a black student a 'nigger,' the offender would be in your office in a flash, but I'll bet nothing would happen to someone calling a classmate a 'faggot.'" Taken aback, I replied, "You're right, Peter, and it's time MCS does something about it."

Indeed, sexist slurs were commonplace in our classrooms and corridors. Boys calling girls "ho's" was a favorite among Peter's daughter's classmates. Though disapproved of by teachers, students passed such name-calling off as teasing, claiming they did no harm. When challenged that they wouldn't use racial slurs so freely, children insisted the two were not the same. Peter's point was that we hadn't taught the children that they *were* the same.

In our initial discussion about Peter's assertion, our seventh/eighth grade English teacher, Carol O'Donnell, who was one of our first openly gay teachers, admitted, "When I entered MCS, I was sure that I had ascended to educational heaven. White, black, Latino, and Jewish kids sit on each other's laps; rap, heavy metal, and rock are played and debated simultaneously. But the same students who discuss the nuances and subtleties of race and culture with confidence and ease, who struggle hard to express and define their heritages, who embrace 'other' as much as any adolescents do—these same dynamos disintegrate when it comes to discussing sexuality and gender. 'Homo' is a constant taunt along with other symptoms of wrist-bending, shrill-voiced homophobia. 'Girl' is a more common insult among younger students. Macho expectations plague boys while standard 'femininity' renders the most powerful girls at times powerless. For the most part, time spent outside in the park is strictly gender segregated, boys playing football and girls talking. I wondered how this could be happening on the front lines of multicultural education."

I had always assumed that in a coeducational progressive school, sexism was not an enemy from within. Certainly it existed, but I gave it little thought. In part, my rationale came from a belief that among the "isms" to be addressed at MCS, racism came first. I would still defend that priority, but Peter's comment opened my eyes to the fact that MCS would have to revisit its founding principles. On the matter of homophobia, we had been blatantly culpable. Though by then tolerant of homosexuality myself, in the school's early years I had stated openly that I would never knowingly hire a gay teacher, and I was not surprised that no one objected to my saying so.

It was clear that gender equity would have to be addressed at MCS. We would have to confront issues of sexism as well as our subtle and not-so-subtle attitudes about sexual orientation. This became possible when, the following March, the school secured a grant from the Beech Street Foundation, a pledge of $100,000 over five years, to be used to develop a gender-balanced curriculum for the elementary-school level and to publish the result through the school's public-outreach program.

Although our decision to make gender equity a priority came late in the school's history, our years of addressing racism had taught us much that could be applied to this new task, which helped qualify us for donor support. In addition, according to Peggy McIntosh, associate director of the Women's Studies Center at Wellesley College, who had coauthored *How Schools Shortchange Girls*, no such work had been undertaken at the elementary-school level; all existing studies had focused on the high school and college levels.

My own interest, and the unique contribution I felt MCS could make, was to examine gender bias within a multicultural context. Inequalities in gender and in race were closely connected, and to my mind, it was the interplay of "isms" that needed to be analyzed. Both racism and sexism rested on an ancient religious fallacy that within a single species some beings were deemed superior to others. If God made man in his own image and God was white and male, as western theology presumed, then white men were supreme. This double fallacy was the canon that supported both male dominance and white supremacy, and it was noteworthy that those who were cast in the most inferior category were black women. Clearly our myth-makers had not heard about the person who, upon asking an angel if God was black or white, was informed, "She's black."

In a community as culturally and religiously diverse as MCS, consensus on gender equity was going to be much harder to achieve than agreement about race. Consensus on issues of sexual preference would be harder still. In the early period of the school's history, when parents and staff met in the racial-awareness seminars, and later on during the more stormy period when we tried to address the Black Caucus's concerns, there had been no argument among us about the injustices of racism. Our divisions were the consequences of our historical separation, and for black people, their deep-seated doubt that white people could change. Nevertheless, in principle we were all integrationists. Not so with our new endeavor. As one eighth grader anguished, "I truly believe in equality, but my priest says that gays are sinners."

The one thing we had going for us was that we all shared the same historical references when it came to gender. And though at best we were recovering sexists, the politics of feminism and our multicultural platform gave leverage to our support of social change, even within religious ranks. When the Muslim parent of an MCS eighth grader was asked if sexism was a subject of concern to her, she replied, "No, but it's on my daughter's agenda."

My own sexist and homophobic upbringing was not derived from religious doctrine, nor were sexism and homophobia expressly taught to me. I simply absorbed these attitudes through observation of countless examples of dominant males who were devotedly served by women. I grew up among males and females who lived parallel lives, separate and dissimilar. From our earliest years, our different clothing defined our separation. As a young boy, I wore short pants, never above the knees; high socks, gray or navy blue; and yearned for trousers. I went to church in a sailor suit. I never saw a girl in pants, and my mother canoed in a long skirt. My sister wore black cotton stockings beneath her Springside School blue tunic. She and her classmates rolled them down on their way home.

Our recreation and schooling were similarly segregated. We went to single-sex schools, at least until I went to Putney. And we played "girl" games like hopscotch and "boy" games like touch football. Noncomformists were "tomboys" or "sissies." Boys only met girls at Sunday school or dancing classes, wearing white gloves. Later on, at well-chaperoned parties, we talked of playing spin-the-bottle, but never did. We whispered about Pamela. She and Joe Smith had kissed; some said more.

My father gave my brother a shotgun when he became a man. I don't know what my sister got, perhaps a string of pearls. The dos and don'ts of my boyhood were the traditional prescripts: "Hold open the door for a lady," "Give up your seat," "Don't fight with girls," "Boys don't cry." And of course: "Men shake hands. They don't kiss."

My father's cooking was limited to boiling a four-minute egg, which he ate from the shell, cracking off a small section from the top. In keeping with their gender roles, my father carved the roast from his end of the table, and my mother served the vegetables from hers. They dressed for dinner, even in summer. On Thursdays, the maids' night out, my mother prepared dinner; "one-arm cookery," she called it, holding her martini in the other hand. Otherwise, she gave the weekly menu to the cook—roast beef after church on Sundays—and ordered the food by phone from Reale's Market to be sent over by the delivery "boy," a man older than my father, in shirt sleeves and a bow tie. On Saturday mornings, my mother and I went to the market while my father wrote his sermon. The food was delivered to our rear door. When my parents entertained, after dinner the men went to the library to smoke cigars, drink their brandy, and tell off-color jokes, while the women, gathering in the living room, drank their demitasses, some smoking cigarettes.

None of my female kin was ever gainfully employed—not my paternal grandmother, whose husband departed each summer for a week of golf with his male friends in Newport, Rhode Island, nor my mother, who labored on the Women's Auxiliary as a volunteer, nor my sister or my sister-in-law, whose spouses were the wage-earners. Once, at Putney, when Marty and I were talking about marriage and careers, I had announced, "I could never marry a woman who works." This was not meant punitively. Convention in my world dictated that women who became wives became mothers. Married men were heads of household and breadwinners. The service of holy matrimony didn't use the word "husband"; it proclaimed that you were "*man and wife.*" Marty would become the first woman in my extended family to file a W-2 form, and although my blind conformity to sexist convention came at a cost to her, this did not deter her from helping me to change my ways. It was Marty's doing that ours was the first double-ring ceremony my father had ever performed. He liked the idea, although my mother thought it was "low class." The symbol of our joint rings was the beginning of my education in gender equity.

Still, I did not question my homophobia for many years to come, at first because I didn't know I had contracted it, then later, because I saw nothing wrong with it. The cure didn't really start until we began our gender-equity project. As a boy, I was aware of effeminate men, whom we called "pansies," and the expression, "Slap me on the bare wrist," which my mother used. "Gay" was an adjective as in "Our Hearts Were Young and Gay." "Homo" was not in vogue, nor was "faggot." Unmarried women of my parents' age were "old maids," a term that carried no connotation other than "single." Even after learning about homosexuality, I didn't know it applied to women as well as men. "Lesbian," "dyke," and "butch" were words I'd never heard.

Reading *Catcher in the Rye* while at Putney, I became aware for the first time of homosexuality as a "perversion." With this awakening came my sudden realization of what my father was talking about when he had called me into his study one Sunday afternoon three years before. He asked me about John, their organist friend, who slept over in my brother's adjoining vacant room when he visited. "Has John ever put his hands on you?" he asked. "No," I answered, "Why do you ask?" "I just wanted to know, that's all, and be sure to let me know if he ever does." I liked John, and I couldn't believe he would ever hurt me. It was when I discovered the cause of my father's fears that I inherited his aversion and was initiated into the prevailing homophobic culture.

THE GENDER-EQUITY PROJECT in its first year entailed a series of required general staff meetings, some with outside speakers, visitations from consultants in the field, and a voluntary discussion group called SEED, which stood for "Seeking Educational Equity and Diversity," an antibias program headed by Wellesley College's Peggy McIntosh. In the summer prior to the project, Carol O'Donnell, and our sixth grade teacher, Amy Bauman, had attended a national training course in California in preparation for conducting MCS's initial SEED meetings.

SEED's approach to developing institutional change was not prescriptive. As metaphorically described by Peggy McIntosh and her colleague, Emily Style, the process was designed to promote personal reflection through "journeys" on which participants would listen to one another's voices and view themselves through the "windows" of others. For our first meeting, we read Jamaica Kincaid's story, "Girl," which recalls the voices of her youth that defined her as a Caribbean woman: "Sundays try to walk like a lady . . . . This is how you smile to someone you don't like too much . . . . This is how you iron your father's khaki pants so they don't have a crease . . . . This is how to behave in the presence of men who don't know you well, and this way they won't recognize immediately the slut I have warned you against becoming . . . . Don't squat down to play marbles—you are not a boy, you know."

Other examples of prepared topics included: "Other than biology, are there differences between men and women and what do those differences mean?" "Why do people feel a clash between affirming gender equity and the aims of multiculturalism?" "Gay and lesbian invisibility in the MCS curriculum," and "Asian and Latino immigrants' insight into gender." Spontaneous topics, which often replaced scheduled ones, included: "Why are more boys in study hall than girls?" "The nature of 'dissing.'" "Boy posturing." And "Was there ever a time when your sense of your own gender differed from what was accepted? What models of female or male behavior, or ways of being did you experience?"

Eighteen faculty members signed up for the SEED seminars, including all our head teachers. In structuring the meetings, Amy had made an unsettling suggestion. She thought that I and other administrators should not join the group. "Why?" I replied. "Because your presence could impede free expression," she answered. "We are going to be talking about very private feelings, subjects that people might be reluctant to discuss if you're there." I appreciated her concern but questioned its wisdom. If we were seriously seeking institutional reform through a process of personal reflections, the "journey" would be incomplete without all of us. I too needed to hear the voices that would enable me to change my own perspective.

I joined SEED, as did Marty and our other administrators, and the seminars became the project's central force. When we struck accord, it was not long before our collective affirmations became school policy. An example of this arose when we were joined by a panel of teachers from Bank Street School for Children, who shared with us the results of their study of gay and lesbian parents' experiences in various schools. Although these parents acknowledged their desire for disclosure, many chose to remain silent for professional reasons or for fear that their children would suffer. The panel also reported that schools, probably unconsciously, erect barriers to disclosure, beginning with their application forms, which ask for the names of the child's "father and mother." "What has Bank Street done about that?" I asked. "Nothing, at least not yet," one of the teachers answered. "We recommended to the administration that the application be changed to use 'parents or caregivers,' but that was some time ago." MCS swiftly made the appropriate corrections to its forms.

Not all changes were this clearly indicated or readily achieved. As with any pathology, the cure to one condition can expose more and often deeper complications. After Peggy McIntosh visited MCS early in the first year of our project, she warned us of this, noting that the process was like "washing the dishes, and washing the dishes." "As you recall," she wrote me, "I said even before I visited the school that MCS was in a position to undertake a gender-balancing project for the simple reason that it had conceived of doing it. As you know, this is how educational innovation often starts: with conception of a vision and then work to implement it over time. Your school has been doing this from the beginning. You also know that more and more dimensions open up as you work on a vision that is in tune with democratic claims but not with societal practices . . . I see the process as taking 100 years because it requires a new understanding of societal and personal systems of perception, meaning, value and power. But people in a committed community can do a very great deal in a decade."

Measured by our funding, the official duration of our project was five years. However, I knew that MCS's commitment to gender equity would be as ongoing as it was with race, and that institutional change should be continuous. Amy Bauman shared this view, saying, "I came to MCS as a self-proclaimed liberal and a feminist, and I thought I knew the politically correct answers. But I have been humbled over and again by the complexity of achieving goals of gender equity. What I wanted to get out of the gender equity project was as much clarity about gender equity as I knew the school had about race."

She then asked me how the school would know that it had achieved its goals for gender equity. "When they're in the bloodstream," I replied.

Seventh- and eighth-grade boys of 1978. *Clockwise from top:* Michael Pope, John Meeks, Arthur Gluck, Michael Colt.

CHAPTER 24

Gender Equity—Tilting the Mirror

DURING THE FIRST three years of the gender project, revisions to the curriculum initiated by teachers appeared throughout the school, with the children voicing a new level of interest in matters of gender equity, sometimes raising questions that teachers had previously been reluctant to discuss. "Can two girls get married?" one four-year-old girl asked. And when a five-year-old boy stated, "A sissy is someone who likes to do girl things like drawing or dressing up," he was corrected by his male classmates, who pointed out that they all liked to draw and dress up and "We're not sissies." On one occasion when girls in the 6-7s staged a protest, they called it a "girlcott." Though a long way from being in the bloodstream, gender equity, like racial awareness in the early years, was becoming a common theme for us all.

It was evident that our SEED meetings were having a positive effect, doing what its name suggested, planting seeds of change. I became convinced that for MCS to do a thorough job, we should make the participation of all staff in the SEED project mandatory. Paula Wehmiller, who served as a consultant to our project, agreed with me. "In the most obvious ways, MCS is supporting what it values in doing this gender-equity work," she said. "But I would like to suggest a deeper expression of the principle 'we support what we value.' That is, we require participation in what we value. Involving one's class in the annual MLK Jr. celebration is not an option. Participation in the farm program is not an option. And so it follows that serious work on the gender-equity issues should not be an option. If the hard work of bringing these walls down is only done by people who sign up to do it, it will inevitably end up being 'owned' by an exclusive and probably resentful little group."

After sharing my intentions with the entire staff, who voiced no objections, SEED project activities became required for all teachers and administrative personnel. In June 1994, at the conclusion of our third year, staff were asked to complete a questionnaire designed to measure their level of consensus on various issues related to our work. In addition, they were to submit "gender narratives," describing their own response to participating in the project.

In keeping with Peggy McIntosh's nonprescriptive approach to institutional change, our staff credited SEED meetings and informal conversations with one another as their most influential experiences, and they assigned a lower rating to readings, meetings with outside consultants, and conferences. By the time we circulated the "consensus questionnaire," all felt that their own knowledge and understanding of the research on gender issues in education had increased substantially.

The questionnaire included fifteen statements covering a wide range of gender-related topics, to which staff were asked to indicate the degree of their positive or negative responses. On nine of the statements given, the staff concurred in their positive responses at a rate of 80 to 100 percent.

One hundred percent of our staff concurred with the statement: "Children need adult encouragement and models to go beyond stereotypic definitions of gender roles so that no aspects of development will be closed off simply because of a child's sex or sexual orientation." My own positive response would have fallen in the negative column before the gender-equity project. Indeed, when I had first met with Peggy McIntosh, I had told her I hoped we could conduct the project without having to deal with issues of sexual preference. She responded by saying, "You can't and you'll find out why."

Not surprisingly, 100 percent of our staff also agreed with the statement: "Examining one's own gender biases is a prerequisite to creating a gender-equitable classroom environment," confirming their preference for self-evaluation rather than indoctrination. On seven additional statements, there was a positive consensus of 90 percent or more of our staff. The statements, and the percentage of our staff that concurred, were as follows:

Ninety-seven percent agreed that "The formal curriculum is a central message-giving instrument of any school. Therefore, it should be examined to ensure that men's and women's experiences are equally represented and that gender inequity is formally brought to all students' attention."

Ninety-seven percent agreed that "Gender-based harassment, whether heterosexual or related to sexual orientation, is a serious equity issue and an institution must develop a uniform policy on confronting it."

Ninety-six percent agreed with the statement "Boys play with guns; girls play with dolls. Boys play football, soccer, and baseball; girls choose to sit on the bench in park. Teachers can have a powerful impact on increasing the willingness of both boys and girls to try other kinds of activities."

Ninety-four percent of respondents agreed that "Language contains messages about gender. Examining the gender content of language with students plays an important role in their increasing awareness of inequities and ability to act on behalf of equity."

Ninety-three percent agreed that "Gender bias is a two-edged sword. Girls are shortchanged, but boys pay a price as well."

Ninety-two percent agreed that "Across the whole spectrum of the curriculum, there is currently more emphasis on the development of assertive rather than cooperative skills, more reward for solo behavior, more reward for speaking than for listening. The curriculum can be strengthened by consciously focusing on the development of reflective, caring, collaborative skills as well as those skills emphasizing individual performance and achievement."

Finally, 90 percent felt that "The formal curriculum should challenge students to form their own ideas and make their own choices about people different from themselves. This necessitates exploring gay and lesbian themes."

A noticeable divergence of opinion among staff occurred in two places on the questionnaire. In response to the statement, "Homophobia and racism are similar forms of bias," there was weak agreement among 84 percent of the staff, with 16 percent answering in the negative. One black staff member said, "There's no way I can liken any other form of prejudice to racism."

To the statements, "A gay/lesbian student would feel comfortable at MCS" and "A gay/lesbian family would feel comfortable at MCS," staff were considerably divided. Sixty-nine percent of us agreed that a gay/lesbian family would be comfortable, but only 48 percent felt that a gay/lesbian child would be. Nevertheless, teachers credited the school for its policy of inclusion and acknowledged that a gay/lesbian student would be more comfortable at MCS than elsewhere. On the other hand, they recognized that negative peer reaction would diminish this positive influence. "Such a student," one gay teacher said, "would feel ostracized here and possibly terrorized, a boy more than a girl."

Division among teachers was strongest over the statement "Gender inequity in any culture is wrong. Although understanding historical and cultural contexts in which gender inequity operates is important, it is possible to determine some universal standards of equity." Although 67 percent agreed somewhat with the statement, consensus was weak.

In SEED meetings, we had heatedly argued this matter more than any other, and in the debate over cultural relativism versus absolutism, our feminist teachers, who had consistently been most vocal in their opposition to sexism, were paradoxically the most reluctant to apply their own values to other principally "nonwestern" cultures. "Who are we to impose our values on another culture?" they asked.

We had anticipated this debate from our initial discussions with representatives of the Beech Street Foundation. At the time, we had noted that the resolution of gender inequity within a multicultural context might lead to societal judgments that could threaten cultural diversity. My own interest in sexism continued to be in its correlation to racism and in its ties to outmoded religious teachings. Those of us who subscribed to universal moral standards argued that cultural acceptance of the oppression of women anywhere was a violation of their fundamental human rights.

In my letter responding to Paula's advice that "we support what we value" I wrote that I felt the issues of gender equity must be confronted in a manner no less committed than that used to combat racial inequality. "We cannot be relativist with sexist teachings and practices even though they be grounded in religious and cultural beliefs," I argued. "It would be easier, I think, to attain equality about gender among atheists than in a community of Muslims, Christian fundamentalists, Roman Catholics or orthodox Jews. I hope I overstate my apprehension, and that being in New York City in the 1990s among persons attracted to its principles of equality, MCS may not be as fraught with division on the matter as I fear."

In response to three statements in the questionnaire, the opinion of staff differed substantially from findings in national studies, including the report from the American Association of University Women, *How Schools Shortchange Girls*. The statements, and the percentage of our staff who agreed with them, albeit weakly, were as follows:

Fifty-nine percent found some truth in the statement "Girls receive significantly less and/or qualitatively different attention from classroom teachers than boys do."

Sixty percent of our respondents agreed with the statement "Girls may start off on equal ground but as they grow older their neatness and silence are reinforced."

And only 8 percent agreed with the statement that "Much of the noise and active behavior in our classrooms is 'boys being boys.'"

It was hard to judge why MCS teachers were generally less prepared to support these commonly accepted statements, especially considering that our own examination of gender inequity, undertaken only two years before by our sex-education specialist, Dr. Cydelle Berlin, had yielded very similar results. Dr. Berlin had reported that starting in the 5-6s, boys were called on more frequently, and were generally louder and stronger in their desire to participate.

She added, "As the children move up in the grades, it is clear that though teachers probably do not recognize this, and certainly are not to be faulted, a more structured curriculum shows the boys off to more advantage than the girls, particularly in science and math."

Then, substantiating both Peter Thom's and Carol O'Donnell's insights, she wrote of our seventh and eighth graders: "These students are sophisticated, concerned and articulate about fairness and equality for both sexes. However, their everyday choices and behaviors reflect more stereotypical notions of how boys 'should be' and how girls 'should be.' There is subtle but real pressure to conform to standardized notions of gender and gender-role stereotyping, no matter how uncomfortable and restrictive their behaviors may be. Boys call girls 'ho's' and 'bitches' and rank them for the size of their breasts. The boys 'posture' and act tough ('cool'). Power issues between the females and males are evident causing the girls to become defensive and adversarial. MCS Director, Gus Trowbridge, is equally concerned about what he characterizes as the 'adolescent bluff' (boys as thugs: boys needing to prove themselves through posturing and 'fronting') which again mirrors societal conditioning."

Adding a forceful voice to our determination to address gender inequity, Dr. Berlin concluded, "This is not news, of course. Literature and research collected for many years support these observations. They merely indicate that even in a school like MCS, societal values impinge. The school still reflects and mirrors society. The challenge for MCS will be to determine how to 'tilt' the mirror, as it were, in order for real change to take place."

The question facing us after three years of immersion in the gender-equity project was whether we had truly tilted the mirror to the extent claimed by our staff's collective opinions. My own belief was that we had begun to generate some fundamental changes, in ourselves for sure, in our treatment of boys and girls, and hopefully in our students' perceptions of themselves and one another. To determine the validity of this belief, we retained another consultant, Dr. Sherryl Graves, a teacher and psychologist at Hunter College, to study MCS classrooms with regard to gender bias in the methodology of our teachers, and gender imbalance in the participation and behavior of our students.

On the matter of teacher performance, Dr. Graves gave high marks. "In general," she said, "favoring male students over female as predicted by research on gender bias was not in evidence in teachers' responses. Girls and boys at MCS are receiving the full range of teacher attention: positive, negative and neutral." Proof that this positive assessment was as a result of the work we had done rested in Dr. Graves' surprising observation that "the most inconsistent and gendered responses to students came from teachers with the least experience in teaching and the least experience in teaching at MCS." In this regard, SEED was not only working, but it was also crucial that it had been required of our entire staff. It was also clear that we needed to continue the process, though hopefully not for the hundred years that Peggy McIntosh had claimed.

Concerning student behavior, Dr. Graves found the school less at variance with national norms than our staff had asserted, with one interesting exception: Our girls did not exhibit the passive or submissive behavior reported at other schools; in fact, they seemed to be faring better than the boys, whose behavior was distinctly more stereotypic. Dr. Graves ended her report on an optimistic note, saying, "At MCS gender is not the best predictor of teacher or student behavior, though it does play a role. In a school that addresses other forms of bias with vigor and determination and puts the students at the center of the learning process, I have no doubt that gender bias will be eliminated."

Unlike Dr. Berlin's study two years before, Dr. Graves found almost no evidence of gender bias in our youngest three or four classrooms, where children had benefited from an awakened sensitivity on the part of their teachers due to the gender project. For my part, I know that during the three years of our SEED project, my courage to take a stand on gender issues had multiplied beyond my expectations. Had I not been challenged by Peter Thom, I would have continued to dismiss the offenses he objected to. I might even have thought of gender equity as a one-way street, encouraging girls to be more assertive, to play more competitively, to be tougher. I now looked for ways to teach boys to be tender, to be more caring, and to shed their defensive postures. Had I not heard the stories of colleagues in countless discussions and allowed their lessons to inform and change my own perspectives, I would not have discovered that I could speak or act as openly and confidently on issues of gender bias.

One example of my enlightenment occurred when an eighth grade parent, Mrs. C., demanded that her daughter be excused from sex education class because it included a unit on homosexuality. It had always been MCS policy that sex education be a required course for eighth graders, so my negative answer to Mrs. C. was readily given, as it was on those few other occasions that parents had made similar requests. Mrs. C. insisted that at the very least her daughter should not have to attend the lessons dealing with homosexuality. When I pointed out that her arguments were contrary to the school's belief in equality, she stated that homosexuals had no claim to equal rights.

I would like to believe that in earlier years I would never have agreed with this statement, but I could not be sure. The confidence to refuse Mrs. C.'s request, however, was fortified by my growing awareness that in issues of equity there was no room for compromise. One cannot be "a little bit equitable," I thought, remembering my father correcting his daughter-in-law when she announced she was "a little bit pregnant."

My convictions on issues of gender equity had come about in a similar way to my convictions about race, through thoughtful and honest sharing, and through the recognition that we were all conscious or unconscious participants in racism and sexism. After the angry eighth grade parent left, I went to our SEED meeting and told my story. And I thanked my colleagues for giving me the strength to act as I did.

This mural, half a block long and four stories high, was created by homeless children from East Harlem in 1991. Entitled *La Calle de Sueños* (The Street of Dreams), it was the inspiration for Gus Trowbridge's talk to parents the following year: "I have always wanted MCS to be *una escuela de sueños*—a school of dreams. We were founded on a dream so well defined and powerful that its force has bound the school in all its diversity with unshakable unity . . . . MCS will greet the year 2000 in good shape so long as it is guided by this dream."

CHAPTER 25

A Covenant for the Future

DURING THE 1990s, I gave much thought to the question of when I would step down as director of MCS, and the process by which a successor would be chosen. I shared my thoughts with our board chairperson Claudia Grose, and at my suggestion in May 1991, she arranged with Peter Buttenwieser to visit the school and meet with me and the board's executive committee to consider the future of MCS. Peter's follow-up report, entitled "Working Out a Solid Future Including a Smooth Transition," was presented to the trustees at their first meeting the following school year, 1991-92. It stressed foremost the need for the board to plan for the transition carefully. The process, Peter cautioned, must be one of "open covenants, openly arrived at."

Noting the key elements necessary for success, Peter cited the need to give "the MCS family" ample notice of my intention to step down, and to choose a specific time "so as not to keep the community off balance and full of behind-the-scenes speculation."

Secondly, Peter identified the need for a solid, sensitive, top-flight board chairperson, who would agree to provide leadership starting two years before I stepped down as director, until two years after. The board chair, Peter emphasized, would be "the only anchor you can count on while the place is in flux, the most important person in both the swing of events and the recruitment of the new head."

Peter then addressed the need for what I subsequently called "de-Gusifying" the school. "Right now," he said, "everything goes through Gus, the central office, and Marty. They have all the 'information keys.' No one else has much of a clue as to how the place works." Turning over the keys, he pointed out, would be my responsibility.

Peter's fourth concern—mastering more firmly the school's finances— was one with which the board and I were keenly familiar. The development committee had already set a goal of building our endowment to the point that, when the new director took over, the operating deficit would be a manageable 10 percent. Peter concurred with this objective, adding that more trustees would have to "learn the magic and feel the weight of responsibility" for fund-raising.

Finally, Peter said, the success of the transition would ultimately rest on the school's educational reputation, particularly in the middle-school years, the extent of parental commitment to the school's future, and the ability of the school to sell itself as an institution, a vision, and an effective educational setting for children—as MCS, and not as "Gus's creation."

Peter ended his report by urging the school to be confident that it could and would find, "with Gus's active help, an educator who is, if anything, more talented than Gus in the business of working with young people and their families—a second-generation leader (perhaps with first-generation vision) who is at least Gus's match, and may bring strengths that Gus doesn't have. If you feel you'll go 'one step down' you will. If you feel you have a chance, with no disrespect to Gus, to go 'one step up,' you just might. That, anyway, should be your goal: to improve."

The first action taken by the board in response to the Buttenwieser report was to instruct the long-range planning committee to set guidelines for the search process itself; namely, the criteria for selection of the next director and the means by which a future search committee would be constituted. Mindful of Peter's first recommendation and after careful consideration with Marty, I promised the board that I would give formal notice three years prior to my retirement. The most likely timing, I suggested, would correspond with the school's thirtieth anniversary in June 1996, five years hence.

Marty and I officially notified the board in May 1993 that we planned to retire in three years. Amply forewarned, the board swiftly drew up a timetable for the transition, with the goal that the search committee it convened would begin its work in the fall of 1994, and appoint a new director by January 1996.

The summer after giving notice, Marty and I each prepared written descriptions of our jobs. Mine was eleven pages; Marty's was much longer, and included a detailed inventory of her myriad responsibilities, together with an appendix of forms and documents referred to in her text. "Marty's Bible," we called it.

In keeping with Peter's comments about the importance of board leadership during the transition period, the board urged Frank Roosevelt to assume the role of chairperson. When Marty and I visited Frank and Jinx that summer at their home in Maine, he was naturally eager to discuss the future. His first question was whether there were any inside candidates that we wanted to recommend. I left the room, preferring Marty to field his inquiry. She emphatically replied that Michèle Solá, MCS's director of special projects, would be an excellent prospect, given her devotion to the school's mission and her involvement in our public-school outreach programs. Later, Frank asked us both if we had any outside candidates in mind. We suggested that Paula Wehmiller might also make an ideal successor, but we doubted she was available.

Frank then expressed enthusiasm about conducting a national search. We did not disagree with him, but found his emphasis curious. Many months later, in her notes about the search process, Marty wrote: "The emphasis on a national search remains puzzling to this day, especially because . . . it wasn't particularly national at all, but merely parochial, encompassing a limited range within the select educational community of private schools. Private school headships are incestuous. All you need to do is keep an updated mailing label file of schools and their heads, as I do, to see how many of these heads keep on moving around within the same, insular private school world.

"There is something else that's interesting about this urge for a national search. It is as if people—trustees and parents in particular—feel that the efficacy of the school can only be borne out to the extent that MCS is able to attract an outside candidate. This is their acid test, and no one from the inside can fully satisfy the need to prove its worth; an insider is seen as only able to maintain the status quo. This attitude and approach have made the road for the inside candidate an undeservedly hard one.

"In recent years, there has emerged a strong, vocal minority at MCS who view it as a commodity rather than a community. 'Go corporate' is the signal that validates the way they live their lives and conduct their business. We need to remember the words of an alumni parent, who said, 'MCS is not like any other school.' But there are still those who act as if they wish it were, with a farm program thrown in for good measure, as if MCS requires standardized testing against other schools, so that everyone can determine if they truly measure up and whether or not they 'bought the right stock.'"

While I had inklings of such a faction within the school as Marty described, I was still utterly confident that the transition would go smoothly. Indeed, during the following year, 1993-94, the school remained remarkably at rest, perhaps because there was no direct opportunity for participation in the search for a new director until the Search Process Committee (SPC) offered its report to the board in June. The SPC called for the establishment of a widely representative search committee, which would include four board members: Frank Roosevelt, our board chair; Walter Christmas, who would serve as chair of the search committee; Pat Carey, the only member who had also sat on the SPC, and Celenia Chévere, a school parent. Three staff members were also elected to the committee: Gloria Brown, Lois Gelernt, and Carol O'Donnell. Finally, the school's parent body chose two representatives from among their number: Ricardo Morales and Kate Shackford. When Walter Christmas became ill the following year, Henry

Drewry, a new trustee to MCS, who was also African-American, assumed the committee chairmanship.

The composition of the search committee was suitably balanced with four men and six women. There were four white, four black, and two Latino members, and at least half of the committee had had long affiliations with the school. The trustees approved the committee's formation with no objection to the addition of parents and staff, although there was some regret that alumni were not included.

The SPC had prepared an MCS mission statement, a budget for the transition process, a job description for the director, and a questionnaire for applicants, all of which were approved by the board. However, the board did not provide the SPC with a written summary of its deliberations. As a result, critical procedural issues that I and other trustees had raised prior to the announcement of my retirement were never formally addressed by the SPC. These included my role in the selection process, whether I would remain a trustee after retirement, the pros and cons of an inside candidate versus an outside candidate, and the weight that would be given to the views of the faculty compared to those of the parents. I believe that we would have reached agreement on these matters fairly easily at this early stage, and had we done so the coming months would probably have unfolded quite differently.

As the search for a new director got underway, MCS trustees recognized that their role in relation to a successor could not be as it had been with a founder. Though overstated perhaps, MCS was slated to change from what I called "a benevolent monarchy" to a "constitutional democracy." Unless founders seriously blunder, the duration of their directorship is generally determined by themselves. In my case, my annual meeting with the chair of the board concerning the terms of my employment dealt exclusively with salary and benefits; otherwise, the board never formally evaluated my performance, and contractual obligations were never specified in writing. Clearly, the board's relationship with the future director would involve a more codified review of performance and consideration of contractual terms.

In preparing for the board's new responsibilities, a number of trustees proposed forming an educational affairs committee, whose purpose would be "to ensure regular, consistent evaluation of the quality of education" at MCS and to determine "which programs are vital to the school's mission." To many trustees who had gone through the quarrelsome years of the policy review committee, the proposal was anathema; under the current circumstances, most trustees saw it as potentially usurping the director's leadership. My own vehement objection to the proposal surprised no one, and when I pointed out that I doubted any candidate for director would accept a position in a school with such governance, the board withdrew the entire suggestion, resolving that the executive committee would undertake responsibility for the evaluation and oversight of the future director.

Concerned about the motives of those trustees who had proposed the educational affairs committee, I sensed for the first time a division over "core values" within the school. It struck me that the challenge the school faced was not primarily the matter of succession, but rather an emerging belief among some parents and trustees that the very mission of MCS was in question.

By the end of 1994-95, the search committee's efforts had produced forty-two completed applications. Michèle Solá's was among them. From this group, the committee would select six to eight semifinalists to be interviewed in September. Marty and I had met with the committee that spring under what she felt were "uncomfortably formal" circumstances. Even so, I felt we had achieved our chief purpose, which was to remain in touch with the process of choosing the candidates. From the beginning, I had made known to the board that I did not expect or want to be a member of the search committee; I did, however, want to be kept informed of their assessment of candidates, and I did not expect that our judgments would be in conflict. Frank Roosevelt had assured me this would be the case, and Marty and I left our meeting with the committee with no specific sense to the contrary.

All of us still felt that the transition would be an unqualified success. As it turned out, my predicted date of retirement would prove to be premature by a year because, against its best intentions, the board was not able to adhere to the principal message of Peter Buttenweiser's report: "open covenants, openly arrived at." Two years later, when all was said and done, *This Little Utopia*, the working title of a book I hoped to write about MCS, would be clearly revealed to be a misnomer.

The stream that runs past the MCS farmhouse is
the east branch of the Delaware River, and is part of
the vast network of Catskill watercourses that supplies
New York City with most of its water.

Chapter 26

"Dear Mr. Annenberg . . ."

MY TALK TO parents in the fall of 1995 was intended to be my last. Unaware that I would still be the director of the school one year hence, I wanted once again to address the significance of the public mission of MCS and to advocate maintaining the unique position of the school within the public and private sectors. In preparing my talk, I struggled for a fitting context, wanting to spare my listeners too preachy a presentation. Slightly abridged, this was the outcome:

"You may recall that in December of 1993, philanthropist Walter Annenberg donated five hundred million dollars to rescue the nation's public-school system. Aside from the unprecedented magnitude of his gift, its most unusual distinction was its purpose: to rid education of its depersonalized bureaucracy and bigness. Annenberg, himself a plutocrat of corporate America, was not following suit with traditionalist solutions such as a longer school day, more tests, and harsher competitive standards; he was aligning himself with those in school reform who were concerned with the cultural climate of schools, with the creation of schools that were to be democratic communities, and with values such as individuality, cooperation, and most importantly, intimacy.

"My opening reference to Walter Annenberg is not to introduce an analysis of the woes and possible remedies of our public-school system. Parents, teachers, and even students of MCS are, one way or another, aware of the failure of public education in New York City and in every major urban area, and they know also the deeper problems of racism and classism that underlie what Jonathan Kozol has called the 'savage inequalities' of our educational system.

"I have selected Mr. Annenberg as my reference for both thematic and stylistic reasons. Surely, it has been a challenge for me to contemplate this last 'Talk to Parents.' And without some editorial controls, I could find myself, after thirty years, ranting and rambling in rhetoric and remembrances that overstep myself. Therefore, I have chosen to proclaim myself an intimate of Walter Annenberg and to speak to him tonight in the form of a letter. You will forgive my author's license, which places me a step aside from you, yet enables me to be more conversational and candid, and I believe, more intimate with you as well.

"I would ask one favor. When I was a boy, I attended my father's church every Sunday. Living in the rectory only a short distance from the church and wishing to remain in bed as long as possible, I would time my arrival to the sermon, for that was the only part of the service that my father regularly brought up for discussion at the midday meal. One Sunday, I was late to the sermon and listened to my father announcing his resignation, confessing that he had failed in his duties, citing shame and remorse. I was mortified and crept away to console myself. Later, I learned that my father was only reading from a letter written to President Lincoln by one of his generals. The favor I ask of you is to explain to anyone who may read my letter to Mr. Annenberg too hastily that my acquaintance with the philanthropist is utterly bogus, and the composition of my letter is totally fanciful.

"Here, then, is my letter.

"Dear Walter:

"I was pleased to hear from you after your visit to MCS, and your offer to be of help prompts me to write you this extended reply.

"You are right in observing that MCS resembles your vision of an ideal public school, and that the makeup of the school mirrors the diversity of our city. When people ask me to describe a typical MCS student, I'm at a loss for words. Sit on any bus going up or down one of our avenues and of the children you see, any one of them could be from MCS. I am less confident, however, that the same could be said of every parent, and I often say to parents applying to the school, 'Choose a school for your child which you would want to go to.' So, while MCS is created to mirror diversity, ours is not a random sampling. Parents who choose us share the desire for a democratic community. They seek a mosaic whose only requirement for conformity is its celebration of differences.

"You are also accurate in observing that we are a progressive school. Our philosophy of education matches the common principles of your Coalition of Essential Schools, and we subscribe to your organization's description of the preferred tone of a school: namely, that it should 'explicitly and self-consciously stress values of unanxious expectation, of trust, and of decency, fairness, generosity and tolerance.'

"I grew up regularly reminded that I could not have my cake and eat it too. This was an annoying admonition, which I have longed to disprove. I believe, now, that perhaps the impetus for school reform as well as the driving force of progressive education is in the aspiration to permit children schools in which they can both have their cake and eat it. There is no reason that disrespect or abuses should arise from trust, that lack of incentive should result from cooperation, that academic achievement should suffer from non-tracked teaching, that informality should undermine authority, or that the acknowledgement of other life-styles should taint one's moral development.

"A good progressive school does not sacrifice excellence when it elects a noncompetitive grading system. MCS students qualify for the most selective high schools in the city. A good progressive school does not sacrifice academic performance when it chooses not to judge its students by tests alone. As in all the best schools, MCS students perform four to five years above grade level on standardized tests. A good progressive school obtains these measures of success at the same time that it provides its students a learning environment that is humane and enjoyable.

"When you commented on the warmth of the school's atmosphere, I was reminded of being told once that the hallmark of a progressive education was in its climate. It is instantly and intuitively felt. You can sense it when you walk into our living room, when you witness the interaction of adults and children, and when you observe students together in work and play. Your interest, of course, is in how such a climate can be achieved within the public schools, and I am glad that you think MCS can be of help.

"When I started our school I wanted it to be a public school. That was not allowed, of course, but the public mission of MCS had always been its principal goal. In the last five years of working closely with public schools, I have been struck by two things. The first is the eagerness and swiftness with which teachers are able to identify and adopt classroom practices that make our model work. Much has been written about muticulturalism, but few examples of it in action exist for teachers to experience and apply to their own classrooms.

"The second response that is common to nearly all those with whom we have worked is their desire to talk honestly and with a sense of safety about matters of race and cultural differences, and to share the frustrations and obstacles of racism that affect their lives as teachers. The experience of MCS in the evolution of its own curriculum of inclusion, and in its institutional growth over thirty years, spanning the flood tide of the Movement and the ebbing and disheartening times that have followed, has taught us to keep talking about the struggle with a continuous sense of hope.

"As a product of the civil rights movement, MCS remains a maverick within the educational order of things. We are a private school, but our origins separate us from the establishment, even though we successfully live up to its standards. Within the public sector, MCS has achieved an uninvited position as an alternative school. Most of our parents and their children and perhaps all of our teachers would be in public schools today if they were not here. And in recent years, since the creation of your Coalition of Essential Schools, many of our parents and teachers are now choosing between us and you. So, in contemplating the offer of your support, I am torn between the impulse to join your coalition, and my desire to have MCS remain poised just outside the public sector and only partially within the private one.

"My reluctance to join your coalition stems from the distrust of the public school system that you and I share. That distrust rests on our objection to bureaucracy and bigness. Your work establishing schools governed collectively by teachers and administrators is, I fear, doomed to fail in a system that belittles educators and manages schools as if they were factories. Your schools are experimental and exemplary, yet as rapidly as they have emerged, they may also dissolve. I want MCS to be here for an eternity.

"We agree about bigness. It obscures the atmosphere. It conceals inconsistencies and contradictions. It diminishes intimacy. Intimacy is obtained through smallness and autonomy, which permit a school to teach the values we share by enabling children and adults to feel a part of the whole. Democracy in education is not experienced alone in the classroom; and it is best experienced when an individual child, or teacher, or parent becomes a valued and integral part of a democratic community, that is, when one sees that the entire institution practices what it preaches.

"Among your imperatives for better schools, you say, 'Keep the structure simple and flexible.' To me, 'simple' suggests a close encounter. One of the reasons MCS works so well is that we function under conditions of forced proximity. We literally work side by side; we have no public corridors; all members of staff eat at an oval table. A parent attending one of our assemblies suggested that MCS rent an auditorium for such occasions. This may have its advantages, but when 250 people crowd into a drawing room once enjoyed by a single family, stand together with hands linked and sing "We Shall Overcome," I cheer for our being so close to one another, and I exalt in the presence of a cohesive community whose unity might not be so apparent in more spacious surroundings.

"I am glad you will be coming with me to visit our farm. I would suggest that we go during one of our seventh-eighth grade trips in October. Our older students are my pride and joy, and in seeing them you can best evaluate everything we do at MCS. There are times when I wish parents of young children coming to the school could experience it in reverse, as one sometimes views a home movie backwards. Observe an eighth grader in rapid descending growth to when he or she was four or five, and you are given more assurance of the results of their education than any brochure could offer.

"The farm is unique to MCS. We struggled with its definition in the early years and debated its relationship to the school's programs. Some wanted the farm to be a school of its own; some wanted it simply as a laboratory to the city's classrooms. As it turned out, the farm developed as a curricular department of MCS. Its program is sequential and geared to its own educational objectives: nature studies, agriculture, textiles, conservation, and so on. Beyond these offerings, the farm provides our children with the most important experiences they share in their years at MCS. It is there that they live together and extend their relationships to dimensions that a day-long program cannot contain.

"While our farm program may not connect directly to our work with your schools, it exemplifies experiential learning at its best and supports the notion that schools need to engage children in lessons that are not simply found in books or transcribed from blackboards. Learning by doing is the essence of progressive education, and somehow urban schools must find more inventive ways to encourage students to be doers as well as thinkers.

"Finally, I want to respond to your personal question about the school's future leadership in light of Marty's and my upcoming retirement. The board has known of this transition now for five years, and it has done everything I can think of to prepare for a smooth and healthy turn-over, including detailed attention to the school's fiscal and managerial stability. The search for the next director is on schedule and is being conducted in a methodical, sensitive, and democratic manner. I'm not uneasy about who might be my successor because the central values of the school no longer rest only on its founder. They are in the school's bloodstream.

"I think I have made headway in convincing others that it will not take more than one person to replace me. Marty's replacement may require that, but not mine. From seeing some of the candidates for director, I know that they are all more qualified than I was when I started the school, and MCS is strong and blessed with a constituency of trustees, staff, parents, alumni and friends who not only deeply believe in the school, but also give their unselfish support.

"Recently a former teacher of MCS sent me a very generous contribution, probably equivalent to a week's salary. Her gift was accompanied by a long letter expressing her indebtedness to the school for its help in shaping her life, personally and professionally. She referred to her gift as a paycheck, and she pledged that she would send it every year. Her affirmation of devotion and commitment is shared by everyone who has been close to MCS. Schools that achieve the collective partnership of a democratic community enroll more than the students they teach. Like this former teacher, I, too, have gone to school at MCS, and it has made all the difference in my life. Our parents, our faculty, and our trustees have also gone to school at MCS, and I hope for them that this has made a similar difference in their lives.

"In celebrating our thirtieth anniversary this year, we are honoring the joining of two generations. In our youngest class there are three children whose parents were in the first first grade in 1966. Their presence among us is a mark of the school's succession. I want our new parents to know that, like our charter parents thirty years ago, they, too, are founders. I welcome them with special thanks because they are the assurance of the school's future.

"Best wishes, Gus."

Michèle Solá joined MCS as its Spanish teacher in 1982.
She later wrote, "MCS remains a community united in its
discontent with injustice and its hope that children may
grow up well educated, knowing who they are and believing in
their abilities to change the world."

CHAPTER 27

A Perfect Storm

IN SEPTEMBER 1995, THE search committee hosted initial interviews with eight semifinalists and swiftly selected the following three finalists for the position of director: David ("Hock") Hochschartner, Michèle Solá, and Karan Merry.

Hock was a natural candidate, closely associated with progressive education, and given his years at North Country School, he was enamored of our farm program. I found him at ease with the school's mission and fully committed to tuition reform. His manner was open and friendly, and our student panel gave him their most favorable rating. Unfortunately, he lacked administrative training, and his experience with multiculturalism was limited. Except when the board later reached an apparent deadlock and he was considered a possible compromise candidate, Hock never gained sufficient support to become the favored choice.

Michèle Solá was the "inside" candidate. She had taught Spanish at MCS for sixteen years and was well acquainted with the school's progressive philosophy. Further, as the director of special projects, she had shown herself to be a tireless advocate of our public mission. Michèle was also the unofficial "dean" of the faculty, regarded by the teaching staff as a good listener and supporter, willing to take their views and concerns and express them to me. Unfortunately, some of the trustees seemed to decide early on that, as director,

Michèle would do little more than maintain the status quo. Given what I would soon recognize as a growing desire on the part of some of the school's parents and trustees to have MCS rank among the blue-chip private schools, Michèle faced an uphill battle from the start.

Karan Merry was the only African-American applicant, although I did not know this when I read her résumé before my first interview. When I asked Henry Drewry, after his search committee had reviewed all the applications, if any were African-American, he had responded, "I believe one is a person of color." "Good," I said, having long felt such a choice would be a logical and desirable one.

Marty, who also read the candidates' materials, had noticed from Karan's résumé that she had been chair of the National Association of Independent School's Multicultural Assessment Team, which had been called upon by Wilmington Friends School after the terrible "Kill the Tar Baby" incident that occurred during Paula Wehmiller's tenure there. Marty suggested we call Paula for insight into Karan's candidacy, and I agreed. But not wanting to make inquiries about a candidate I had not even met, I decided I would do so following my interviews with her.

Karan's qualifications were of the highest caliber, and since she was an active candidate for at least two other head-of-school positions, it was by no means certain that she would accept an offer from MCS. She had eighteen years experience—five as a teacher and thirteen as head of Chestnut Hill School, located in an affluent suburb of Boston. She also had a highly successful record in fund-raising and a visible national presence within the private school sector, in which she participated as a member of the NAIS board.

My first interview with Karan left me with an entirely positive impression. She exuded energy and spark, and I could tell that she cared deeply about children. "The MCS mission is like going home," she said. "You walk the walk and talk the talk." It was during the three-day period of her second visit that I began to have misgivings. When staff members asked about her commitment to the school's priorities, Karan's statements were ambiguous and superficial. She likened multiculturalism to a buffet, and she considered Spanish simply as a foreign language. In response to a question about the school's public mission, she stressed only the importance of the role of MCS as a model to private schools. Particularly troublesome to the faculty was her exchange with a teacher, who asked, "What will MCS look like next?" To which she replied, "I want to take you to places you've never been." Asked to explain, she responded, "I'm not ready to tell you." To a similar question I posed, she said, "I can refine MCS, give it more polish. I am thoroughly respected; any school I head will gain in its reputation."

In the course of future debate over Karan's candidacy, it was on the basis of this discussion with her that I inferred she intended to remake MCS into a school more in keeping with the private establishment. The places we had never been, I believed, were those very places from which MCS had deliberately chosen to depart.

When I asked Karan what her feelings were about the racist incident at Wilmington Friends, she hesitated, and then said, "Oh yes, the poor thing. I felt very sorry for her"—meaning Paula Wehmiller.

That night I called Paula to ask what she knew about Karan Merry. She asked why, and I said, "Because she's a candidate for my job." I told her I had just met Karan for the second time and was uneasy about her. Paula replied, "When you first mentioned her name, my heart sank. You're like my dog. You have a good sniffer." According to Paula, the NAIS team had not satisfactorily addressed the school's responsibility for what had happened at Wilmington Friends. No wonder, I thought to myself, that her heart sank. As the only black administrator in the school facing such a deeply painful experience, Paula had naturally expected a more proactive response.

When Henry Drewry heard about my conversation with Paula and my reservations about Karan, he accused me of witch-hunting and character-assassination. He said I played the race card by pitting one African-American woman against another. He stated further that the matter was now in the hands of the search committee, and I was not to mention it again without his approval.

After learning that Henry told Karan of my conversation with Paula, I concluded that she was his hand-picked candidate. Although I did not fault Henry for his interest in Karan, I would have better understood his investment in her candidacy had he been forthright about it. Instead, he became increasingly secretive about the search process. From then forward, the political climate of MCS bore the markings of a perfect storm, with two frontal systems driven in opposite directions and destined to collide. In fairness to the candidates, though they suffered the brunt of the storm, they were not its principle cause.

At its root, the schism was ideological, but it caused a power struggle between two quickly aligning groups. One, comprised of the head of the search committee and the majority of its members, sought to move the school away from its founder's influence and to take it in new directions; the other included the founder-director, supported by the faculty and the chair of the board, all of whom sought a successor who would firmly sustain the school's mission.

The first group, as Henry said, saw Karan as a "prize catch," a leader who would enhance the school's academic distinction and its prestige within the private sector. The second group knew Michèle's dedication to the school's mission and her ability to administer and organize. It was the second group, excited by Michèle's deep knowledge of the school and her activist spirit, that was largely responsible for her candidacy. This group regarded Karan as someone who was too closely allied with the private-school establishment.

Had our two groups been engaged in ongoing communication, the intensity of our disagreement might have been averted. The search committee, however, began to function with deliberate disregard for me, Marty, and the faculty, and until the day before their vote on which candidate to recommend to the board, I was not invited back to meet with them. Henry Drewry later told the board, "Gus was out of the loop. He was never meant to be in the loop."

To add to the storm's fury, the vacuum created by the absence of such dialogue was filled by an intensely vocal group of anti-Michèle parents, prompted by a few key members of the search committee and the board. Rather than waging their campaign on the merits of Karan's candidacy, they focused entirely on undermining Michèle. They blamed her for faults they cited in the Spanish program, even though our graduates qualified for advanced classes in high school. They attacked her style of interpersonal relationships, saying she did not "reach out to be inclusive and nurturing," and they alleged that her academic standards, as demonstrated by the school's Spanish program, lacked "rigor."

This latter charge never failed to get a rise out of Marty, a lover of dictionaries and an accomplished doer of crossword puzzles. Peeved by repeated references to the need for "rigor" at MCS, Marty had this to say in a column for the monthly parent newsletter:

"One Monday morning, the clue for number 51-Down in the *Times* crossword was 'Hardship.' I puzzled over possibilities for the five-letter answer. The answer turned out to be 'Rigor.' That's interesting, I thought, recalling articles, even in MCS newsletters, in which the authors chose the word 'rigorous' as the aim for a good school's curricula. I consulted *Webster*, and, sure enough, the *Times* had it right; 'rigor' is defined as: 'rigidity, stiffness, strictness, severity, harshness; an act or instance of severity, oppression or cruelty. (Also see 'rigor mortis.')' A Dickensian institution for sure!

"Seeking a more appropriate word to describe a school's curriculum, I made a one-letter change and came up with the word 'vigor.' Aha! (a popular crossword palindrome), this is more familiar territory: 'Vigorous' is defined as 'possessing vigor; full of physical or mental strength or active force; strong, lusty, robust; exhibiting strength, either of body or mind, energetic.'

"Spell-check programs can't caution you that 'rigor' and 'vigor' have very different meanings; this critical ability resides in the human mind. If in doubt, we are blessed with dictionaries.

"The word 'rigorous' has often appeared in the press to describe the ideal American education. It has rolled off the tongues and pens of the late Albert Shanker, Chancellor Rudy Crew, members of central and local school boards, as well as critics propounding sundry cures for what ails our schools.

It even made it into the *Porter Sargent Handbook of Private Schools*. I wonder if any of these people have thought about what this word really means. Are we (or they) being BAM_O_ZL_D onto a B_NDW_G_N without even a BL_NK?"

How I wished that MCS's critics would take to heart the message of Marty's column!

BY THE END of November, word got out that in one of her trustee interviews Karan Merry had stated that she would not want me to remain on the board should she be the next director. While she had obvious reasons for feeling as she did, I never understood why she chose to reveal them at that time. I thought a declaration so antagonistic on her part would only hurt her candidacy, perhaps even among her supporters. If nothing else, it gave her opponents cause to be fighting mad.

On December 19, 1995, by a vote of six to three, the search committee nominated Karan Merry for director. Adding insult to injury, they named Hock as their second-choice candidate, and Michèle as third choice.

The search committee agreed that Frank Roosevelt should be the one to break the news to Marty and me the following day, with the proviso that I not disclose the results to Michèle or others on the staff. Henry also told Frank that he wanted the official announcement of the search committee's choice not to be made until January 17, when the board was scheduled to vote on their nomination.

Determined to counter the committee's recommendation, and to rally the faculty in Michèle's support, I disregarded Henry's wishes.

Taking a similar course, Frank convened the executive committee of the board on December 27; the committee met for three hours in my absence. With Henry and one other member abstaining, the committee voted that I should remain a trustee after my retirement. The same motion was later carried unanimously by the full board. Frank also informed the executive committee in detail of my story concerning Karan's connection to Wilmington Friends

School. Although Frank stated that as board chair he would prefer to remain neutral in any trustee discussions prior to casting their secret ballot, the executive committee urged otherwise; at which point, Frank declared that he would vote to reject the search committee's proposed slate. Finally, the executive committee concluded that the full board should be notified immediately that Karan was the search committee's first choice.

Pete Seeger at MCS's thirtieth anniversary celebration. The singer tells the
story of meeting a young student in an anti-Vietnam War rally. The
student was waving a placard in protest. Seeger asked, "Do you think
you're going to change the world with that sign?" The student replied,
"Maybe not, but I'm going to make sure the world doesn't change me."

CHAPTER 28

Deadlocked!

OVER THE NEXT two weeks, the executive committee met with the faculty in an effort to mollify their sense of betrayal at the search committee's nomination of Karan Merry, and to hear their opinions of all three candidates. Knowing that some trustees based their opposition to Michèle on the presumption that I would remain too strong an influence after her succession, I addressed a memo to the board, outlining my preferred role as retiring founder-director. I proposed that the areas of my participation be restricted to: 1) fund-raising; 2) public relations; 3) the public-school outreach program; 4) alumni relations; and 5) organizing the school's archives. The areas in which I would not serve were those which fell under the direct authority of the director, such as curriculum, staff development and supervision, and school management. Similarly, I preferred not to serve on any board committee overseeing the educational program or personnel matters. Finally, Marty and I would reside in Maine for as long as five months, and my presence in the school would be limited, with the majority of my work taking place away from the premises.

The bottom line of my memo was: "For over five years I have been looking forward to a change of leadership at MCS. I am keenly aware of the generic hazards of founders haunting their successors. During this period, I have made every effort to de-Gusify MCS. On June 30, when I turn over the keys, I will be letting go."

All twenty-four trustees took part in the January 17, 1996, meeting, with one member participating by speaker phone from South Africa. Results of their secret ballots, cast in three parts were:

Karan Merry: eleven in favor, thirteen opposed.

Michèle Solá: eleven in favor, thirteen opposed.

Hock Hochschartner: nine in favor, fifteen opposed.

After the voting was over, Henry asked, "May I call Karan tonight and tell her she's not a candidate?" Frank, joined by several other trustees, replied emphatically, "No." The conversation that followed was lengthy and acrimonious. "Gus tried to control the outcome," one trustee said. "Don't belittle Gus's work. This is his baby," someone countered. "Karan is a black woman. How can she not know what social justice means?" another challenged. "I'm prepared to accept Karan. I'm prepared to accept any candidate," a fourth trustee said. And: "Let's just put Hock in the job as a compromise. Then we'll be able to say we've done our job." "The board's vote to overturn the search committee is a charade." "I've stayed awake nights worrying about Gus and Marty, and this is a terrible way to end their thirtieth year." "Real democracy is really ugly."

Given the tone of that meeting, I could see that continuing the debate on ideological grounds was not going to break the deadlock, and I was not willing to entertain the growing interest among some trustees that Hock's appointment would save the day. For either Karan or Michèle to win, five out of the thirteen opposing trustees needed to switch sides. We knew that one of these was the trustee who had said, "I'm prepared to accept any candidate."

At the board's follow-up meeting on January 24, Frank allowed me to present the opening remarks. My approach was to argue the case on strictly practical grounds, urging that the board choose the path that would cause the least damage.

First, I warned that acceptance of the search's committee's recommendation would result in faculty resignations. And given the committee's note that Karan was "probably out of our price range," I predicted that she would not accept an offer from MCS anyway. Also, I could not imagine her serving under a chairperson who had opposed her, or in association with a founder whom she had declared should not be a trustee. In addition, I stated, if Karan and the board were to scrap the public-school outreach program, MCS would lose substantial financial support.

I knew that my warnings would be regarded by my strongest opponents as threatening, but to the extent that they indicated likely hazards, I was banking on winning over those additional votes. On a more compatible note, I then restated my preference for Michèle Solá, acknowledging her need to join us all in mending fences.

My effort failed, and the voting that followed was a replica of the first meeting, a total deadlock. In perhaps its only unanimous vote of the year, the board thereupon instructed the executive committee to seek an interim director for MCS.

Our adjournment was delayed because Henry had two additional motions. His first, that the three search committee candidates be excluded from consideration for interim director, passed by seventeen to five votes. His other motion, aimed specifically at me, excluded the current administration from consideration as interim director. Mike Pope promptly proposed a counter motion to elect me as interim director. Given such a messy turn of events, I asked to be excused from the meeting. After I left, the board voted sixteen to five to reject Henry's motion and delegated the matter of succession back to the executive committee.

I suppose that night was the culmination of the storm. At least, I thought, it couldn't get worse. The opposition had no candidate, the search committee had been effectively dissolved, MCS was still in the hands of a supportive executive committee, and unless she chose to resign, Michèle Solá was still on board.

The executive committee and I felt that the appointment of an outside interim director had too many drawbacks. It would be an extremely hard job to fill, and unless a person of extraordinary skill took it on, the school would remain divided, and by all appearances, leaderless. An internal solution was preferable. With Michèle out of the running as interim head, the logical potential candidates were Cynthia Rogers, upper-school director, and Lois Gelernt, lower-school director, both of whom were highly experienced educators with long MCS associations. However, both declined, leaving the executive committee with the inevitable choice: to ask me to stay for one or two more years. Marty and I talked at length about this, knowing it was a team deal. Ultimately, we agreed. Even Henry Drewry favored this solution, and on February 12, sixteen trustees approved the recommendation with two abstentions.

My memo to the staff the next day began with the word "Amen" and ended: "The immediate future for the school's leadership is now clear, and it is my hope that this course of action will enable you all to be put at ease after a long and difficult time of disappointment and uncertainty. Specifically, I hope you will choose to remain on the staff next year. We are, as you know, behind schedule in making plans for the future, and I am resolved to catch up as quickly as possible and to forge ahead with solidarity."

Before accepting the board's decision, I told the executive committee I had two conditions, the first being that Marty and I would work three days a week with our salaries prorated. My resolution to the staff that I wanted to "forge ahead with solidarity" alluded to my second condition: to have Michèle's candidacy reconsidered. Michèle knew of and shared this objective, as did the staff. Three of the five members of the executive committee also endorsed it, knowing that we would still need to secure a majority vote from a highly divided board.

On Saturday, March 16, 1996, the executive committee hosted a day-long meeting of the board to hammer out the dos and don'ts of the new search. For the most part, the meeting was productive, with a substantial majority of trustees agreeing that Michèle, or any other inside candidate, should be considered prior to outside candidates. They also agreed that thereafter, should an external search be required, the committee appointed to do so would be restricted to trustees only.

The discussion then turned to what had gone wrong the first time around, and few trustees could refrain from casting blame. I, of course, was a target, as was Henry. The following day he submitted his resignation, as did another black trustee, Margaret Haynes. Sadly, and perhaps inevitably, the board had become deeply divided by the racial bitterness of those members of color who had supported Karan.

A month later, I attended a meeting of the parent association to talk about the way the search for a new director had unfolded. I recounted the story of Paula Wehmiller's connection to Karan Merry, and acknowledged the presence of a racial divide in the school. I explained that I had wanted the full story told from the very beginning so that people could judge for themselves what had transpired. Later that month, at the April 30, 1996, board meeting, the executive committee resolved to proceed with the reconsideration of Michèle Solá's candidacy, promising to make a recommendation by the following spring.

The year ended better than it began as, to everyone's relief, the skies brightened. On May 5, 1996, we celebrated MCS's thirtieth anniversary with a triumphal concert featuring Pete Seeger. "I knew the MCS magic was still alive," said one alumna, "when I looked around as we were singing 'We Shall Overcome' and saw that the ushers were singing with us." Elizabeth Kitzinger, an MCS parent and trustee, known fondly as the school historian, wrote: "The event was a benefit, which raised over $100,000, but, even more, it was a moment of grace. After a year of wrenching discourse it was good to feel unity, to be with old and new members of what is now a large family with deep roots of common experience, and awe-inspiring to look around and see the hundreds of people, some once MCS schoolchildren and now themselves parents, whose allegiance to the dreams of this small elementary school is a cornerstone of their lives."

Among those present was Kenneth B. Clark, there at age eighty to receive the school's mentor award in recognition of his great contribution to MCS in its founding years. I sat next to Dr. Clark, who smiled and squeezed my hand, murmuring, "Congratulations." Dr. Clark even cried during Frank Roosevelt's speech, as if the history of MCS were intricately tied with his own.

"We began this effort with the sense that we were part of a strong tide of history, a tide carrying us toward the racial justice and equal opportunity that many of us believe is the promise of America," Frank said in his speech. "We soon realized that it wasn't going to be easy and, starting in the early 1970s, the tide of history began moving in other directions . . . . One shocking report on where we are today was the cover story of last week's issue of *Time* magazine (April 29, 1996). It was titled: 'Back to Segregation' and it carried the subtitle: 'After four decades of struggle, America has now given up on school integration.' . . . If there is one thing that is more than anything else at the core of the philosophy of the Manhattan Country School, it is that 'separate but equal' just won't do . . . . We cannot move forward if we go our separate ways; we can only make progress if we join together . . . to push for national policies that will benefit us all. One of the main goals of MCS-style multicultural education is to prepare our children to engage in this kind of concerted action. So, even though we are swimming against the tide these days, we will keep on swimming. At the very least, we may be able to persuade some others to 'Come on in, the water's fine.'"

In his additional remarks directed to Marty and me, for whom the occasion had been initially intended as retirement "hoopla," Frank conveyed an extra message of hope to all of us whose thoughts were fixed on the fragile state of the school. He spoke of MCS as "an enduring institution" in which "all of us could actively seek to define ourselves and to discover capacities we did not know we had." Echoing Coretta Scott King, he concluded, "As a result of your efforts, Manhattan Country School has come to reflect what is best in America: its democratic ethos, its activist spirit, its diversity, and its inclusiveness, enabling all who have come through the doors of MCS to go back into the world with a renewed sense of possibility and hope."

That May had another banner day in store for me. Two weeks later, I stood on the dais of the Cathedral of St. John the Divine, with *New York Times* columnist Bob Herbert and education writer Lisa Delpit, to receive an honorary doctorate of humane letters from Bank Street College of Education. The citation read: "The Manhattan Country School is the tangible expression of your unfailing vision, your wholehearted commitment to democratic ideals, and your dynamic leadership. The school's lived experience of diversity, of learning about and working for social justice, make it a beacon for educators who believe that social justice and equality for all must be central to education if they are to be achieved in society at large."

When I shared the news of my honorary degree with the MCS faculty, I wrote, "Dear Staff, We earned this together! Thank you for keeping your eyes on the prize! Yours, Gus." In return, the faculty gave me—using my alias, Caesar Hurlpont (a play on Augustus T[h]row bridge)—their own citation. It was an honorary DDS in recognition of my thirty years of removing the loose baby teeth of children in the school. "Extraordinary Extractions," the staff called them, giving credence to the MCS child who once said, "Gus used to be a dentist."

Kenneth Clark at MCS's thirtieth anniversary celebration,
receiving a Living the Dream Mentor Award from
Carl Flemister and Frank Roosevelt.

Chapter 29

An Invented Community

ALTHOUGH I HAD agreed to extend the search for the next director for two more years, I was both determined and optimistic that Michèle Solá could win the necessary support. Michèle and I talked about the forthcoming year. "What I need," she said, "is a campaign manager." "Then, that's what I'll do," I said. "We need to get you away from being on the defense. Your role in the school next year should be more prominent than mine. You should be out on the front lines, speaking for MCS, setting educational policy, and shaping the school's future. I'll do the politicking."

In my year-end meeting with parents in June 1996, I spoke about the programmatic and practical needs for MCS the following year. The school was due for its ten-year NYSAIS evaluation for New York State certification in 1998, and in September we would begin the comprehensive process of self-assessment. I pointed out that the educational objectives that I listed— improving the school's computer technology, strengthening its math curriculum, and further initiatives in our gender equity project—were all designed by Michèle in keeping with her long-term goals for MCS.

I reminded the parents that Marty and I would be working three days a week, and said that in June I would announce changes in the administrative organization to take effect in September. I ended by saying, "The spring dinner meeting of the Guild of Independent Schools always invites heads of schools to bring their former heads as guests. Each year I am amused by my orphaned condition, being the only school director in New York City without a predecessor. I look forward to accompanying my successor to this annual affair in the not-too-distant future."

Two weeks later, the eighth graders graduated, a class of twenty-one students, thirteen of whom had attended MCS since the 4-5s. As with other graduation talks, my message to the children was also intended to apply to their parents. On this occasion, among those present were several of my more vocal opponents throughout the search process.

I began by apologizing to the children that we were not graduating together as I had promised them when they were in fifth grade. "Things have changed," I said. "They held me back." I went on to say that as a class, the power of their presence at MCS had not simply been in their longevity. "Your distinction as a group rests in the fact that you all fit together so closely," I told them. "That is why I was especially looking forward to being in the class of 1996.

"You should know," I continued, "that Marty and I are avid and expert doers and connoisseurs of the jigsaw puzzle. The most complex jigsaw puzzles are interlocking ones, meaning that pieces are neatly and firmly joined. Puzzles cut along color lines are also particularly satisfying. In these puzzles, sections of the puzzle appear separate from one another until you notice that they combine as a whole, revealing thematic connections in the picture that had been concealed. Among my favorite puzzles are those that contain figurals or special shapes of people, animals, letters, or numbers.

"Thank you for giving me the metaphor of the jigsaw puzzle. Like the best of puzzles, each of you as pieces of the whole is different, and the picture you portray is not the making of hallmark mediocrity. For each of you, there is also a distinct and memorable figural that you have contributed to your collective portrait. Most importantly, as separate parts, you have joined as one. The finest interlocking puzzles, when fully assembled, can be lifted up without a single part falling loose. I will not attempt to demonstrate your qualifications along these lines, but I know that should I try to do so, you would meet the standards of a puzzle maker's dream.

"Thank you for coming together and for being such a perfect example of MCS at its best. Most Americans live in worlds that barely touch. That is our national ailment. You are in a uniquely preferred position to help remedy this ailment because you know how to bring worlds together. May your lives continue to interlock with others to spread the dream."

AT THE FINAL board meeting of the year, I announced that all head teachers had signed contracts to continue at MCS and that I had appointed Michèle full-time assistant director in charge of daily operations of the school. When school reopened in September, she would sit at my old desk.

The stage for Michèle's succession was set, but the outcome was far from certain as the opposition was also hard at work. In their year-end meeting, the parent association had held the first hotly contested election for president in the history of MCS, which resulted in the election of copresidents who were known as ardent "anti-Gusites."

The following September, preparing for what I again hoped would be my last talk to parents, I decided to meet the opposition head on, addressing two of their mistaken views about MCS: first, their failure to recognize the uniqueness of MCS within the private-school sector, and second, their desire for a more traditional approach to education.

"I want once again to speak about what makes MCS so different from other schools," I began. "The uniqueness of MCS rests in our joining together two legacies: the legacy of progressive education going back to the early decades of the twentieth century and the legacy of the age-old struggle for freedom and equality, which found such powerful expression in the civil rights movement.

"There is a profound difference between progressive and traditional schools. The gulf is so deep that a teacher or head of school could not tolerate working in both camps. What people who are not educators do not understand is that the difference between the two camps is not in their academic goals or standards. Send identical twins with identical aptitudes to a traditional school and a progressive one, and I am convinced that their SAT scores would be the same in twelfth grade. What would be different about them would show in their values and their social relationships—specifically, in the company they keep. Traditional schools tend strongly to maintain the existing order; progressive ones, to undo it.

"More than any other institutions, including perhaps the family, schools today make children the people they become. Progressive schools, and surely MCS, welcome an extended purpose in this function. They choose to educate children to become committed to social change."

Nine months later, when I repeated my message to the graduating class, I concluded, "My hope for the future of MCS and for all of us inspired by the prophetic longings of progressive education is that we can educate others who can help us fulfill the dream. I want our children to live with respect in many worlds, to touch and be touched, to be unafraid to be themselves, to keep company with whomever they wish. And when they have come of age, I want them not only to have shined on their SAT scores but also to know what levers to pull when they enter the voting booth."

IN THE PERIOD from the board's first meeting on September 25, 1996, to February 12, 1997, the date on which the board would put Michèle's candidacy to a final vote, the trustees met more frequently than at any other time in the school's history, including during the era of tuition reform. At the first board meeting, the opposition to Michèle was full-blown. Many trustees, frustrated by the decision to reconsider Michèle, were hoping for a swift outcome. One trustee went so far as to inquire, "Doesn't Michèle realize she will be a battered, worthless individual if we go on? She should withdraw her candidacy."

Michèle's meeting with the board on October 17 was attended by fifteen trustees, five of whom were adversarial. The meeting was planned as an interview, structured to begin with questions posed by all trustees, followed by an extended period for Michèle's response, then time for additional questions. The format gave those opposed to Michèle's candidacy the opportunity they had been waiting for, and to no one's surprise, they dominated the evening. Of the twenty-eight questions, Michèle fielded eighteen contentious ones. Ten trustees did what they could to mitigate the antagonism by asking helpful questions, but to avoid creating a deeper division within the board, they refrained from taking issue with Michèle's opponents, or speaking out in her defense. Michèle handled the aggressive questioning with remarkable composure, and when it was over, she understood that the worst was behind her. Further, as pro tem chief administrator of MCS, she had four months ahead to prove her worth.

I weighed Michèle's prospects. In the fall of 1997, the active membership of the board was twenty-two trustees; fifteen of their votes would be required to obtain a two-thirds majority. I was fairly certain that twelve board members would vote in Michèle's favor and that six would oppose her. We would therefore have to win over three of the four undeclared votes, which at the time did not seem likely.

Fortunately, the board had agreed the previous June to elect two or three new trustees, specifically people of color, to replace those who had resigned. Over the summer, the nominating committee had enlisted the following nominees: Debo Adegbile, an MCS graduate and an associate with a prestigious New York law firm; Alma Carten, a former MCS parent and teacher, and professor at the New York University School of Social Work; and Awilda Perez, a school psychologist with a public school in New Jersey, and a former staff member of MCS. When they were presented to the board for approval on October 22, the opposition was naturally concerned, correctly surmising that they would be pro-Michèle.

One trustee moved to postpone the seating of the new trustees until after the February 12 meeting. His motion was defeated eleven to six. The next motion, to accept or reject the nominating committee's recommendation to elect three, rather than two, new trustees, was approved by fifteen to two, and finally the board voted sixteen to one to seat all three candidates immediately.

Although the numbers game had shifted in our favor, we still had insufficient cause for confidence. With the enlarged board, seventeen trustees were now required for a two-thirds majority. Adding the three new trustees to the twelve who supported Michèle, we remained shy by two votes. In the months ahead, at least two of those four trustees who were undeclared would have to join the majority.

At the October 22 board meeting, the president of the parents' association, Barbara Barnes, distributed a letter, calling for the trustees to reverse their course. With twenty-seven signatures, including sixteen current MCS parents, the letter appeared to represent less than one tenth of the school. But it ended by stating that substantial numbers of parents had chosen not to add their signatures "for fear of the effect it might have on their children's opportunities and their own financial relationship with the school."

The letter did more than rehash the opposition's view that, under Michèle's leadership, the school would remain a "mom and pop" operation. It went on to criticize the governing board of the school, including those trustees who also held dissenting views. It accused the board of manipulating the search process and delaying its outcome, of stacking its membership in the majority's favor, and of withholding information concerning the reasons for Henry's resignation. The letter also questioned my authority in appointing Michèle as "the day-to-day director of the school," and alluded to past assertions of mine as "uninformed, intolerant, and divisive."

"At this juncture, in this highly-charged atmosphere," the letter summed up, "we strongly believe that it is impossible for the board to make a decision on Michèle's candidacy that will appear fair and unbiased; one that will not leave deep and long-lasting divisions within the school community. The wisest course for all concerned would be for her name to be withdrawn."

The letter sparked indignation on the part of both parents and trustees. One trustee noted, "We can't appease the people who wrote this letter. When we do vote, we will consider the fact that there are parents who are against Michèle. In the meantime, we need to act in a steady, clear way, and to defend our actions." Before the meeting ended, I asked who had written the letter. Barbara replied, "This is not my letter. It was a group effort and all signers should receive a reply." With no objections, Frank adjourned the meeting, turning the matter of a reply over to the executive committee.

In the end, the letter did more harm than good for those whose cause it represented. In challenging the actions of the board and doubting its integrity, the letter gave the executive committee an opportunity not only to explain in detail the basis of the board's authority, the rationale for its decisions to date, and its future plans, but also to share with the entire parent body and faculty the full contents of the opposition's stated position. This was done on November 4 in a three-page memorandum, attached to which was a copy of the October 22 letter, with the signatures removed to preserve privacy. In the memorandum's last paragraph, the executive committee stated that while it was still open to suggestions regarding process, it chiefly wanted "input reflecting actual experiences that parents, faculty, and alumni/ae have had with Michèle, particularly as an administrator."

The faculty, who were eager to be heard, wrote over thirty letters to the board, with ten more submitted from former teachers who had worked with Michèle, and one composed collectively on behalf of the faculty council, representing the staff's endorsement of Michèle's candidacy. Their letter closed with the glowing comment: "Michèle has experienced MCS from the basement to the roof, from the youngest children to the oldest . . . Each day she lives and breathes the school's energy and spirit with us. We know her strengths and we recognize, in her, the next director of MCS."

The board meeting with the staff on January 16, attended by almost every member of the faculty, lasted an hour and a half. There were prepared statements from three teachers and two administrators, as well as from the farm director and the director of the upper school. Unfortunately, four board members known to be opposed to Michèle were absent. This may have accounted for the generally cordial reception on the part of those trustees present. With less than a month left, the staff answered all the questions posed to them by the board; whether the answers were to the trustees' satisfaction remained to be seen.

One staff member absent was Gloria Brown, whose views on the selection of a successor were the only known exception to those of her colleagues'. Gloria had been on the search committee and voted for Michèle on the first ballot, switching to Karan Merry thereafter. While influenced by Karan's candidacy as a fellow African-American, Gloria explained to me that after she had been sent to visit Karan's school in Chestnut Hill, Massachusetts, she came back entirely won over. In recent months, however, she had again changed her mind, and she wanted the board to know where she now stood. Knowing she would be away in Florida "rocking my first grandchild" on January 16, Gloria wrote the board to go on record that she now fully supported Michèle. "For the last eight months I have worked very closely with Michèle. Boy, was I wrong in my vote!" her letter said. "Under her leadership, I see MCS's future secure, its mission singing from the tree-tops."

Gloria's change of heart was increasingly shared by others. After the executive committee distributed their memo with the October 22 letter attached, two parents who had signed the parent association letter wrote to withdraw their endorsement of its contents, and two trustees, one of whom had been on the search committee, told the board that they would be voting for Michèle. Indeed, the tide seemed to be turning. As one new parent said after a December 4 parent association meeting, at which faculty members explained their support of Michèle, "Most people were very moved by the passion of the faculty and staff for Michèle's candidacy. I've never heard a faculty group speak as one but with different voices, a group of faculty who are so devoted to their children. If they want her, I do too. You must have faith in your faculty, or why would we be here?"

By the time the board met with the parents' association on December 12, parents who favored Michèle outnumbered those who opposed her by perhaps five to one. A month later when the opposition was down to a small but rancorous handful, one parent, who was active among the leadership of the parents' association, explained the turning of the tide as follows: "It is time for us to move on from discussion of the process. Flawed or not, it was a process, a learning experience; mistakes were made. I believe most of us are ready to put this issue aside and work toward creating the next era in the history of MCS. We approach this new era with excitement and confidence—confidence in Michèle, confidence in the ability of this community to heal, confidence in the board of directors, and confidence in Gus and Marty's continuing relationship with the school."

Michèle's second and final meeting with the board was on February 5, 1997, a week before the election, for which her prospects had begun to look hopeful. In consultation with the executive committee, she prepared a speech to cover four topics: 1) the school's academic priorities and challenges; 2) internal challenges, including healing the division within MCS; 3) MCS's future role in the public and private school efforts to reform educational institutions; and 4) the school's fiscal priorities over the next three years. In addition, she spoke about the assistance she would need from the board, what she had learned from being assistant director, and why she wanted to be MCS director.

Throughout her speech, Michèle offered assurances that every area of the school's program would be subject to scrutiny by the faculty, and that the curriculum would be "innovative, replicable, and of the highest academic quality." In particular, she announced her plans to address the merits and weaknesses of the school's Spanish program, for which she had been so sorely criticized, and its math curriculum. Finally, she promised to develop a comprehensive plan for the use of computer technology.

In her remarks, Michèle characterized herself as both a keeper of the school's proven traditions and a builder of bold initiatives, saying, "As all of us contemplate the future of MCS under new leadership, I think we must set bold new priorities which will continue to position MCS as an innovative social experiment, at once an exemplary school and an invented community. We must reject the temptation to see MCS as an institution isolated in time and place and chart the next era by understanding it as a 'learning institution.'

"MCS was founded as a community whose very nature was intentional," she continued, "embracing diversity and democracy, and with the understanding that achieving both would involve struggling with the segregation and hierarchy so prevalent outside its walls. For thirty years, that vision has remained at the core of a community that has been inventing and reinventing itself through sometimes messy moments. What beckons now is not nostalgia for a perfect past, but keeping alive the sense that each of us is part of reinventing the original vision."

Michèle ended by telling the board about a panel of alumni that had recently convened to evaluate the school's impact on their lives. Ten graduates from the first thirteen classes of MCS, who had each visited the school on separate days in December and early January, met together with two outside facilitators for eight hours over the weekend of Martin Luther King Jr.'s birthday. The alumni were asked to bring an artifact that captured for them the meaning that MCS had had on the rest of their lives.

"Their response to that assignment," said Michèle, "has absolutely rekindled my passion for this place and this job. It is because of them that I urge you tonight to think boldly about the future of MCS. Individualized diplomas, a yearbook, and now-ratty pillows woven at the farm, led to amazing stories about how each of them had gone beyond the green door to face challenge after challenge and apply the lessons they'd learned here. Acknowledging that it had been hard to reproduce the diversity they'd known at MCS, they agreed that each had become 'secret missionaries' for justice in their places of work and community. Therein seems to lie the basis of my renewed passion for having the job of director."

Before the board adjourned, there was a brief exchange introduced by one trustee who spoke about the need for "unbuilding walls." This prompted Walter Christmas to say, "We must deal with what's happened, with our bruises. We must become more creative and take MLK downtown. I still love this school; I want it healed. This is the only board we have and some terrible things have happened to it." Michèle was the last to speak. Seemingly in response to Walter, she said, "The New Dawn—that was the name of my mother's favorite rose. I want to take us there."

With a week to go, the certainty of Michèle's election was suddenly threatened by the absence of trustee Jo Levinson, who was in Israel. Our bylaws prohibited an absentee vote except by direct telephone, and the quorum we required was seventeen members. Without Jo, we were sure of sixteen votes. Frank Roosevelt faxed Jo to convey the urgency of her participation. She called him back to say that she could not be present and she did not want to place an extended phone call during the predawn hours from Tel Aviv. Prepared for this impasse, Frank asked her if she was willing to resign from the board. "Yes, if that would help," she answered. Jo's resignation, sent by fax the next day, lowered the quorum to sixteen.

When the February 12, 1997, meeting convened, the opposition seemed resigned to defeat, although no less angry, particularly when they learned of Jo's resignation. "I can count," said one of them. "It's been a long and a masterful campaign."

"The orchestration was unprecedented," another added. "People were dug up from under rugs." In a gesture of goodwill, one trustee pointed out, "It's not a lifelong appointment. If she doesn't do her job, I'll be the first to ask her to leave."

The vote was taken at 8:30 PM by secret ballot. Its result was eighteen in favor of Michèle, five opposed, and one abstention.

The annual sixth grade performance at the MLK assembly
is held in the music room—"the heart of the school."

CHAPTER 30

Renewal

MICHÈLE'S VICTORY WAS met with widespread approval and relief throughout the school. For Marty and me, the relief was more like restitution. The demands of the search process had been so brutal that for two years our daily pastimes had been reduced to a minimum. I read the morning newspaper and glanced at the cartoons in the *New Yorker*, but never read a book. I was on the phone too often and too late every night, and in the early evenings, when we once enjoyed doing a jigsaw puzzle together, we would be at the computer at work on our running chronicle of the events of the search. Ever since I first started giving my own hand-cut jigsaws to our grandchildren, Christmas 1996 was the only year they did not receive their annual "Poppy Puzzle."

Although we had agreed to suspend our retirement for one or at the most two years, I think the prospect of the second year was one we would have found intolerable. I wagered that, sensing prolonged instability, Michèle would have resigned, as would have many staff members. Indeed, many parents on both sides of the aisle would have fled the school, and the prospect of an entirely new search with a lasting positive outcome was slight.

So for me at least, February 12, 1997, represented a return to normality and an opportunity to move on. We would graduate with the class of 1997, and I would find a new and welcomed role as founder-director, a role not unlike that of grandparent, which I had come to enjoy. Most important, MCS had survived the storm. It was ready to resume its work, and in my judgment, it was in good hands.

Others seemed to agree. Contrary to the predictions of the opposition, there was very little fallout. Only a few parents chose to leave, and others who had opposed Michèle stayed on to have their children graduate. No other trustees resigned. The fighting ceased, and with Michèle taking the appropriate lead, the healing began.

A month after her appointment, in an article for the *MCS Sampler*, Michèle wrote about the school's past and future, including its recent struggle and its need for reconciliation. Her message both acknowledged her awareness that the school was now in her hands—"I feel a somewhat daunting task awaits me"—and invited the entire MCS community to join in a reaffirmation of the school's mission. "Of the many issues and questions facing the school," she said, "there is one thing I am certain about: We must find the answers together."

One search for answers was through the alumni forum, which was held at the school in the fall of 1996. As it had done for Michèle, the results of the alumni forum, which I helped organized but did not attend, had rekindled my own passion for MCS. Coinciding with the final weeks of the search, the forum was a resounding tribute to the school at a time when its future seemed most at risk.

We had invited participants from the first half of our graduating classes who lived in or near New York, and who, together, reflected the diversity of the school. In selecting which graduates to invite, I gave no consideration to their future schooling or fields of employment. My choice was based only on a subjective appraisal of them when they were MCS students. To my gratification, their accomplishments after MCS disproved the criticisms voiced so strongly during the search process that our school lagged in its academic standards.

Aiming for a group of ten when I extended the initial invitations, I did not have to place a single additional call. Everyone said yes. Of the group assembled, there were two white males, three white females, one African-American male, one African-American female, one Latina, one Latino-Korean, and one African-white American female. The average age of the group was about the same as the school's—the oldest being thirty-nine, the youngest twenty-six.

These ten alumni met for six hours on Friday, January 17, and Saturday, January 18, 1997, with Emily Style, codirector of the National SEED Project on Inclusive Curriculum, and her cofacilitator, Betsy Hasegawa. Betsy, who had never visited the school before, said later that the group "seemed to feel that their MCS experience was especially unique and not to be treated casually. It was their 'secret' source of strength in the world, knowing they had attended this private school with a public mission." Emily described the conversations of the alumni as a "Quilt of Voices," many patches of which we recorded in our *Sampler.*

These were the ten who comprised the forum:

CRIS GARCIA ('84) attended Bronx High School of Science and Fieldston High School, and graduated from Connecticut College in 1992. He founded and directed an Asian-American community organization in Lower Manhattan, and is currently a vice president at Banker's Trust Company. "Personally, I was never made to feel by anyone at MCS that my own multiracial heritage was anything but a blessing, and my background was a nonfactor in terms of the treatment I received."

SABRINA KING ('73) went to Trinity School, graduating from the University of Pennsylvania in 1981. She received masters and doctorate degrees in education from Teachers College, Columbia University. Sabrina is a professor of education at Hofstra University. "Music had gotten me through my life, and through lots of struggles with the kinds of things that MCS was talking about. I recall lots of experiences in the music room singing freedom songs. Since then, I have not had similar types of experiences in school where that part of me, my blackness, could be expressed."

ROBIN LEVI ('82) attended Stuyvesant High School, graduated from Georgetown University School of Foreign Service in 1990, and attended

Stanford Law School, where she received her JD in 1993. Robin is a staff attorney and Sophie Silberburg Fellow with the Women's Rights Project of Human Rights Watch in Washington, DC. "I remember thousands of ways in which I had positive reinforcement about my racial identity, my ethnic identity, my religious identity; I didn't feel the same way about my gender, although I would say that the building blocks from here led me to be able to do women's rights work in the way that I do it."

MEGHAN MCDERMOTT ('84) attended Elisabeth Irwin High School and received a BA in East Asian Studies from Barnard College in 1992. She is research assistant with the Education Development Center's Center for Children and Technology, conducting research on media literacy in the classroom, and she assists the Access by Design project to investigate issues of diversity and equity of access to technology in underrepresented communities. "I was thinking about the term 'utopia.' There is a lot of hard work going on every day in the school, and there's a lot of struggle. I think MCS seems to become more of a utopia, given the challenges we face once we leave the school, struggling to put our values to work. But with utopia also comes a remembrance that certain communities are possible."

KATE MILFORD ('84) graduated from Stuyvesant High School and Brown University, where she received a BA in 1989. She studied film-making in Berlin for a year, and is a professional freelance photographer. "I get the sense that there's this 'secret missionary' purpose. 'Missionary' is pushing it a bit, because I'm not really trying to convert anyone, but in a sense I do feel like I have something really important from having been here, which would be really valuable for someone receptive to it to have too. It's that understanding that we have to look at ourselves in a much broader context than the messages in our culture at large tell us."

LIAM PLEVEN ('79) attended Lenox School and graduated from Swarthmore College in 1987. Formerly on the staff of the *Herald Tribune* in Paris, Liam is now a journalist with *Newsday*. "In my personal life, when I am confronted by an issue, I feel I've either succeeded or failed by whether I'm being true to what MCS taught me."

JUDITH ANN SOLIVAN-HASPIL ('75) attended Martin Luther King Jr. High School and graduated in 1983 from John Jay College. She received a JD from New York Law School in 1986 and is an attorney with Arawak Consultant Corporation. "When I left here I felt very confident that I could be in any environment, socially, culturally, economically, and feel like I belonged. MCS fostered my wanting to be part of something, a movement, a project, a school community that could build better educational values."

KATHERINE WEBBER ('80) went to Friends Seminary after MCS. She graduated from Smith College in 1988, and in 1992 received a master's degree in social work from Hunter College. Most recently she has been a counselor and therapist with the Rape Crisis Intervention and Victims of Violence Program of Long Island College Hospital. "Going back through papers my parents saved from MCS, I found a copy of Gus's graduation speech to my class. In this speech I noted that he singles out every student. This is what being a community is about. It is appreciating everyone's individuality and acknowledging its impact on the whole. One incident I remember well at MCS that I had difficulty processing took place in the 9-10s. I remember learning that if you were White Anglo Saxon Protestant you were afforded a certain privilege in our society. The disturbing part about this discussion for me was that I remember feeling secretly happy that I was in this category, but I also remember thinking that it was bad that I felt this way without knowing why. Now, as an adult looking back at this, I think it was natural that I felt that way, but that if it had been talked about, I would have understood that everyone deserves to feel a sense of entitlement in our society."

DAVID WILCOX ('71), one of MCS's first eight graduates, attended Midwood High School and graduated from Boston College in 1979. A sales manager for many years at Xerox Corporation, David now manages his own business. "MCS was a bold move. It helped me to better understand the lifestyles of the economically privileged, and how the parents of many children think. It showed me the possibilities that can happen when people are committed to an equitable community. We were taught to think 'out of the box' and to be independent as well as community-minded. On the other hand, the stark reality of life as a black man in America can never be fully understood or taught unless you experience it. The dynamics of privilege are always underestimated, and in many cases, minimalized."

SASHA WILSON ('84) went to Friends Seminary after MCS and graduated from Wesleyan University in 1988. He was an assistant in the senatorial campaigns of Paul Simon and Carol Moseley-Braun, and has been a member of the teaching team for VISTA's Ravenswood 'I Have a Dream' Project. He was currently in Nicaragua with his sister, Elizabeth ('87), helping former MCS Spanish teacher Alejandro Obando with his own new school, MCS-Los Chavalitos. "Having Dr. King's portrait towering over the living room, the gateway to the school, made a strong impression on me, reinforcing the idea of the school being his."

In reporting on their individual day-long visits to MCS, the alumni expressed agreement that the school had developed a stronger and more comprehensive academic program. The earliest alumni were amazed that MCS had become "a real school." "When we were here," David Wilcox commented, "this was really an experiment, now it's much more serious. I can't believe the schedule, and all the courses they're taking."

While acknowledging that the curriculum was more demanding, the alumni noted that their hardest adjustment to high school was the shock of realizing that the outside world did not share the values of equity, social justice, and a participatory community that they had experienced at MCS. Pointing to the snow on the fire escape, Cris said, "The analogy would almost be like walking outside here without a coat. I wasn't steeped in, or aware of, the lack of a real correlation of what goes on inside these doors and what goes on outside. You sort of get the wind knocked out of you. Eventually you come around, but still I think the school could do a bit more to lessen that shock."

Liam answered, "Maybe having the world inside MCS be such a good, cohesive community and having the initial shock be such a difficult transition is a worthwhile price to pay." Meghan joined in, saying, "In ninth grade we all had a reality shock, but then a moment came when we realized that, 'Yeah. I am right. I know I'm right about this issue, but how come they don't get it.'"

Later, in an article for the *MCS Sampler,* titled "What Is Still to Be Overcome?", Emily Style shared her impressions of the alumni weekend and addressed what she called "the work of the next season at MCS." Speaking in metaphor about "the politics of location," she invited the reader to imagine that the product of the alumni forum was a tangible quilt instead of a metaphorical "Quilt of Voices." She then posed the question of where such a collective work of art should be displayed or located in the school.

"The quilt could certainly hang in the kitchen of MCS," she wrote. "The kitchen is the organizational hub of the school. The help and the hierarchy, such as they are, eat together at the table in the working kitchen. One of the most provocative and oldest women-of-color publishing presses in this country is called Kitchen Table Press, bearing witness, as does MCS, to an alternative sense of where the heartbeat of work and discourse can be located in an organization.

"I could also make a case for hanging the quilt in the library of the school, where the alumni conversations actually took place. MCS is an institution where there is balanced attention to knowledge on the shelves and to knowledge in the selves, what I like to call 'the textbooks of our lives.'

"But I would not hang the quilt in the kitchen or the library, nor would I put it on display in the magnificent entrance way or in the cozy, fireplace-lit living room on the first floor. It's true that there it would be most visible to visitors and perhaps work to keep Martin Luther King, Jr. company. But I'd suggest that the quilt of this event could find a home in the spacious heart of the school's large music room on the second floor. I believe such a testimonial quilt of voices belongs in an interior place capable of holding the whole school, because the work of the next season of MCS belongs to the whole school and its community."

In the same article, Emily summarized the connections made by those MCS graduates who attended the alumni forum: "Their conversation revealed how the institutional memory in the room held both commonalities and differences. While there was clear appreciation of the world created by equity and excellence at MCS, it was also clear that there were other worlds outside to be navigated, worlds that did not always share MCS's values. It also became clear that students brought with them their experiences of that outside world when they reentered the school. Life in the outside world was not always comfortable, but the alumni said they had acquired a reservoir of self-affirmation and an experience of community-in-action that helped them navigate other places . . . . [They] appeared to be nourished, body and soul, by the weekend event, even as they seemed to hold themselves more accountable, perhaps, than ever before to living out the MCS mission."

In terms of our own accountability to the MCS mission, Marty and I feel much the same. In the years following our official retirement, our connection to MCS has remained close, our commitment to its principles unshaken. Our younger daughter, Mary, is now director of the lower school, and her daughters, Sophie and Caroline, are students. I am still on the board, serving as treasurer, and I meet weekly with Michèle to work on fiscal matters and fund-raising. Marty was correct; it took more than one person to replace her, and her time spent in the school during our initial retirement years was devoted to training her successors. A good portion of our time together in the building has been spent organizing the school archives.

Now in our eighth year as retirees, the generational shift is happily complete. All but the oldest students currently enrolled in MCS are new to us, and the last of those whose baby teeth I extracted will soon be graduating. Annually, Marty and I are interviewed by the sixth grade in connection with their study of the civil rights movement and the history of the school, and for the last few years I have shared my knowledge of stamp collecting with the 6-7s, who run the school post office. To some of the younger children, I am "the philatelist person" who showed them a Penny Black, Great Britain's first stamp. Others know us now not as Gus and Marty, but as Sophie's and Caroline's grandparents. After all, it's their generation's school now. As it should be.

Congressman John Lewis, the writer David Halberstam,
and Michèle Solá, director of MCS since 1997, sing "We Shall Overcome"
at the thirty-fifth anniversary celebration.

Epilogue

A Homecoming

IN MARCH OF 2000, President Bill Clinton went to Selma, Alabama, to deliver the keynote speech commemorating the thirty-fifth anniversary of Bloody Sunday. Standing on the Edmund Pettus Bridge, where so many years before Southern blacks had marched to protest racial discrimination, Clinton spoke of other bridges yet to be crossed. In closing, he stated that "whites have gained at least as much as blacks from the march to freedom."

"My fellow Americans," he said, "this day has a special meaning for me, for I too am a son of the South, the old segregated South. And those of you who marched thirty-five years ago on Bloody Sunday set me free too. Free to know you, to work with you, to love you, to raise my child to celebrate our differences, and hallow our common humanity."

In helping to plan the thirty-fifth anniversary of MCS, I was especially inspired by this acknowledgement by President Clinton on behalf of white America that the civil rights movement was about setting free not just black people, but *all* people. Dr. King had known this well. "It is history's wry paradox," he once said, "that when Negroes win their struggle to be free, those who have held them down will themselves be free for the first time."

My copy of *Playbill's Broadway Answers Selma*, an exclusive performance commemorating the first Selma march in 1965, became the template for Manhattan Country School's own thirty-fifth anniversary celebration in April

2002, which we called, "Today's Children Salute the Children of the Movement." We asked that John Lewis, one of the leaders of the Selma march and now a U.S. congressman, be our honored guest, and we invited others to join us in a partnership that spanned nearly four decades. To our minds, the occasion would be a kind of family reunion. As Michèle Solá explained in her speech to those gathered, "From the vantage point of MCS, our thirty-fifth anniversary year has been a time to review our own history, to invite people who have lived that history to return and share their stories."

And, indeed, it *was* a reunion, appropriately held at Riverside Church. Congressman John Lewis attended, as did David Halberstam, who hosted the program. Other honorees included Harry Belafonte, the actor and civil rights activist; Ruby Bridges, the first black child to desegregate a public school in the Deep South; Charlayne Hunter-Gault, the first African-American student to attend the University of Georgia; Carolyn Goodman, the mother of slain civil rights activist Andrew Goodman; the singer Odetta; and Bob Zellner, the first white field secretary of SNCC. In her introduction to our publication of "Today's Children Salute the Children of the Movement," Elizabeth Kitzinger wrote, "As it marks its thirty-fifth year, Manhattan Country School is doing publicly what it has done institutionally: invoking its link to the Civil Rights Movement and reaffirming the applicability of the values of social justice and collective nonviolent action in today's world . . . . Manhattan Country School, more than anything else, has been and continues to be an example of what can happen when the possibilities embedded in historical moments are seen and seized."

When John Lewis got up to speak, he began by relating the opening story from his 1999 book, *Walking with the Wind: A Memoir of the Movement*. It is the story of a Sunday afternoon when he was twelve and living in Troy, Alabama, with his Aunt Seneva in a "shotgun house." "An unbelievable storm came up," he said. "The wind started blowing, the thunder started rolling, the lightning started flashing and the rain started beating." His aunt called him and his dozen or so siblings and cousins into the house, and told them to hold hands. She then instructed them that when the wind began to lift any corner of the house, they were to walk to that corner and hold the house down. "We were little children walking with the wind," Lewis said. "And we never left the house."

In a generous tribute to MCS, Lewis ended his speech by saying, "For more than thirty-five years, the Manhattan Country School, like many of us in America, have been walking from Selma to Montgomery, trying to hold the American house together. But this school did stand, just like the civil rights movement stands. We all live in the same house. We're one family, we're one people . . . So I say to each of us—hold on. Walk with the wind, and let the spirit of Manhattan Country School be our guide."

Afterward, as the children of our school joined hands and led the rest of us in the civil rights anthem, "We Shall Overcome," I understood that this was an extraordinary homecoming for all of us. And I knew as surely as I had ever known it that our mission would continue to guide future generations. As one of our eighth-graders, Tanisha Colon-Bibb, had said at our annual MLK Walk just three months earlier, "It is important to me to be part of the world that Martin Luther King Jr. dreamed of. People we never met fought for us to live in a world where children of different skin colors could learn side by side. However, our world still has homelessness, poverty, diseases, racism, and other problems. Just learning about what happened in the past makes me believe even more that any obstacle can be overcome. We have to fight for the generations that will come after us, who will live in a world we dream of today."

The children hold the dream now. They will lead the way.

A view of the Martin Luther King Jr. trees,
35 years after their planting by MCS children in 1968.

About The Author

AUGUSTUS TROWBRIDGE received his BA and MA in Literature from Brown University and was awarded an honorary doctorate of humane letters from Bank Street College of Education in 1996. He taught at Dalton School in New York City for eight years before founding Manhattan Country School in 1966. He retired as director of MCS in 1997, but is still active as a trustee. He and his wife Marty live in New York City. They have three children and six grandchildren.